DISCIPLES AND PROPHETS

Francis J. Moloney, SDB

DISCIPLES AND PROPHETS

A Biblical Model
For the Religious Life

CROSSROAD · NEW YORK

1981
The Crossroad Publishing Company
18 East 41st Street, New York, NY 10017

Printed in the United States of America

Library of Congress Cataloging in Publication Data

Moloney, Francis J.
  Disciples and prophets.

  Bibliography: p.
  Includes indexes.
  1. Monastic and religious life—Addresses, essays,
lectures. 2. Bible—Criticism, interpretation, etc.—
Addresses, essays, lectures. I. Title. II. Title:
Biblical model for the religious life.
BX2435.M58   1981   248.8'94   81-573
ISBN 0-8245-0049-0   AACR2

To
the Salesians
of the
Australian Province

The dream I have today, my Lord,
is only a shadow of your dreams for me;
only a shadow of all that will be
if I but follow you.
(From a popular hymn by Carey Landry, *Only a Shadow*)

Contents

Preface

This book has come into existence because of a desire on my part to avoid schizophrenia. Let me explain. As a professional biblical scholar, my working day is spent analysing the sacred texts, reading the major works written about those texts and communicating my own intuitions through teaching and publication. This is a most exciting, even though exacting, profession. The biblical renewal, which came rather late in the Catholic Church (initiated by Pius XII in 1943), has opened up some wonderful new avenues of research, and a powerful rebirth of interest in biblical questions. Nowadays, Catholic scholars are second to none in this field.[1] However, I am not only a professional biblical scholar; I am also a Salesian priest. This means that my life is spent attempting to live a particular vocation in the Church which is not exhausted by my being a biblical specialist, and it was here that the danger of schizophrenia arose. As I read contemporary works on spirituality and Religious life and listened to homilies and retreat preachers, I found that there was a continual use of certain biblical material which proceeded as if the biblical renewal had never happened. For example, I shuddered when I heard and read Matthew's version of the story of the Rich Young Man (Matt. 19.16–22) used as a proof that there was a more perfect way of life in the following of the evangelical counsels, and Paul's suggestion that the unmarried should remain so in I Cor. 7.32–5 as a proof that celibacy was a life-style which brought the celibate closer to God. This could not be. Thus, over the years, I have attempted to approach all of these classical texts once again, to show that they often do not mean what they have been taken to mean, but to show further that contemporary Religious life has nothing to fear from a modern critical approach to these traditional texts. The following book is the way in which I have resolved my problem of schizophrenia.

The problem, however, has not only been mine. In one form or another, the following pages have been given as lectures to Religious in Australia, Italy, Israel, Germany, France, England and the United States over the past four or five years. Wherever I have given them I have inevitably had the reaction: 'At last! I always felt that somehow these texts were not being used properly. We have so much to gain from what you have said.' Encouraged by this reaction, I am now offering them here in a published form in the hope that they will be of use to a still wider audience.

The structure and limits of the book will be seen from a glance at the contents. This is not a full-scale theology of Religious life.[2] I have limited myself to an attempt to identify a biblical model for this particular life-style within the context of the universal call to sanctity. My reflections on contemporary Religious life arise, I hope, directly from the biblical material. Much more could, and should, be worked out in a systematic theology of Religious life. Religious life has come into existence to respond *publicly* as a community living the vows of poverty, chastity and obedience. All of these aspects of the Christian response are found in the Scriptures and thus they are not reserved to Religious life, which had its beginnings some centuries after the New Testament period. We must ask what the specific role of the poor, chaste and obedient Religious community within the Church might be. It seems to me that the answer lies in the models of discipleship and prophecy. Whether or not I am correct in this I will leave to the reader to judge.

As this book is an attempt to find a *biblical* model it is necessarily idealistic. I am well aware that there is a huge gap between the reality of the Religious life which most of us live as individuals and in community and the ideals presented here: but this must not deter us in our attempt to find the *ideal model* against which we should continually examine our efforts to live as disciples and prophets of the Lord. The Scriptures never apologise for their idealism. St Paul does not say: 'Love *should be* patient and kind; love *should not be* jealous or boastful.' He says: 'Love *is* patient and kind; love *is not* jealous or boastful' (I Cor. 13.4). This book also attempts to avoid the conditional and to present a biblical model as an imperative, idealistic though that imperative may be.

Although I take responsibility for all that follows, I have depended, heavily at times, on the work of others in this field. Given the history of this book, it is often difficult to retrace just exactly where I first encountered some particularly suggestive line of thought, but I have attempted to give credit to my sources throughout. Informed readers will recognise a great deal of Fr J. M. R. Tillard, OP and Fr J. Murphy-O'Connor, OP,[3] and I am most grateful to these two scholars, even though my point of view differs from theirs on occasion. One further remark on sources. I have tried to limit myself to fairly basic works, especially in the area of contemporary biblical scholarship. Thus, instead of giving long notes which listed all sorts of scholarly positions, I have sent the reader back to basic commentaries and reliable handbooks.[1] It is my experience that a careful reading of the text, aided by a modest library of up-to-date guide-books, can open up the sacred text for any intelligent reader.

I would like to thank the many Religious from all parts of the world who have listened attentively to what follows. Without their encouragement and criticism this book would never have seen the light. Sister Mary Bernard, OSB, worked very hard typing a first draft of the book from reams of my almost illegible handwriting, and my sister, Mrs Pauline Cullen, in the midst of her duties as a wife and mother, undertook the task of providing a final typescript from the much-corrected version of that first draft. To these two women, upon whose affection and support I have so heavily leaned over many years, I would like to express my deepest gratitude. Thanks are also due to one of my students, Brian Ferme, SDB, who gave the typescript a careful and critical scrutiny before it finally left my desk.

The mention of Brian leads me to thank all the Salesians of the Australian Province. Although my vocation to scholarship has caused me to be absent from my home province for eleven of the past thirteen years, their love, loyalty and support have shown me more than anything else that life in Christ is not just a preached doctrine, but an achievable reality. To them this book is dedicated.

Francis J. Moloney, SDB

I

The Religious in the Church

1. *The Universal Call to Sanctity*

It is well known that Vatican II gave more time and more documentation to the Religious life than any other previous Council of the Church. Not only did the Council Fathers issue a complete document on the renewal of Religious life *(Perfectae Caritatis)*,[1] but various other Conciliar documents also devoted space to the same question (see *Lumen Gentium* 43–7; *Christus Dominus* 33–5; *Sacrosanctum Concilium* 80, 98, 101; *Ad Gentes* 18, 40). The first number of *Perfectae Caritatis* describes Religious as: 'Men and women who strive to follow Christ more freely and imitate him more nearly by the practice of the evangelical counsels', hinting, by the use of the word 'more' that there is a comparison to be made between the Religious and 'the others'. Although this does not reflect the mind of the Council Fathers, there is a danger that the number might be understood as an indication that there is some sort of *qualitative* difference between the Religious life and the life of the other baptised who are attempting to imitate and follow Christ.[2]

When we turn, however, to *Lumen Gentium* we find that such a danger is very clearly avoided. Here there is no doubt about the teaching of the Council:

> The Lord Jesus, the divine Teacher and Model of all perfection, preached holiness of life to each and everyone of his disciples, regardless of their situation. . . Thus it is evident to everyone that all the faithful of Christ *of whatever rank or status* are called to the *fullness* of the Christian life and to the *perfection* of Charity *(Lumen Gentium* 40).[3]

It is interesting to notice what William Abbott, the editor of the English version of the documents, has to say in his note on this number:

Not only those who live according to the evangelical counsels but all Christians are called to 'the fullness of Christian life and to the perfection of Charity'. *It would be an error* to think of holiness as the special preserve of some one class of Christians, e.g. the religious.[4]

The same commentator makes a general remark on chapter 6 of *Lumen Gentium*: 'It deals with a *special manner* of following the *universal* call to holiness. The religious are not a third state in addition to the clergy and the laity.'[5]

With this teaching Vatican II buries once and for all some of the strongly held concepts of Religious life which have made Religious some sort of Gnostic stream within the Church, a group of *illuminati*, specially gifted people who had special calls, special means to holiness and above all a special privileged way to the perfection of love which was not available to the ordinary Christian. Many, in fact, have long argued that there is a 'qualitative' distinction between the Religious and the non-Religious.[6] It is well known that Vatican II refused to condemn anything, as Pope John XXIII insisted that the teaching of this council had to depart from the traditional form of condemnatory canons and present the wealth of the Catholic tradition in an exclusively positive sense.[7] I would suggest, however, that the positive statements which we have just considered are implicit condemnations of anyone who wishes to give Religious life a qualitatively superior standing within the context of the universal call to holiness.[8]

While the teaching of the Council is very clear on this question, and most contemporary works on the theology of the Religious life accept it as a point of departure,[9] many Religious, formed in a tradition which insisted that they were 'called to perfection', and many of the baptised who, in the midst of their 'worldly' concerns, see themselves as second-class citizens in the Kingdom, fail to grasp the significance of this very important premise for a correct under-standing of their particular vocation. As Christians, radically open to 'a word from the other side', we must listen carefully to God's Word on this question.[10] Of course, the Sacred Scriptures are not the *only* authoritative word of God through history.[11] We must also listen carefully to tradition, and my brief presentation of the state-ments from Vatican II has shown that the teaching Church has left

little room for doubt in this matter. Nevertheless, doubt still remains, and the pages that follow will be an attempt to show how contemporary biblical exegesis had led the Church to her present position. We must sketch out answers to two basic questions:
1. What is the biblical teaching on the call to sanctity?
2. Is there any biblical background for the traditional idea of the qualitative distinction between the Religious and the baptised?

THE BIBLICAL MESSAGE: A CALL TO UNIVERSAL HOLINESS

It should be said, at the outset of this section, that one should simply read the whole Bible to find this message. It is impossible to present all the evidence for this basic biblical idea; the biblical call to holiness is a universal call. I will have to limit myself to a few outstanding passages which show, even at a first reading, that God's call to his creation cannot be understood as 'more' for some and 'less' for others.

What was the original plan of God? There are several answers to the question since various Old Testament authors grappled with this fundamental problem. It is best summarised in a passage from Genesis which comes from the hand of the author of the last of the various traditions, both written and oral, which over many years were moulded together to produce the Pentateuch, Gen. 1.26–8:[12]

> Then God said, 'Let us make man in our image, after our like-ness; and let them have dominion over the fish of the sea, and over the birds of the air, and over the cattle, and over all the earth, and over every creeping thing that creeps upon the earth.' So God created man in his own image, in the image of God he created him; male and female he created them, and God blessed them.[13]

Men and women are created in the image of God, appointed lords over all creation and blessed by God. This is the vocation of *all men*, called to reproduce in themselves that image in which they were created. We know from Genesis 3 that man turned away from the original plan of God, and was separated from the very sense and purpose of his existence, but this does not alter man's basic structure and purpose. The whole of the history of salvation is the story of

God's continual intervention among men to call them back to his original purpose, until this is made an achievable reality by Jesus Christ. St Paul best summarises the situation when he writes to the Romans:

> As one man's trespass led to condemnation for all men, so one man's act of righteousness leads to acquittal and life for all men. For as by one man's disobedience many were made sinners, so by one man's obedience many will be made righteous (Rom. 5.18–19).

The matter at stake is too central to be conditioned by qualitative difference. Either man *is* created in the image of God and even in his sin offered the possibility of a restoration of that image 'in Christ' or he *is not*. There can be no notion of 'some more than others'!

With this ancient, but basic biblical teaching in mind, we can turn to see how the New Testament presents the situation of men and women who have God's image 'restored' in their lives through Jesus. Again we must go to a famous text which Paul wrote to the Romans:

> The creation waits with eager longing for the revealing of the sons of God; for the creation was subjected to futility, not of its own will but by the will of him who subjected it in hope; because the creation itself will be set free from its bondage to decay and obtain the glorious liberty of the children of God. We know that the whole creation has been groaning in travail together until now; and not only the creation, but we ourselves, who have the first fruits of the Spirit, groan inwardly as we wait for adoption as sons, the redemption of our bodies (Rom. 8.19–23).

This famous, and much discussed, Pauline passage is bristling with difficulties, and has been the source of a great deal of scholarly consideration.[14] For example:

What is meant by 'the creation'?

What does it mean to say that it is subjected to futility?

Who is the 'he' who subjected it – God himself, or some power of evil?

In what sense are those who already have the first fruits of the Spirit still 'groaning inwardly' in a way analogous to 'the creation' which 'has been groaning in travail until now'?

These are serious problems, but for our purposes the passage has a general sense which is quite clear, although my explanation already presupposes some answers to the questions which I have just posed. Not only does Paul see those of us who have been baptised (those who have the first fruits of the Spirit) as still struggling with the task in hand, but he extends this profound search for divine sonship to the whole of creation. The creation may mean only all men and women, but I believe that Paul presents the whole of creation as somehow unfulfilled. It will be in pain until it achieves 'the glorious liberty of the children of God'. Already in Genesis 3.14–19 does the Jahwist indicate that not only have men and women 'lost their way' in sin, but also the animals, the plants and the earth itself become rebellious. Only in the restoration of God's original plan can this disorder be set right. The redeeming activity of Christ does not only restore man, but also the whole of creation. A later follower of Paul, spelling out all the implications of Romans 8 will write:

> For he has made known to us in all wisdom and insight the mystery of his will, according to his purpose which he set forth in Christ as a plan for the fullness of time, to unite *all things* in him, things in heaven and things on earth (Eph. 1.9–10).[15]

Returning to Romans 8, it is important to notice the parallelism drawn between v.21: 'the creation itself will be set free from its bondage to decay and obtain the glorious liberty of the children of God,' and v.23: 'we ourselves, who have the first fruits of the Spirit, groan inwardly as we wait for the adoption as sons.' The second statement is a part of our experience. We, already graced by the presence of the Spirit through baptism and insertion 'into Christ', are still yearning for the fullness of life, which we believe will make ultimate sense out of life and death. Paul says in the first statement that the same destiny will eventually make sense of the whole of creation, at present so ambiguous in its beauty coupled with its continual tendency to lead us to sin and destruction.

This is a breathtaking and surprising vision of God's plan for

mankind and his world: all are destined to return to what God had
originally planned. As in Genesis, here there is no qualitative distinction. No one will be 'more' a son of God than any other. There
can be no special group inside the wider context of the baptised.
On the contrary, the whole of creation is called to a perfection
which can already be experienced by some who have been 'given'
the first fruits, but which will be finally enjoyed by all, in the
ultimate restoration of God's order.

Another 'Pauline' text which needs little comment is found in
Ephesians 1.3–6:

> Blessed be the God and Father of our Lord Jesus Christ, who
> has blessed us in Christ with every spiritual blessing in the
> heavenly places, even as he chose us in him before the foundation
> of the world, that we should be holy, and blameless before him.
> He destined us in love to be his sons through Jesus Christ,
> according to the purpose of his will, to the praise of his glorious
> grace which he freely bestowed on us in the Beloved.

This 'purple passage' is taken from the beautiful hymn which opens
the letter to the Ephesians and if this hymn belonged to the joyful
praises of the early Church, then it was a *community of baptised* who
sang it! They praised God, the Father of Jesus, because he had
called them to a fullness of life, a perfection which is now possible
through Jesus Christ. Paul, or his successor, or a community of
enthusiastic members of the early Church, had no concept of any
high-powered, special groups among the brethren. All were called
to: 'be holy and blameless before him in love'. This was the vocation
of the baptised!

We have glanced at three texts, but the whole of the Bible – and
especially the New Testament – is written in the belief that God
made man in his image, that man was culpable in going his own
way but that God persevered in his love and: 'so loved the world
that he gave his only Son, that whoever believes in him should
not perish, but have eternal life' (John 3.16). The only *qualitative*
distinction known by the New Testament is between those who
believe and those who do not believe – and here the gap is wide
– and tragic.

MATTHEW 19.16–22: THE SUPPOSED BIBLICAL BACKGROUND
FOR THE TRADITIONAL DISTINCTION BETWEEN THE
RELIGIOUS AND THE BAPTISED

If, as seems apparent, the biblical books know nothing of this 'way
of perfection' among the baptised, why has the idea been so central
in the history of Religious life? Is there any biblical background for
such a notion? At first sight, there certainly appears to be a very
clear 'proof text' in the Matthean version of the Rich Young Man
(Matt. 19.16–22).[16] The man asks what good deed he must do to
have eternal life, and Jesus answers that he must keep the commandments: the precepts of God from the Old Testament. When
the young man asks which particular precepts, Jesus gives a list of
commandments which are particularly concerned with his attention
to his neighbour: adultery, theft, false witness, honouring his parents
and loving his neighbour. A wealthy man may fulfill all the commandments as far as his ritual observance of religious practices is
concerned. His greatest temptation will be to offend his weaker
neighbour. The young man replies that he has always fulfilled these
commandments. It is important to notice that so far all that has
been asked of the young man is the fulfilment of Israel's Law,
known to us as the Ten Commandments. Matthew has used Exodus
20.12–16; Deuteronomy 5.16–20 and Leviticus 19.18. The Laws
cited all belong to the Word of God to Israel found in the Torah.
When the young man asks for something more, Jesus answers: 'If
you would be perfect, go, sell what you possess and give to the
poor, and you will have treasure in heaven; and come, follow me.'
No longer is Jesus asking the young man to live out the Jewish
commandments, but he is asking him to embrace poverty, and then
follow Jesus. This action is described as becoming 'perfect'.

What could be clearer? This has been long accepted as the classic
proof text that there are two qualitatively different ways of following
Jesus:[17]

1. The performance of the Commandments. This will bring the
Christian to eternal life (see vv. 16–17).

2. If anyone wants to be 'perfect', he must go a step further and
follow the evangelical counsel of religious poverty (see v. 21).

It would appear, then, that there is at least one very clear statement
in the New Testament of a qualitative distinction between the life
of those who are called to 'eternal life' by means of an observance

of the Commandments, and those who are called to the practice of the evangelical counsels, and thus to 'perfection'. This seems to contradict everything we have seen so far and thus merits our particular attention.

It is very important to remember that Matthew 19.16–22 is not a tape-recorded account of what Jesus said to the man, and Mark's account (10.17–22, closely followed by Luke 18.19–24) shows us that there were at least two versions of the story available for the early Church. The second point that we must remember is that Matthew wrote a Gospel, not just Matthew 19.16–22. The story of the rich young man has to be understood in the light of these two factors:

1.   What was the situation in Matthew's community which caused him to take up this story from Mark and use it in a slightly different way?

2.   How does the story fit into the theological message of the whole of Matthew's Gospel?

It is commonly agreed that Matthew's Gospel is written for a largely Jewish audience, and this conditions a great deal of the argument of the Gospel. One can imagine easily enough the pain of a group of Jews who found that their acceptance of Jesus of Nazareth as the Christ was the cause of their being ostracised by their fellow-Jews. Above all, it was the cause of their being prohibited from their synagogue worship. Thus they would have begun to wonder just who Jesus was in relation to a Law which had supported the life and faith of a people for 2,000 years. Was this now valueless? The question was probably put to them by their ex-friends from the Synagogue. One of Matthew's most serious problems was to show his Jewish Christians that Jesus had not done away with all that God had revealed in the Law, but he had brought it to its perfection. The clearest example of Matthew's technique in doing this is found in the Sermon on the Mount.[18] To start with, Matthew has Jesus going up onto a mountain (Matt. 5.1), while Luke has Jesus giving the same discourse 'on a level place' (Luke 6.17). Matthew deliberately presents Jesus as a law-giver in chapters 5–7 of his Gospel, but as Moses, the giver of the old law *received* the Law at Sinai, so Jesus, the new and perfect Moses *gives* the new and perfect Law on a new Sinai to a new people of God.

The major part of chapter 5 shows Jesus, the new law-giver,

presenting his Law over against the Law of Moses. Six times he quotes the old Law to them, introducing it with the phrase used by the Jewish Rabbis to quote the Law: 'You have heard that it was said to the men of old . . . ' (v.21) and similar fixed phrases (see vv. 27, 31, 33, 38, 43). After quoting from the Torah itself (Exod. 20.13; Deut. 5.17; Exod. 20.14; Lev. 19.12; Num. 30.31; Deut. 23.22; Exod. 21.24; Lev. 24.20; Deut. 19.21; Lev. 19.18), he then says; 'But I say to you . . . ' (see vv. 22, 28, 32, 34, 39, 44). It is important to notice that Jesus never *denies* the Law. He carries it much further, and asks of his followers that they do not stop at an external observance of the Law, but realise that they are called to the fullness of the law which must strike at the depths of their existence. In other words, vv. 21–47 are merely an application of what Jesus promised in v. 17: 'Think not that I have come to abolish the law and the prophets; I have come not to abolish them but to fulfill them' (see also vv. 18–20). In this way Jesus answers the problems of the Matthean Church. The Law has not been abolished, it is being brought to its fullness. Matthew uses a Greek word *plereō* to indicate Jesus' relation to the Law. The Christians are called to a 'fullness' which exceeds the righteousness of the Pharisees: 'Unless your righteousness exceeds that of the scribes and Pharisees, you will never enter the kingdom of heaven' (Matt. 5.20). It must be remembered that these 'scribes and Pharisees' were real people for Matthew's community in the 80s of the first century. They were 'the Synagogue across the street'[19] who refused to have them in their midst because of their belief in Jesus as the Christ. The solution of this problem was to show that the Christian was no longer called to observe the 'precepts' so carefully guarded by late first-century Judaism, but he was called to a 'fullness', a 'higher righteousness'. The radical nature of this 'higher righteousness' is summarised at the end of chapter 5 when Matthew rounds off his contrast between the Law of precept and the Law of Christ in v. 48: ' "You, therefore, must be perfect, as your heavenly Father is perfect." '[20] This remarkable statement takes us back to Matt. 19.16–22 where the Rich Young Man was also called to 'perfection'.

There are only two places in the whole of the Gospel of Matthew where the word 'perfect' (Greek: *teleios*) is found, in 5.48 and 19.21. We have just seen that the context of the first of these 'perfection' sayings (Matt. 5.17–48) is a continual presentation of the Law of

Moses brought to perfection in Jesus, and an indication of the radical nature of the vocation of all who would follow Christ to a 'higher righteousness' – a call to a radical 'perfection', as God is perfect. *Exactly* the same system is being used in Matt. 19.16–22. The Rich Young Man has fulfilled all the precepts. He is able to say honestly that as far as the Law of Moses is concerned, 'All these I have observed.' Jesus then calls him to 'perfection' as he calls all Christians to perfection. The condition which Jesus imposes is that he sell his goods and give to the poor. The significance of this condition will be given further consideration when we discuss the vow of poverty, but it must be said that *any* follower of Christ (see v. 21: 'and come, follow me') must abandon *any* obstacle that stands between himself and Jesus (see especially Matt. 8.21–2) and *this man's* problem was his riches. Matt. 19.16–22 is primarily a message about the radical nature of the faith required from anyone who wishes to embrace the 'perfection' which is to be found uniquely in the following of Christ. It is to do violence to Matthew's message to find here an example of 'precept Christians' and 'perfect Christians'. The Rich Young Man was not called to Religious life – but to Christian life, and Matthew calls that life, both in 5.48 and 19.21, a life of perfection.[21]

SOME CONCLUDING REMARKS

Even though we have looked only at some 'sample texts', it is important to notice where these various biblical passages came from. The text from Genesis 1 was from the Priestly tradition, which was attempting to summarise the whole of the Old Testament teaching on creation in an ordered and systematic way.[22] The Priestly work, itself based on ancient traditions, runs through the whole of the Pentateuch, tying it together, developing a logical (sometimes boringly over-logical as, for example, in the books of Leviticus and Numbers) re-statement in a later era (after the return from Babylon) of the religious thought of Israel which had been earlier worked out in the more moving and expansive narratives of the Jahwist and the Elohist (the creation story, the Joseph story and the exodus stories, for example). What is important for us is that Genesis 1.26–8 is a most valuable *summary* of Old Testament thought on creation.

Turning to the New Testament we went to the letter to the Romans. Again we are dealing with what could be called a major doctrinal statement. The letter to the Romans was written to a Church which Paul did not know. He does not appear to be doing battle with opponents, as he is, for example, in the letters to the Corinthians and Galatians. In Romans, more than anywhere else in Paul's letters, do we find the earliest Church's theological developments presented. Thus, in the mid-50s of the first century the Church's first major theologian has taken up the message of universal failure and death from the Old Testament to write now of the *universal* significance of the death and resurrection of Jesus, already participated in by the baptised, and eagerly awaited by the whole of creation.

The passage from Ephesians shows that Paul's thought was not betrayed. In this hymn from a church later in the first century, we find that the idea of a universal call to sanctity, made possible by the death and resurrection of Jesus, was not just the subject of theological preaching and writing, but it was caught up into their Christian hymns of praise. This is important as it shows how central the idea of a universal call to sanctity was to the apostolic and earliest Church.

Perhaps the latest document which we examined was the Gospel of Matthew.[23] We saw that the use of the term 'perfect' in this Gospel is important. It is used twice (5.48; 19.21) and on both occasions it is an indication of the radical nature of the Christian vocation. The vocation to perfection cannot be limited to a select few, but is the vocation of all who wish to follow Christ. Our texts have been few, but they have all been key texts, and we can be sure that they represent the heart of biblical thought on the universal call to sanctity.[24]

There is no need to labour this point any further as it should be clear from our summary presentation of Vatican II and a few central biblical passages. It must also be said that the point has generally been accepted by Religious Congregations (in theory, if not always in practice) since the Council. The problem, however, which has arisen sharply out of this biblical and conciliar teaching is: just what is the Religious all about if he or she is not called to a life of perfection which somehow makes him or her 'different' from the other members of the Church? In other words, over the last fifteen years we have experienced somewhat of an identity crisis.

Once we could claim that our identity could be found in the vows of poverty, chastity and obedience. However, as we will see in our examination of the classical biblical texts behind these 'evangelical counsels',[25] the Scriptures offer no foundation for the widespread idea that these three 'counsels' are the particular reserve of the Religious.[26] The impression used to be given that the married state was somewhat of a 'second-class' Christian life. Following a certain line of Patristic thought it was suggested that couples could almost become fully Christian in spite of being married. Now we seem to be faced with an equally ridiculous situation where some suggest that the Religious can almost become fully human, in spite of being celibate! This questioning attitude, of course, can have a positive effect as it forces us back to our sources (*Perfectae Caritatis* 2: the Gospel, our Founders and the needs of our times) to take a fresh look at the significance of a vowed life; but we all know bishops, priests and laity who practise the virtues of poverty, chastity and obedience *at least as well* as we Religious. Those of us who have lived the Religious life for some time have all had the experience of fellow-Religious for whom the vows may have been means of putting off the old man – only to put on the old woman!

The habit and a strictly literal observance of a written rule used to provide some sort of identity, and the loss of these things in recent years has been a cause of great pain to many.[27] No matter what one's persuasion is in these matters, liberal, conservative or 'middle of the way' (and there should be room for all of these opinions in a Church where the law of love is supposed to rule), to insist that the Religious must find his *identity* in the external sign of a habit and the public observance of a written law is to place him in the company of only one biblical group: the Pharisees, so roundly condemned in the Gospels (see especially Matt. 23.1–36).

As these traditional marks of the Religious – the vows, the habit, the rule – seem to be taking on a different function, it is clear that the identity of the Religious and his role in the Church cannot be found here. Many, therefore, turn to the apostolate, claiming that it is in nursing, teaching or social work etc. that a particular religious community finds its identity and plays a role in the Church and the world. Even here we must be realistic. The work can be done, and is being done, by lay people. Very often these lay people are far more professional than the Religious with whom they work, and the Religious discovers that even here he does not find that 'something special' which he is contributing to the Church and society. One then argues that it is in the fact that it is 'a Religious' who is doing the work which makes the difference, and here we are at the heart of the matter. This *should* be the case, and if it is, then we must go further back, behind the fact of the work which is being done, and ask *why* the Religious has 'something special' to offer, and *what* that 'something special' is. One does not have to be particularly observant to notice that in the midst of decreasing numbers and increasing work, some of us are so busy working that we simply do not have the time to ask just what the significance of our work *as Religious* might be. The rest of this book is an attempt to find that 'something special' by an examination of the biblical model against which, it appears to me, Religious life should be measured.

II
A God who Calls . . .

2. *The God of the Old Testament*

In any study of Religious life it is most important to consider the notion of 'religion'. This term can be defined in various ways, but there is a unifying element which stands behind all the definitions and, in fact, behind all the various forms of 'religion' that the history of mankind has known, from the most primitive to the most refined. All 'religions' attempt to find an answer to the deepest needs and questions of men and women – birth, love, death, suffering, joy, ambition, hope, failure, depression etc. – by turning to some explanation which lies outside a man's immediate control. In other words, they all look to some sort of transcendent principle which governs the deepest longings and experience of mankind. Although the names given to this principle are manifold, we can justifiably say that all 'religions' look to gods, goddesses or a god or goddess.

This may appear to be a serious digression from the task in hand, but I am convinced that one of the basic reasons for the current difficulties in both Christian and Religious life and practice is that we have lost touch with our God. By 'our God' I necessarily mean the God of the Bible. As Christians we are followers of Christ, and as followers of Christ we must necessarily find the sense of our lives, as he did, in the God who sent him, the God of the Old Testament, whom Jesus called 'Father' (see especially Matt. 11.25–7; Luke 10.21–2). Not only did he call God 'Father' but he brought about a new situation in which we also can now turn to that God and call him 'Father' (see especially Matt. 6.7–15; Luke 11.2–4. See also Mark 11.25–6; Gal. 4.1–7). Our God is the 'Father' of Jesus – the God of the Bible whom Jesus has revealed to us as a unique creating, loving and saving 'Father'. This is the God who created us and calls us to himself. Unless we keep this God and his demands continually before us, we will rapidly fall into 'the ways of the other peoples'. Thus, as a basis for any consideration of Christian, and therefore, Religious life, we must preface our more specific considerations of community, vows and discipleship with the question of God.[1]

THE GOD OF ABRAHAM: GENESIS 12.1–3

We have already seen that the book of Genesis must not be read as a 20th-century history book, as our written accounts are the product of a long literary development. This has led some scholars to pay little attention to the historical aspects of the Patriarchal stories.[2] They claim that these stories are the later imaginative reconstructions of the past by a people, already settled in the land of Israel, who had the experience of a faith in one God whom they called 'Jahweh'.[3] Despite this school of thought, there is every reason to believe that the traditions which stand behind the Patriarchal stories of Gen. 12–50 come from ancient traditions and that they were already in their present form as early as the 10th century BC. It would be out of place to discuss the literary and historical questions which lead many scholars to this conclusion,[4] but we can claim to be on safe ground in maintaining that Abraham was a historical individual who, as the head of a clan, migrated from Upper Mesopotamia to the land of Canaan. He set out on this extraordinary adventure because he believed that he was called to do so, and that he was protected by a unique God. This God will later (as in Gen. 12.1–3) be called Jahweh, but that Abraham moved in obedience to a call from a God can hardly be questioned.

This event, which took place somewhere between the 19th and 17th century BC, is seen by the biblical authors as the starting point of a divine revelation, the first act of the God of Israel in the history of the salvation of mankind. No Semite of the second millenium BC would dream of risking the radical change of life involved in abandoning his home and pastures unless he felt the overwhelming presence and protection of a God. So must it have been for Abraham.

However, there was something unique about the call and the response of Abraham, and this uniqueness is caught by Gen. 12.1–3. It is well known that Gen. 1–11 forms a prologue, not only to Genesis, but to the whole of the biblical story. These beautiful chapters tell us of a creating God, the origins of man and woman and the nature and consequences of their sin, in an inspired use of the myths of the Near East.[5] This section of Genesis is a profound theological statement, without parallel in its contemporary literature, about the origin and purpose of man, largely told by the oldest theologian of the Bible, the Jahwist, and finally edited by the school responsible for the final form of the Pentateuch, the Priestly School. We must be careful, however, not to separate Gen. 1–11 from Gen. 12 as they belong together. Throughout Gen. 1–11 the theme of 'promise' – fall – a gesture of grace' has been continually developed:[6]

1. Adam and Eve sin and are banished from paradise, *but* God gives them clothing and promises that the offspring of the woman will do battle with the serpent (Gen. 3).

2. Cain is jealous and kills his brother Abel, *but* he is given a sign which will prevent his being killed (Gen. 4).[7]

3. In the deluge God destroys a wicked and sinful world which, marked by sin, has turned away from him, *but* in Noah, God shows his mercy, grace and the promise of a new covenant (Gen. 5–10).

4. The story of the Tower of Babel is again the account of man's pride and sinfulness, *but* Gen. 12.1–3 begins a further story, the story of God's gracious intervention in the history of mankind (Gen. 11).

It appears to me that the Jahwist did not intend chapters 1–11 to be read as 'the brute facts' of history. Once we have recognised the pattern of fall and a gracious reply from God, then it appears probable that Gen. 1–11 is above all a systematic use of current myths to present a unique God who saves in the midst of failure. It is the same Jahwist who concludes his account of the primeval drama with the story of the Tower of Babel – pride, ambition and sin, leading to the division and scattering of men across the face of the earth. Where is God's gracious reply to this fall? In *history*, especially in the history of God's presence among his chosen people which the Jahwist begins with Gen. 12.1–3.

Let us now analyse Gen. 12.1–3 to find out what sort of a God reveals himself to Abraham. I will set out the text in a structured form, as this will make the author's point much clearer:

Now Jahweh said to Abraham:

(a)   'Go from *your* country
                    and *your* kindred
                    and *your* father's house

to the land which

(b)   *I* will show you
                        and *I* will make of you a great nation
                        and *I* will bless you
                        and *I* will make your name great
        so that you will be a blessing
                        I will bless those who bless you
        and him who curses you *I* will curse;
        and by you all the families of the earth
        shall bless themselves.'

Notice that all the elements which Abraham had gained ('your') for his own security are the usual elements which were the yardstick for the wealth and power of a Mesopotamian landowner of the second millenium BC: family, land and beasts, a father's house. In short, Abraham is asked to abandon his human security. In place of this security Jahweh offers a security which must come uniquely from him (the continual repetition of 'I'): a promised land, father of a nation, blessings, a great name, a blessing for those who bless Abraham and punishment for those who curse him. All of these promises could well have been achieved by a powerful man by virtue of his own efforts. By his own power, authority or wealth he could possess land, show forth his manliness by his fertility and see to it himself that others were blessed or punished, according to their acceptance or refusal of his authority, power and wealth. Abraham, however, is commanded: no longer is this to be your way. If you will be obedient to me, your God, I will see to it!

Here, for the first time, since the Fall, God and man enter into an 'I-thou' relationship. Among the religions of the Near East this was impossible. The gods and goddesses were distant and impersonal and had to be appeased and besought with rites and sacrifices. Not so here. Jahweh does not simply proclaim or predict. He calls upon Abraham as 'Thou' and promises as 'I'. A God who is a person treats Abraham as a person. He is asked to co-operate in the plan of Jahweh, and this plan is entirely for Abraham's benefit and the benefit of 'all the families of the earth'.[8] There is no indication that Jahweh will gain any profit from the pact which is being established. Again this is an extraordinarily new concept of God. In the Mesopotamian and Egyptian myths it is always the God who is the beneficiary. Even the victories of the Assyrian Kings were not for the benefit of the King, but the means of glorifying (and appeasing) the vengeful power of the god Assur.

The God of Abraham enjoys an unrestricted freedom of action, both at the time of Abraham, to whom he makes his explicit promises, and for all the future, as Abraham is told that 'by you all families of the earth shall bless themselves.' Eventually the plan of Jahweh could affect all mankind. However, we must stress that this God Jahweh calls for a 'loss of self' right from his very first intervention in history. All that Abraham would have seen as his security, his land, family and house, must be left behind. It is not the works and achievements of the 'I' of Abraham that ultimately matter, but the trust and hope which he places in a 'Thou' called Jahweh.

This same point of view is again expressed in another famous passage, Gen. 15.5–6:[9] 'And Jahweh brought him outside and said "Look toward heaven, and number the stars, if you are able to number them." Then he said to him, "So shall your descendants be." And he believed Jahweh, and Jahweh reckoned it to him as righteousness.' Here Jahweh gives a command and makes a far-reaching promise (v. 5). The choice of the skies and the stars is neither mere poetry nor practical – it is used because ancient man looked to the blackness of the sky and the stars blinking through the blackness as a source of great wonder and mystery, surely the domain of the gods. Jahweh subjects this mystery to himself by using it as an example for the splendour which would come to Abraham if he would take the risk of accepting the promise of the God who was dealing with him in a unique 'I-thou' relationship. He does, and the development of this relationship between Abraham and his God make up the rest of the story of the Old Testament, and is prolonged into the New Testament. Indeed, perhaps the best summary of all that I have been trying to say is found in Hebrews 11.8–10:

> By faith Abraham obeyed when he was called to go out to a place which he was to receive as an inheritance; and he went out, not knowing where he was to go. By faith he sojourned in the land of promise, as in a foreign land . . . For he looked forward to the city which has foundations, whose builder and maker is God.

For the first time a God comes forward as a person who enters into an 'I-thou' relationship with man. The consequences are risky from man's point of view: faith and commitment to a unique God of history, with the subsequent loss of self, possessions, authority and the glory among men which comes from human achievement. The God of Abraham is a truly personal God who makes himself known to the man of his choice, and that man will discover his God only in the loss of himself.

JAHWEH: THE GOD OF ISRAEL (EXODUS 3.13–15)

Our study of Abraham's encounter with his God was often phrased in terms of 'Jahweh', as both of the passages (Gen. 12.1–3; 15.5–6) come from the Jahwist account. However, these stories were *written* by the Jahwist in the 10th–9th century BC, telling of events which happened between 2000 and 1700 BC. The Fathers of Israel certainly did not call their God 'Jahweh', but most probably 'El Shaddai'.[10] However, by the time the Jahwist came to write, a profound development had taken place in the faith of Israel. Now there was only one God, and his name was Jahweh. If we can understand what that name meant for Israel, then we will understand Israel's concept of God.

We must, of course, examine Exod. 3.14 where, in answer to Moses' request God reveals himself as 'I am who am'. There are many books and articles on this subject, but we will have to limit ourselves to an attempt to see what the name 'Jahweh' meant for the faith of Israel.[11]

Again, to bring out the most salient points I will give the texts of Exod. 3.13–15 in a structured form:

Moses: 'I shall go to the children of Israel and say
to them:
The God of your fathers sends me
    and they shall ask
"What is his name?"
    "What shall I say to them?" ' '

Jahweh: '*I am who am*

Thou shalt say:
"*I am* sends me"
Thou shalt say:
"*Jahweh, the God of your fathers,*
the God of Abraham, the God of Isaac
and the God of Jacob sends me."
This is my name forever;
thus shall I be named
from generation to generation' (Author's Translation).

There are two very important aspects which we must point out immediately:

1. The writer is at pains to show that the God who reveals a new name to Moses is the God of Abraham. The opening words of Moses already indicate that he recognises that he is dealing with 'The God of your fathers', and in v. 15 the words of God himself spell this out in greater detail: 'The God of Abraham, the God of Isaac and the God of Jacob.' There must be no room for doubt here. Israel does not change its allegiance from a God of the Patriarchs to a God called Jahweh. It is the same God, but he reveals himself further by means of a new name: Jahweh.

2. This new name comes from the Hebrew verb 'to be' (*hyh*). God, speaking in the first person singular, speaks of himself as 'I am'. Israel, speaking of that God in the third person singular, must call him 'he who is'. Thus, it is from the Hebrew verb 'to be' that we arrive at the name 'Jahweh'.[12]

On other occasions in the Old Testament, God refuses to give his name: on Jacob's encounter with the stranger at the Jabok (Gen. 32.23–32. See esp. v. 29) and in Manoah's vision of an angel before the birth of Samson (Judges 13. See esp. vv. 17–18). Jacob, Manoah and Moses all ask for the name of the visitor, but only Moses receives an answer. Moses recognises from the start of his encounter that he is dealing with God. In Exod. 3.6 he is already told: 'I am the God of thy fathers', and Moses hid his face, not daring to look. Moses' problem was not that he did not recognise God – but he wanted 'a name'. There is something tremendously new in this revelation. If Moses had said to his people: 'The God of your fathers sends me' (v. 13) the people would have wanted to know more. They want to know his 'name'. The question would not be 'Who is he?', as they were familiar with the God of the Patriarchs. Something more was needed now as the usual name 'El Shaddai' was not enough. 'As El Shaddai this God has certainly guided and helped the patriarchs (see Exod. 6.3), but he had apparently left the descendants of the Patriarchs in Egypt for four centuries without help.'[13]

At the time when this account came to be written down, the God of Israel was called Jahweh, but from the distant past Israel recalls the events of the Exodus, the encounter with their unique God in the desert, and the formation of the people of God in and through that desert experience. It is through this experience that Israel discovered a God called Jahweh, and the revelation of this name has been placed within the context of that all-important moment in the history of God's people.

The God Jahweh 'is', i.e. 'I am who am' is an ever-present and active God among his people. Those heedless of God's commands would claim 'There is no God' (Ps. 10.4), but the God 'Jahweh' *is* always. Jahweh's *being* was an active and effective state of being present, a presence made clear by his actual intervention in the affairs of men to such an extent that Israel came to see Jahweh as a God who ultimately saved the good and punished the wicked (see, among the many examples, Judges 7.21; Joel 2.17; Pss. 41.4; 78.10; II Kings 2.14 and especially the encounter between the arrogant Sennacherib and Jahweh in II Kings 19.8–19).

Yet, 'I am who am' is not really a name which can be grasped and dominated by men or the affairs of men. Jahweh is, despite his active presence in the lives of men and women, a transcendent God. His very 'name' escapes the categories of men. This absolute independence of Jahweh is central to the Old Testament concept of God. He is never a God to whom one can dictate terms, whom one can cajole or lead. Ultimately, he is in no way dependent upon what men can do. He is always before Israel, calling them away from themselves towards himself. He was, and always remains, a God of the Exodus. As this is the case, the conflict with the 'other Gods', especially in the book of Isaiah, but throughout the Prophets, is really no conflict at all. All 'the other Gods' are ultimately subject to human whims and fancies, but Jahweh transcends all this:

For what he hath cast is false,

and there is no spirit in them.
They are vain things and a ridiculous work:
in the time of their visitation they shall perish.
The portion of Jacob is not like these:
for it is he who formed all things
and Israel is his tribe and inheritance.
Jahweh of hosts is his name (Jer. 10.14–16, see vv. 3–16 and the
whole of Isa. 43–6).

Thus, the name 'Jahweh' – 'I am who am' – is, at the same time
'there' and 'not there'. He can be experienced in all the events of
mankind, but he cannot be limited to these events:

> The fact that Jahweh is not and cannot be defined serves to
> accentuate, all the more strongly, the one thing that can be said
> positively about Jahweh – the fact that he 'is'. And, in the Bible,
> Jahweh's 'being' is nothing more or less than his all-embracing
> and all permeating immanence. Jahweh was a God far off, and
> a God at hand (see Jer. 23.23). Israel's faith in God was, so to
> speak, suspended between the opposite poles of divine transcend-
> ence and divine immanence.[14]

Cardinal Ratzinger has stressed the new 'availability' of God
which is expressed in Exod. 3.15. Reacting to the traditional use of
this passage as a 'proof text' for the philosophical understanding of
God's being,[15] he writes that the 'naming' of God was 'not so much
expressing his inner nature as making himself nameable; he is
handing himself over to men in such a way that he can be called
upon by them. And by doing this he enters into a co-existence with
them, he puts himself within their reach, he is "there" for them.'[16]
However, to this we must add that when Israel finds him 'there',
she finds a demanding God who insists that she must shed all
pretensions and the desire to 'be like the other nations'. They must
be led uniquely by Jahweh, a God at hand, but also a God whom
they cannot grasp, a transcendent God of the desert experience who
leads them into a future which only he can determine.

This notion of God is manifested with remarkable consistency
throughout the whole of the Old Testament, through historical
writings, poetry, wisdom literature and the legal books. This hap-

pened because the God of Israel's faith was a God called 'Jahweh'. It has been worked out most systematically (and one could almost say that it is the major thesis of the book) in Deuteronomy where the themes of a 'present', loving God, but a demanding, all-powerful and transcendent God, run side by side.[17]
A few passages must suffice:

> For what great nation is there that has a god so near to it as Jahweh our God is to us, whenever we call upon him? (Deut. 4.7)

> Take heed to yourselves, lest you forget the covenant of Jahweh your God . . . for Jahweh your God is a devouring fire, a jealous God (Deut. 4.23–4).

THE EXPERIENCE OF JAHWEH'S PRESENCE (JER. 20.7–13)

Thus far we have glanced briefly at two major expressions of Israel's faith: the God of Abraham and Jahweh, the God of Moses and the Exodus. Before concluding we must, however briefly, glance at an example of the active presence of this God among his faithful ones. There are many passages of the Old Testament which could be used, the book of Job or some of the Psalms (see, for example, Pss. 8;22;41 which come immediately to mind), but we must limit ourselves to the experience of one of the most sensitive of the sons of Israel: the prophet Jeremiah.[18] In his famous 'confessions' (Jer. 11.18–23; 12.1–6; 15.10–21; 17.9–10; 17.14–18; 18.18–23; 20.7–13) the prophet bares his soul. These passages were not written for a public. They are the attempts of a poet, as well as a prophet of Jahweh, to understand the mysteriously demanding, ever-present but ever calling further into pain, difficulty and persecution, not-to-be-escaped God of Israel. We have seen that God revealed himself as such in Gen. 12.1–3 and Exod. 3.13–16. In Jer. 20.7–13 we will find the action of that God in the life of his faithful one.

All of the confessions were written during the reign of King Jehoiakim (608–598 BC), a frivolous and despotic character who would not be crossed. Jeremiah was called to preach God's ever-demanding word – and he was forever at cross-purposes with Jehoiakim who wanted the prophet to preach what he wanted to hear. In this situation Jeremiah wrote a scroll condemning the current rule in Judah. He dictated this scroll to Baruch and it eventually came into the hands of Jehoiakim. The king threw it furiously into the fire and attempted to lay hands upon the prophet (see chapter 36). From that moment on Jeremiah's life was in danger and he faced a series of unmerited, humiliating punishments at the hands of Pashhur, the superintendent of the Temple: a night in the stocks, banned from the Temple etc. . . . (see chapters 7–20). It is during this period that the prophet, in the midst of his anguish, wrestles with God in deep, heart-searching prayer.

Once we have grasped this background, the text hardly needs comment:

> O Lord, thou hast deceived me, and I was deceived;
> thou art stronger than I, and thou hast prevailed.
> I have become a laughingstock all the day;
> every one mocks me.
> For whenever I speak, I cry out, I shout,
> 'Violence and destruction!'
> For the word of Jahweh has become for me
> a reproach and derision all day long (20.7–8).

The lament arises out of Jeremiah's consciousness that his words and actions flow from his dependence upon Jahweh. Under the pain of the scorn which his hearers heap upon him he feels that Jahweh has seduced him, leading him away from the proper course of action in the eyes of men, because of his overwhelming presence. It is important to notice that Jeremiah's suffering comes about 'because of the word of Jahweh' (v. 8). 'If I say "I will not mention him, or speak any more in his name," there is in my heart as it were a burning fire shut up in my bones, and I am weary with holding it in, and I cannot' (20.9). Whenever he yielded to the temptation to keep silent, the word of Jahweh burnt within him like a fire. It could not be contained. Jahweh, as we have already seen, will not be dictated to. He will lead, and the faithful one will ultimately go where Jahweh wills. Jeremiah 'stands under the divine compulsion'.[19] 'For I hear many whispering. Terror is on every side! "Denounce him! Let us denounce him!" say all my familiar friends, watching for my fall. "Perhaps he will be deceived, then we can

overpower him, and take our revenge upon him" '(20.10). Here we
have a closer description of the situation of the prophet. There was
a malicious whispering campaign being carried on against him in
Jerusalem, and he is constantly under suspicion. Those who were
once his friends are now attempting to catch him out. Overpowered
by Jahweh he has preached and written a scathing criticism of
contemporary Jerusalem and he has condemned the Judean leaders
in Jahweh's name. Now they await their opportunity to catch him
out and to humiliate and denounce this preacher of God's
righteousness:

> But Jahweh is with me as a dread warrior;
> therefore my persecutors will stumble,
> they will not overcome me.
> They will be greatly shamed, for they will not succeed.
> Their eternal dishonour will never be forgotten.
> Sing to Jahweh; praise Jahweh!
> For he has delivered the life of the needy
> from the hand of evildoers (20.11,13)[20].

Now we come to see the other side of Jahweh, Jeremiah's God. The
prophet concludes his confession with a profound confidence in that
same Jahweh who had seduced him. Jahweh transcends! Yes, he
had called Jeremiah away from all that he would see as basic to his
human security (as he called Abraham from Ur, and Israel from
Egypt) so that he could experience the mystery of a God whom he
could never fully grasp and understand. This was the cause of the
anguish expressed in vv. 7–10. However, that is not the end of the
experience of Jeremiah. Jahweh is also a God who is near at hand,
a God who 'is available'! However strong the forces lined up against
Jeremiah may have been, still stronger was the prophet's consciousness of the presence of Jahweh in his life, and he compares his God
to a powerful warrior who will put down the evil ones and raise up
the needy.

It is a profound consciousness of this God which, as Luke opens
his story of the appearance of Jesus among men, we find the Mother
of Jesus proclaiming:

> He has put down the mighty from their thrones,

and exalted those of low degree;
He has filled the hungry with good things
and the rich he has sent empty away. (Luke 1.52–3)[21]

The God of the Old Testament does not cease to exist and act among his people with the appearance of John the Baptist. On the contrary! We must turn now to see in what way Jesus of Nazareth calls those who wish to follow him to an even more radical commitment to the God who asks us: ' "Am I a God at hand", says Jahweh, "and not a God afar off? Can a man hide himself in secret places so that I cannot see him?" says Jahweh. "Do I not fill heaven and earth?" says Jahweh' (Jer. 23.23–4).

3. *The New Testament: God is Love*

The New Testament presupposes the fundamental concepts and consciousness of a God which we have traced in the Old Testament, but there is, of necessity, an all-important newness. In the Old Testament God revealed himself through his active presence in the affairs of Israel, and through the prophets who announced: 'This is the word of Jahweh'; in the New Testament the Word has become flesh, and has dwelt among us (John 1.14).

While the study of the New Testament is full of scholarly difficulties and varying opinions (some of which we will meet as we progress further) there is universal agreement that Jesus of Nazareth revealed the God of Israel, whom he called 'Father', in a unique and 'once and for all' way (see Rom. 6.10; I Cor. 15.6; Heb. 7.27; 9.12; 10.10).[1]

In order to present a coherent picture, and not to lose the reader in a variety of texts and opinions, I will limit my consideration of the God of the New Testament to one of the last of the New Testament documents, the Fourth Gospel. I believe that there is nothing in the concept of God in this Gospel which is not a coherent development along a trajectory which ran from Jesus of Nazareth into the earliest Church. This was carried further by the theological reflections of Paul, Mark, Matthew and Luke, and is probably most clearly spelt out in the Fourth Gospel.[2] The relationships which existed between the communities which produced these various writings are difficult, probably impossible, to establish, but the Fourth Evangelist in no way betrays the teaching of Jesus, Paul, Mark, Matthew and Luke. They all present Jesus as a Son of God. In all of the New Testament books Jesus' relationship with his Father is of vital importance.[3] John stands at the conclusion of this fundamental, but developing, consciousness in the earliest Church, and his Gospel depends entirely on Jesus' being the Son of God (see especially John 3.16–21; 5.19–30).[4]

THE FOURTH GOSPEL

John's Gospel was written in the last decade of the first century for a largely Jewish community which had been 'cast out' of the Synagogue (see 9.34) because they believed that the Messiah had already come in the person of Jesus of Nazareth. In John 9 the drama of the whole of the Johannine community is played by the man born blind. After the man has had his sight given to him (vv. 6–7), 'the Jews' (see v. 18; this group forms the opposition to Jesus throughout the Gospel[5]) call for evidence from the parents of the man. They do this in an attempt to prove that the man was never blind, and that Jesus was therefore an impostor. Naturally, in the case of someone *born* blind, the best people to interrogate are the parents who bore him (vv. 18–23).[6] The parents have to admit that he was born blind (v. 20), but they are in no way prepared to compromise themselves by saying that Jesus had given their son sight (v. 21). The Evangelist then comments, reflecting the situation of his own Church: 'His parents said this because they feared the Jews, for the Jews had already agreed that if anyone should confess him to be Christ, he was to be put out of the synagogue' (v. 22). In fact, when the man who was once blind tells the Jews that Jesus must be 'from God' (v. 33) they heap abuse upon him 'and cast him out' (v. 34. See also 12.42 and 16.2). The Johannine community, committed to faith in Jesus of Nazareth, had to cross the threshold from the old and sacred ways of Judaism which they had loved and in which they had been brought up, into a strange new cosmopolitan world in Asia Minor in which they now had to live their Christian faith. This world was full of many religious creeds and cults which the blending of Greek, Roman and more eastern religions produced in Asia Minor in the first century.

Faithful to the message of the life of the historical Jesus, the Johannine community, like all the other communities of the early Church, had to believe and preach the ridiculous message of a God who became a man, a man who had been crucified, or as the Johannine community preferred to say, a man who had been 'lifted up' on a cross. The Greek world had its own ideas about incarnate deities. Generally one of the hierarchy of gods merely 'pretended' to take on human form – very often for some sort of sexual motive – but they only 'seemed' or 'appeared' (Greek: *dokeō*) to be human. They could never be regarded as truly incarnate, and there could

never be the idea of a god 'giving himself' so that mere men might
have life. No Greek god could become a man to such an extent that
he could suffer death on a cross. Some would be prepared to accept
that Jesus 'appeared' to have done so, and thus the heresy of
'docetism' is born. In the midst of these currents of thought, John
insisted that 'the Word became flesh and dwelt among us,' and that
'we have beheld his glory' (1.14).

At I John 1.1–4 he argues very strongly for the *human* Jesus:

> That which was from the beginning, which we have heard, which
> we have *seen with our eyes*, which we have *looked upon* and *touched
> with our hands*, concerning the word of life – the life was *made
> manifest*, and we *saw it*, and testify to it, and proclaim to you the
> eternal life which was with the Father and was made *mani-
> fest to us*.

Through a long series of very concrete, human and visual expressions, the author insists that God has manifested himself in the
unique but eminently human event of Jesus of Nazareth.[7]

WHAT SORT OF GOD?

It was not enough, however, simply to affirm the fact that Jesus
was the human revelation of God, as John's audience would quickly
run on to the question which logically follows that affirmation: Why
did God act in this way? What sort of God would do such a strange
thing? Gods do not reveal themselves by sending their sons to a
cross! The answer to these questions is to be found in John's presentation of God as a God who is love. As he also tells us in his first
letter: 'He who does not love does not know God; for God is love'
(I John. 4.8. See also 4.16). The whole of the Johannine literature
(the Gospel and the Letters) has a basic conviction about God: God
is love.

This must be our point of departure in our attempt to understand
the God of the New Testament. This so-called 'definition' of God
is the only such 'definition' in the whole of the New Testament.[8]
No other author of the early Church attempts to describe God.
They write about how God has acted in and through Jesus of
Nazareth. It must also be admitted that John does not really

describe him either, as a definition in terms of 'love' is hardly a reduction of God to our categories. We would do John a grave injustice if we were to think that this 'definition' was all he gave us. He certainly arrived at his understanding of God as a God of love only after a long and profound experience of the significance of Jesus. He too was primarily concerned with what God did in and through Jesus. If Jesus, sent by a God whom he called Father, had spent his life in an attempt to reveal the sense and purpose of life and love to mankind then, John must have concluded, the Father who sent him, whom Jesus sought to reveal, must be love.[9] But even if John and his community arrived at this explicit statement about God as a consequence of their reflection upon Jesus, we must work in the opposite direction, and take it as our starting point: God is love. With this premise it is possible to trace John's thought and argument about who God is, what he does in and through Jesus, and how we are to respond.

Early in the Fourth Gospel there is a passage which almost summarises John's thought. In fact, scholars have called this passage 'a miniature Gospel'.[10] 'God so loved the world that he gave his only Son, that whoever believes in him should not perish, but have eternal life' (3.16). God is love, but love can never remain some inner virtue. So must it also be with God. The love of God could not simply remain some part of the inner life of the God of the Bible. If it were thus, it could hardly be called love. Love necessarily shows itself, and a God who *is* love moves into action when he shows that he loves the world[11] so much that he gives his only Son so that those who believe in him may come to eternal life. Over the centuries, particularly in the scholastic debates, there has been a great deal of discussion over the 'motive for the Incarnation'. This means that scholars argued over various explanations of just why the Incarnation took place. In the theology of the Fourth Evangelist there is only one possible solution. The Incarnation took place because a God who is love loved the world *so much* that he gave his only Son. It is not as if God grudgingly conceded something to the world, but he 'gave' his Son . . . he freely handed him over.[12] This 'giving' of the Son, however, is for a purpose. By our acceptance or refusal of what Jesus reveals – and we shall shortly see what that is – we either perish or have eternal life. A new possibility is offered to all men: we can now come to 'life'. All of this has been made possible because a God who is defined as love has shown his love. He has shown, in Jesus, just how much he loves the world.

JESUS: THE REVEALER OF A GOD WHO IS LOVE

Throughout the Fourth Gospel, Jesus speaks of his 'task' (see 4.34; 5.36; 6.29; 9.4; 10.25,32,37; 14.10–12; 15.24). As he begins his public ministry he announces: ' "My food is to do the will of him who sent me, and to accomplish (Greek: *teleiōsō*[13]) his work" ' (4.34). At the conclusion of his ministry, speaking in the context of the upper room as if everything had already been accomplished, he prays to his Father: 'I glorified thee on earth, having accomplished (Greek: *teleiōsas*) the work which thou gavest me to do' (17.4). Just what was this 'work' of Jesus, which he felt that he had somehow 'accomplished'? He explains it himself as he prays to his Father: 'Thou hast given (the Son) power over all flesh, to give eternal life to all whom thou hast given him. And this is eternal life, that they know thee, the only true God' (17.2–3). The task of Jesus was to make God known, or in our theological terminology, to reveal God. The whole purpose of the presence of Jesus among men, according to the Fourth Gospel, is to reveal God to them. Nobody from among men has ever seen God, yet we have a desperate need to come to know our God. It is Jesus who makes him known: 'No one has ever seen God; the only Son who is turned in loving union towards the Father, he has made him known' (1.18).[14]

If God is love, and the task of the Son is to make this God known, then somehow he must reveal 'love'. There are basically two ways in which Jesus reveals this God of love: he speaks about him in his discourses, and he lives a life which shows what love is all about. Jesus reveals the Father in word and action. One can talk about love forever, and never make an impression, but if the one who speaks of love also loves greatly, then his message will make sense and will have an impact. For this reason, the highest moment, the climax of Jesus' revelation of his Father as 'love' does not lie in something which he *said*, but in something which he *did*. The high point of Jesus' revelation of a God who is love is described in John 15.13–14: 'Greater love has no man than this, that a man lay down his life for his friends. You are my friends.' Because the total gift of self for the other is the greatest sign of love, the Cross of Jesus is the climax of God's revelation of love. The Cross, in the Fourth Gospel, is not a place of misery, suffering, humiliation and sorrow (as it is, for example, in Mark's passion story, or in Phil. 2.5–11), but it is, above all, the place where Jesus is 'lifted up'. Three times in this Gospel Jesus speaks of his death as a 'lifting up':

> As Moses lifted up the serpent in the wilderness, so must the Son of Man be lifted up, that whoever believes in him may have eternal life (John 3.14–15)[15].

> When you have lifted up the Son of Man, then you will know that I am he (8.28).

> Now is the judgement of this world, now shall the ruler of this world be cast out; and I, when I am lifted up from the earth, will draw all men to myself (12.31-2).

Just in case the reader still has not grasped what Jesus means when speaks of the necessity of his being 'lifted up', the Evangelist adds a short note of his own, explaining to the reader, after this third reference to the 'lifting up' that the Cross is being announced: 'He said this to show by what death he was to die' (12.33). The 'lifting up' is not some sort of human glorification. It is the moment of a physical lifting up on a stake. However, John deliberately uses a word which has two meanings. The Greek verb 'to lift up' (*hupsoō*) also means 'to exalt'. In Jesus' prophecies of his death on the Cross through a 'lifting up' we are already given a hint that this death is, somehow, something more than a death.

What this 'something more' is finds further expression in the beautiful passage which opens the Johannine version of the last supper: 'Now before the feast of the Passover, when Jesus knew that his hour had come to depart out of this world to the Father, having loved his own who were in the world, he loved them to the end' (13.1). This statement from the Evangelist comes at the beginning of the second half of the Gospel, commonly called 'the book of glory'. In this part of the Gospel the meaning of Jesus' death, his being 'lifted up', is first explained in chapters 13–17 (the last discourse) and then it takes place in chapters 18–20 (the passion and resurrection). His glorification in death has a meaning for Jesus

and also for us. Both of these elements are summarised in this
opening statement to the book of glory. The 'hour' has come. The
moment of death, the lifting up to glory on the Cross is at hand,
but it is also the 'hour' through which Jesus passes over to the
Father. In and through the Cross Jesus returns to where he was
before (see 6.62 and 17.5). This is what it means for Jesus, but what
does it mean for us? We are told here: it is the moment when we
shall see that Jesus loves 'his own' to the very end. The phrase 'to
the very end' (Greek: *eis telos*) does not have, primarily, a chrono-
logical sense. It is an indication of the quality of the love that is
revealed. In his hour of the Cross Jesus shows a love which is
completely without limit, without measure. When, at the end, Jesus
bows his head in death and pours out his Spirit, he is able to
proclaim: 'It has been accomplished' (Greek: *tetelesthai*). Earlier we
found that Jesus saw his role as the accomplishment of the task
which the Father had given him. That task was to reveal God, his
Father, a God of love, to the world. Now he claims that he has
accomplished his task. We have seen that Jesus continually looked
forward to this accomplishment, speaking of it as the fulfilment, the
very end, the perfection of all that he was called to do, using a
Greek word which conveyed to his readers the perfect nature of the
task (*telos*). Now it is all accomplished, and a form of the same word
is used for the last time in the Gospel: it has been brought to its
perfection (*tetelesthai*)). A less literal translation, but perhaps a better
rendering of what John is trying to tell us would be: 'I have brought
to perfection the task which my Father gave me to do.' All this has
happened so that the world may see 'love': 'I do as the Father has
commanded me, so that the world may know that I love the Father'
(14.31). We saw above that Jesus spoke the words of 17.3 to describe
how he would fulfill his task by making known the only true God,
but I did not cite all of that verse. Now we are in a position to
understand all the implications of these words: 'And this is eternal
life, that they know thee the only true God, *and Jesus Christ whom
thou has sent.*' We are told, not only of the necessity to know God to
have eternal life, but also of how we come to know this one true
God: through the revealing love of Jesus' gift of himself on the
Cross, and we have come a full circle from the very first passage
which we considered: 'God so loved the world that he gave his only

Son, that whoever believes in him should not perish but have eternal life' (3.16).

In order to see the logic of John's argument, we can pause a moment here and summarise all that we have found so far:

1. God is defined as love.

2. This God who is love acts in history because he loves the world so much; he sends his Son: the Incarnation.

3. Jesus has the task of revealing his Father, the God who is love, to the world. For this purpose he came into the world (see 12.27).

4. He does so in word and deed, and supremely in an ultimate gift of himself on the Cross, so that he might reveal love to us: 'They shall look upon him whom they have pierced.' In the 'lifted up', pierced one is the ultimate love revealed.

THE TASK CONTINUES

The message of the Fourth Gospel concerning the revelation of a God who is love does not cease with Jesus' accomplishment of his task. This task is passed on from Father to Son, as we have seen, and then from the Son to 'his own'. Those who wish to be known as disciples of Jesus must show, through the quality of their lives of love, what stands behind the mystery of their faith in Jesus: a God who is love: 'A new commandment I give to you, that you love one another; *even as I have loved you*, that you also love one another' (13.34). Notice that the model and basis of the love of one Christian for another is the gift which Jesus made of himself in love: 'as I have loved you'. The Christian is now asked to repeat the love which Jesus has shown for his own and thus, ultimately, to continue the task of revealing the God of love to the world. Christian love is not just a moral imitation of a great leader. It is being fired by the same radical openness to the same God of love who stood behind all that Jesus said and did: 'By this *all men* will know that you are *my* disciples, if you have love for one another' (13.35).

We must take seriously the logic of what is being said here. Jesus has been sent because the Father loved the world. In his own turn he has revealed love in his love for us – being 'lifted up' so that he could draw all men to himself (see 8.28). Now he states that the hallmark of his disciples is that they love one another. What we must notice, however, is the purpose of this love which must unite the followers of Jesus. It is not so that they will all be safe and happy within the loving ghetto of the Christian Church.[16] On the contrary, it is so that '*all men* will know'. The purpose of a life of love among the disciples of Jesus is to 'preach' and teach all men that behind the mystery of a Christian life stands a God who is defined as 'love'.

In his priestly prayer Jesus prays to his Father first for himself and his task (17.1–8), then he prays for the sanctification in love of 'his own', i.e. those disciples gathered around him in the room of the supper (vv. 9–19) and finally he prays specifically for us (vv. 20–4): 'I do not pray for these only, [his immediate disciples], but also for those who believe in me through their word' (17.20). The prayer which he prays repeats exactly what had been stressed in the earlier parts of the Gospel: a unity of love is prayed for. Again, however, the unity of love which is requested is not an end in itself. It must make the world sit up and take notice, asking just what it is that stands behind such love: 'That they may become perfectly one, *so that the world may know* that thou has sent me and hast loved them even as thou hast loved me' (17.23. See v. 21). As Jesus closes his prayer, and moves off to speak no longer, but to show the world how much he loved in the event of the Cross, he sums up all that I have been trying to say in his closing petition: 'I made known to them thy name, and I will make it known, that the love with which thou hast loved me may be in them, and I in them' (17.26).

We can now complete the cycle from a God of love to a Christian community, following Jesus, which reveals that God by the quality of its uniting love.

1. God is defined as love.

2. This God who is love acts in history because he loves the world so much; he sends his Son: the Incarnation.

3. Jesus has the task of revealing his Father, the God who is love, to the world. For this purpose he came into the world (see 12.27).

4. He does so in word and deed, and supremely in an ultimate gift of himself on the Cross, so that he might reveal love to us: 'They shall look upon him whom they have pierced.' In the 'lifted up', pierced one is the ultimate love revealed.

5. Those who wish to follow Jesus are called to carry on the same task, to reveal a God of love. They are called to a quality of a life of love that will reveal a God of love to 'all men', 'to the world'.

Summarising all that I have been trying to say by means of a diagram, it would come to something like this:

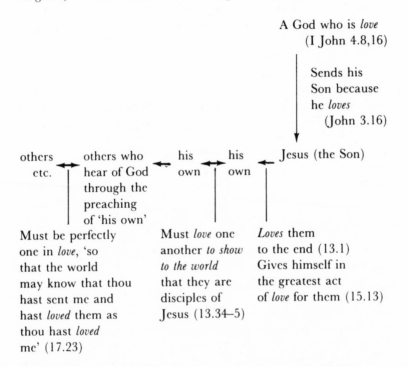

A God who is *love*
(I John 4.8,16)

Sends his
Son because
he *loves*
(John 3.16)

others · others who · his · his · Jesus (the Son)
etc. · hear of God · own · own
through the
preaching
of 'his own'

Must be perfectly · Must *love* one · *Loves* them
one in *love*, 'so · another *to show* · to the end (13.1)
that the world · *to the world* · Gives himself in
may know that thou · that they are · the greatest act
hast sent me and · disciples of · of *love* for them (15.13)
hast *loved* them as · Jesus (13.34–5)
thou hast *loved*
me' (17.23)

The common and consistent factor in Jesus, 'his own' and those who hear the word from them (i.e. us), is that they must show 'all men' (13.35) or 'the world' (17.23) that they live lives which reflect the God that they believe in.[17] This means that Christian life is of necessity marked by an outstanding quality of love, as it reveals a God who is love. Again it is I John which provides us with a synthesis of what is said throughout the Gospel:

Beloved, let us love one another; for love is of God, and he who loves is born of love and knows God. He who does not love does not know God; for God is love. In this the love of God was made manifest among us, that God sent his only Son into the world, so that we might live through him. In this is love, not that we loved God but that he loved us and sent his Son to be the expiation for our sins. Beloved, if God so loved us, we also ought to love one another. No man has ever seen God; if we love one another, God abides in us and his love is perfected in us. (I John 4.7–12).

CONCLUSIONS

We have found that the God of the Bible is a questioning, all-demanding, leading God who cannot be questioned. He is a mysterious God who insists that his faithful ones must never be 'like the other nations'. Yet, despite the mystery of this God who calls his faithful ones away from themselves into the mystery of *his* designs, he is also an 'ever present' God. He will never leave his people alone; in their faithfulness and also in their infidelity he is always *there*. This, in itself, only leads us further into mystery. Our God – the God of the Bible – can in no way be compared to the whimsical, fickle gods 'of the other nations'. What sort of God can this be?

The answer, as we have seen, comes to us from the 'once and for all' event of Jesus Christ, who has made God known (John 1.18). Our God is a God of love. Precisely because he loves so much, he can question, demand and lead; precisely because he loves he can ask that we be 'unique' for him, and not 'like the other nations'. Most importantly, precisely because he loves is he a jealous God, a God who is always *there*, constant in his love despite unfaithfulness.

Jesus has revealed this God of love to us in the supreme gift of himself, when he loved us with a love that knew no limits (John 13.1), being 'lifted up' (3.14; 8.28; 12.32) so that he could draw all of us to himself, that we might gaze upon this physical revelation of love (John 12.32; 19.37). This is what our God is – and we are called to repeat in the world what Jesus did for us: 'A new commandment I give to you, that you love one another; even as I have loved you, that you also love one another' (13.34).

Now we can see why the vocation of the Christian is to 'the perfection of charity' (*Lumen Gentium* 40). This affirmation from Vatican II is not open to any 'more' or 'less' interpretations. The perfection of love is the vocation of all Christians, and ultimately, of all mankind. This means that the life of the Christian should reveal a God of love to the world by the visible quality of the love in his own life. This is also the function of the Religious within the context of the universal call to holiness. He is in no way superior or different.

Again we find ourselves faced with the question which will return again and again throughout these pages: why Religious? It is the task of the Religious community within the heart of the Church to make sure that this *preached* doctrine becomes a *lived* reality. All are called to this perfection because we are all created, loved and called by the God of the Bible. Can it be done? Each of us has the experience of people from all walks of life, families or various other groups, who show us that it can be lived, but a Religious has declared *publicly* to the world that he or she wants to show *publicly* that it can be done.[18] Only when we understand our public profession as a shouting out to the world that we believe in a God who is love, and when the world can see that this love has swept us off our feet, will Religious life make sense. Then our communities, our apostolic endeavours and above all our vowed life will be understood (both by ourselves and by others) as *the means by which*[19] this God is revealed to the world . . . and Religious life will be seen as having an urgently important function within the context of the universal call to a holiness which the Church has described as 'the perfection of love'.

It is an easy and even a moving experience to *talk* about a God who is love. However, it is often a waste of time, or worse, a dangerous 'double-talk'. If we are to reveal a God of love it is not sufficient to talk about him. Words have been cheapened by the massive contemporary production of the printed page and the interminable lists of courses, conferences and institutes which seem to be springing up all over the world.[20] While these phenomena have their value, it is only lives marked by an *outstanding quality of love* which will raise eyebrows and eventually make the world ask: 'Why?' The answer must be: 'Because of the God I believe in!'

A Neil Diamond can reduce thousands of people to tears as he sings of man's basic openness to love and hope. Contemporary man is looking for an answer to why he has this void in his life. We believe that we have the answer, but we do not seem to be making any great impact. In recent years the Neil Diamonds have certainly been 'stealing the show', closely followed by various oriental mystical groups, especially among the young. Where do we go wrong? Too often the answer is given that the world is wicked and will not listen. I do not think that this is the whole truth. Perhaps we should start looking less at what we say, and our skill in saying it, and much more at the quality of our love.

I would suggest that we listen closely to the warning given by John: 'He who does not love does not know God; for God is love' (I John 4.8). Do we Religious really know this God that we talk so much about? Ultimately, that means asking the question: 'Do we really love?' There is another statement from John which is more positive, and which should spur us on in our attempts to know this God of love and to accept our publicly professed responsibility to reveal him to the world: 'No man has ever seen God; if we love one another, God abides in us and his love is perfected in us' (I John 4.12).

One cannot understand or live a life of love unless one has some knowledge and understanding of the object and source of that love. In the human sphere this statement would never have to be made. It is self-evident. This is not the case when it comes to man-God and God-man relationships. Because of this, I have chosen to begin this book on Religious life with a consideration of God, the source and object of all love. Notice that I speak of the source and object of love. All authentic situations of love are made up of this interplay. Someone inspires someone else to love (and is thus the source of love) and is then loved (thus becoming the object of love). In the meantime, the same interplay takes place in and through the other partner. He or she is in turn 'the source and object' of love. Too often Religious life misses this point and degenerates into a situation marked by rigidity and an idea of each Religious 'getting on' with his or her job. They forget that their primary 'task' is to reply to the God of Sinai and the God of Jesus Christ who has called them. Religious life, therefore, is like Christian life, made up of a loving partnership where God has taken the initiative. If this mystery is forgotten (or never known!), then the Religious sees his task as one of getting on with a life 'serving God', and the mystery of our Christian vocation is absorbed by the 'task' to be performed, as if this is what determines our knowledge and love of God. When this happens, as it often does, we have lost touch with the God who loved us first (see I John 4.9–10; Rom. 5.8). These first chapters, dedicated to a pen-picture of how the Bible reveals our God to us, are fundamental to my understanding of why we attempt to live in community, why we take vows and why we live and work in and for the Church and mankind. These 'activities' are not ends in themselves; they are merely attempts on our part to respond to a God who is love, by losing ourselves in the wonderful mystery of his demanding, restless, urgent but loving presence in the world, in men and women, in his Word and in his Church.[21]

III

A Community which Answers . . .

4. The Old Testament 'Community'[1]

Thus far we have attempted to discover just who God is, or at least, how the revealed word presents him. One could say we have been looking at one side of the story, now we must look to see who it is who responds to the God who calls. Naturally, all that we have found out so far about our God will be most important for an understanding of what the biblical books have to say about the community which answers the God who calls. I will follow the same logic as the previous chapters, attempting to see the divine pedagogy involved in the gradual formation of a 'People of God'. Thus I will attempt to trace a picture of the Community of the Old Testament, the Community of Jesus himself and finally, the Communities of the Early Church.

THE CALL TO BE JAHWEH'S PEOPLE

You are a people holy to the Lord your God;
the Lord your God has chosen you
to be a people for his own possession,
out of all the peoples
that are on the face of the earth.
It is not because you were more in number
than any other people
that the Lord set his love upon you and chose you,
for you were the fewest of all peoples;
but it is because the Lord loves you,
and is keeping the oath which he swore to your fathers,
that the Lord brought you out with a mighty hand,
and redeemed you from the house of bondage,
from the hand of Pharoah, king of Egypt.
Know therefore that the Lord your God is God,

the faithful God who keeps covenant and steadfast love
with those who love him and keep his commandments,
to a thousand generations (Deut. 7.6–9).

In these words from the book of Deuteronomy we have the *ideal*
expression of the way in which Israel herself understood her role as
God's people. Notice, however, that behind Israel's presentation of
herself in these words stands a conviction about Jahweh. Israel had
been chosen by Jahweh – not because of her own greatness – but
because of Jahweh's immeasurable love; she had been led out from
Egypt so that she could come face to face with a God called Jahweh
in the harrowing experience of the desert, an experience dominated
by the events at Mount Sinai. There Jahweh called them to be his
own. He would be faithful to them in his love – but he demanded
that they be faithful to him:

Hear, O Israel: Jahweh our God is one Lord; and you shall love
Jahweh your God with all your heart, and with all your soul,
and with all your might (Deut. 6.4–5).

And I will walk among you, and will be your God,
and you shall be my people (Lev. 26.12)[2].

This is the basis of any understanding of the Community of the
Old Testament: a people chosen by God, and called to love and
serve God in reply to that love. The Old Testament knows only one
such 'Community' – Israel. However, she did not become a nation,
much less a community, overnight by some wonderful act of divine
providence. She had to struggle through history, facing difficulties
of various types and dimensions from both inside and outside her
own ranks as she strained on to reach that ideal community towards
which Jahweh her God was continually calling her.

Every page of the Old Testament shows a profound and deeply
felt consciousness in Israel, and these pages reflect a continual
interaction of 'Call and Response'. It is an interesting and beautiful
experience to consider the whole history of that people with the
tensions of this 'Call and Response' in mind. A shapeless band of
nomads are slowly welded into God's people. 'A wandering Ara-
mean was my father,' Moses tells his people in the book of Deuter-

onomy (Deut. 26.5),[3] but, from these humble origins, the great prophet of the nation promises: '[God] will set you high above all nations that he has made, in praise and in fame and in honour' (Deut. 26.19).

So far I have quoted from the book of Deuteronomy. It is important for an understanding of this book to know that it took on its final form, not in a moment of great glory in Israel, but after the cataclysmic collapse of the Northern Kingdom before the troops of Assyria (721 BC). This tragic event caused Israel to stop and reflect upon the reason for these happenings. How could such a thing happen to God's own people? It seemed impossible, but the ruins of Samaria, the dead, and the people who had fled from the north to crowd into the city of Jerusalem left no doubt: it had happened! The question that had to be asked again was: what does it mean to be God's people? Thus the book of Deuteronomy, which certainly had a long and complicated history before it came to its present form,[4] became a meditation on the divine vocation of Israel: the wonder of a little nation called to be a people of God. He had called them, he had subjected them to the fire of the Egyptian enslavement, and then, in the desert, when they came face to face with him, they began to understand what it meant to be his people. All of this happened, according to Deuteronomy, because this was the plan of Jahweh, Israel's God. He had led them out of the fiery furnace of Egypt, and had taken them by the hand into the desert. There they began to live that unique experience that was never forgotten by the faithful of Israel. She encountered her God – at Sinai. This moment is the beginning of a 'people of God'.[5] He gives them his Law, and they experience his presence among them.[6] The idyllic moment of belonging to the loved one was experienced.

Why did the book of Deuteronomy have Moses tell this story, and ask Israel to respond to it? The whole point of this book is to recall the nation to the original faithfulness that was required by the loving, but all-demanding and jealous God of the Sinai experience.[7] If Israel is in pain and confusion (as she was after the fall of Samaria and the Northern kingdom in 721 BC), then she must examine her conscience. She will find that *she* has failed – *not God*. Israel was the cause of her own pain, because she wanted to be 'like the other nations'.

THE FAILURE OF A PEOPLE OF GOD

The book of Deuteronomy is closely associated with the reign of
King Josiah, a king who is presented as one who did 'what was
right in the eyes of the Lord, and walked in all the way of David
his father, and he did not turn aside to the right hand or to the left'
(II Kings 22.2). According to the author of the books of Kings,
Josiah, in his eighteenth year, began a programme of repair work
on the house of the Lord. This was already an indication of his
holiness, but during the repairs 'the book of the law' was found by
the High Priest Hilkiah 'in the house of the Lord' (II Kings 22.8).
Josiah has it read to him:

> And when the king heard the words of the book of the law, he
> rent his clothes. And the king commanded Hilkiah the priest,
> and Ahikam the son of Shaphan and Achbor the son of Micaiah
> and Shaphan the secretary, and Asaiah the king's servant, say-
> ing, 'Go, inquire of the Lord for me, and for the people, and for
> all Judah, concerning the words of the book that has been found;
> for great is the wrath of the Lord that is kindled against us,
> because our Fathers have not obeyed the words of the book, to
> do according to all that is written concerning us' (II Kings
> 22.11–13).

This 'book of the law' is the basis of the book of Deuteronomy and
stands as the norm used by Josiah to reform the nation.[8] From the
Josian reform onwards, the book of Deuteronomy is used as a
criterion for judging the personalities and the people who appear in
the books of Samuel and Kings:

> It was for the sins of Jeroboam which he sinned and which he
> made Israel to sin, and because of the anger to which he provoked
> Jahweh, the God of Israel (I Kings 15.30).

> He (Zimri: 7 days in 885) died because of his sins which he
> committed, doing evil in the sight of Jahweh, walking in the way
> of Jeroboam, and for his sin which he committed, making Israel
> to sin (I Kings 16. 19–20).

> And he (Ahaz: 736–716) did not do what was right in the eyes

of Jahweh his God, as his father David had done, but he walked in the way of the kings of Israel. He even burned his son as an offering, according to the abominable practices of the nations whom Jahweh drove out before the people of Israel. And he sacrificed and burned incense on the high places, and on the hills, and under every green tree (II Kings 16.2–4).

So the list goes on, for all the kings of both the Northern and the Southern Kingdoms, after the division of the nation under Rehoboam (931–913:South) and Jeroboam (931–910:North) which took place immediately after the sinful period of the last years of Solomon. Only two kings are given unconditional praise:

And he (Hezechiah: 716–687) did what was right in the eyes of Jahweh, according to all that David his father had done. He removed the high places, and broke the pillars, and cut down the Asherah (II Kings 18.3–4).

And he (Josiah: 640–609) did what was right in the eyes of the Lord, and walked in all the way of David his father, and he did not turn aside to the right hand or to the left (II Kings 22.2).

A reading of the history books of Israel shows that there are very few who 'do right' and that the criteria for this 'doing right' are the laws laid down in the book of Deuteronomy. The continual failure of Israel, personified in her kings, to meet the demands of the God of the Exodus is clear from the historian's long list of failures.[9] However, the story does not end there, as even in the midst of this failure God was still active, especially in the prophetic movement in Israel (to which the Deuteronomist really belongs). What is the ideal to which Israel is called? It has been finely expressed in Deut. 6.4–5: 'Hear, O Israel: Jahweh our God is one Lord; and you shall love Jahweh your God with all your heart, and with all your soul, and with all your might.'

THE MEN WHO SPOKE FOR JAHWEH: THE PROPHETS
The very existence of the prophetic movement in the history of Israel is a further indication of the faithfulness of their all-demand-

ing God. Their presence among the people is to remind Israel continually of her vocation, but also to remind them that Jahweh, the God of Israel, was a loving God. In the midst of the unfaithfulness of the divided Kingdoms in the latter half of the eighth century, Hosea can still cry out in the name of Jahweh:

> When Israel was a child, I loved him,
> and I called my Son out of Egypt.
> I myself taught Ephraim to walk,
> I took them in my arms . . .
> I was like someone who lifts an infant close
> against his cheek
> Stooping down to him I gave him his food.
> (Hos. 11.1,3–4, Jerusalem Bible)

God set up a people and made them his own – but they were *never* faithful. The idyllic presentation of the desert experience referred to in the passage from Hosea which I just cited comes back, again and again in the Prophets (see Amos 2.9–11; 3.1–2; 9.7; Hosea 2.14–15; 13.4; Micah 6.4; Jeremiah 2.2–7; Ezek. 20.5–6) but this ideal is a long, long way from the reality of the Israel which they knew. However, the memory of an all-important encounter with their God kept the faithful ones, the Prophets, straining forward. They knew that they were his people, and they suffered all things in order to lead their people towards Jahweh, the God of Israel.

It is vitally important to see what the prophet did in the midst of God's people. They were men who lived lives which were intensely taken up with the Covenant, the union between God and his people. They were like lovers who were deeply hurt because they saw that the Covenant was being violated, as the people of Israel lived in division, alienated from one another and from their God, seeking the gods 'of the nations'. Therefore, they spoke to remind the establishment of Israel why she had been established. Prophets are not primarily people who speak about the future. They address themselves to the waywardness of the present, pointing back to the radical demands of their desert God, Jahweh. A blessed future lies in store for Israel only if she will be faithful to her faithful and loving-jealous God. The role of the prophet is to criticise the present failure to meet the past demands of a creating, calling God. That they bear the authentic word of that God is shown by the fact that their promises and their threats come true (see Deut. 18.15–22).[10]

The strange tension of a past Covenant, a present unfaithfulness and a future promise were very strongly felt at the time of Jesus of Nazareth, when a group of pious men lived apart from the rest of Israel. They went back to the desert and settled there in the hope that they would once again recapture the spirit of the true Israel. This group and their way of life have been revealed to us only recently through the discovery of the Dead Sea Scrolls and the excavation of the Essene monastery beside the Dead Sea, close to the place where the Scrolls were found. But the prophets and the Essenes were the odd men out. When we speak about the Old Testament community, the people of Israel, we are forced to the conclusion, especially in the light of the very existence of the prophetic movement, that there is only one constant amongst all the vicissitudes of love and unfaithfulness, and that is the faithfulness of the loving, creating but jealous God of the desert experience. The God who called Israel to himself at Sinai *never* goes back on his promise. One side of the bargain is always kept: 'You shall be my people and I shall be your God.' How rightly Hosea interprets this situation when he again announces in the name of Jahweh:

They have not understood that I was the one looking after them.
My people are bent on turning away from me;
How can I give you up, O Ephraim!
How can I hand you over, O Israel!
My heart recoils from it,
my whole being trembles at the thought.
I will not give rein to my fierce anger,
I will not destroy Ephraim again,
for I am God not man;
I am the Holy One in your midst
and have no wish to destroy (Hosea 11.3, 7, 8–9).

THE OLD TESTAMENT COMMUNITY?

Can we say that our reflections so far have established some fixed points concerning an Old Testament community? There is a community which has come into existence because of the initiative and love of God. This community stays in existence because this God is not capricious. He is true, he is faithful.

This idea is not new to us. We saw in our chapter on the God of the Old Testament that a jealous faithfulness was perhaps his most outstanding characteristic. What this meant to the community of Israel has been beautifully spelt out in the passage just given from Hosea 11, but the same idea stands at the heart of Israel's understanding of her own history.[11]

1. God blesses his people (e.g. David: 1010–970)

2. but they fail to respond (e.g. Solomon: 970–931)

3. and this leads to dire punishment, both of individuals and of the nation (e.g. the division of the nation into Northern and Southern Kingdoms under Jeroboam and Rehoboam in 931. Hatred now rules, and the people suffer).

4. The promise, however, is never withdrawn (e.g. the Davidic line continues in Jerusalem, and this is highlighted by the reforms of the two good kings Hezechiah and Josiah).

5. But Israel as a community still fails to respond (e.g. the ultimate sinfulness of this line in the persons of Jehoiachin [598] and Zedekiah [598–587])

6. and they are destroyed (the destruction of Jerusalem and the exile in Babylon: 587–538).

7. But even this is met by a further blessing (e.g. the return from the exile and the promise of a future).

The message is an overpowering portrait of a faithful God in the midst of his unfaithful community. This God is not passively faithful, he is *active* in his faithful love, and this is what stands behind the periods of punishment. Israel's God was a jealous God, but his great jealousy arises from his great love.

Why did God remain faithful in the midst of all this unfaithfulness? To answer this important question, we must know why this particular community was formed in the first place. The community of Israel was never to be an end in itself. It was formed by God as a pilgrim people, moving towards a future which Israel herself sensed from her earliest days. In the first chapters of Genesis we find a ninth-century sage of Israel writing: 'I will put an enmity between you and the woman, and between your seed and her seed; he shall bruise your head and you shall bruise his heel' (Gen. 3.15). Evil has come into the world, but Israel knows that the powers of evil will not always hold sway. Out of the woman, out of the people themselves, will come someone who will lock himself in bitter struggle against the powers of evil, personified in the snake. For the author of these words, this event was still to happen, and he is telling Israel to look forward to this moment, when God's love, which is always with his chosen people, will be *fully* restored over the hatred and division which sin has engendered. The community of God must remain 'open ended', as it moves forward to the supreme moment in a relationship of love which has been set up between a loving God and a weak group of men and women. When Israel forgets this – she fails in her task; she fails in her role as the people of God.

A look at the history of the people can show us this. When Israel sees herself as self-sufficient, when she thinks she has 'made it' – prepared to accept the *status quo* as normative for her life as God's people – then she fails in her love of that God who keeps calling her to look forward and to move forward to meet him in the moment of supreme union of that God with his people, in the person of Jesus Christ.

The Israel which has taken possession of 'the land', as they themselves call it, is continually liable to fall into the ways of her neighbours. This unique and demanding God whom they cannot quite reach out to and touch, is not sufficient for them . . . or rather, he calls for a risky plunging into the darkness of a future which they themselves cannot fully determine. Eventually they ask for a king and Jahweh tells Samuel: 'Hearken to the voice of the people in all that they say to you; for they have not rejected you, but they have rejected me from being king over them' (1 Sam. 8.7). So Samuel listens to them as they call out: 'Appoint for us a king to govern us like all the nations' (1 Sam. 8.5), and they fall into the chaos of the rule of their first king, Saul.

Jahweh, however, does not let them slip away from his love; he raises up David, only to see his people turn away from him again. With the strength of the kingdom comes conquest, wealth and splendour and the consequent falling away of Solomon, the division of the land into Northern and Southern Kingdoms and an ever-growing desire to be 'like the other nations'. This is betrayal. This is a total abandoning of the essential forward-looking openness to risk, to which their desert God had called them. Prophets come and call to them, telling them of Jahweh's love, only to be rejected and persecuted. This must come to an end – and it does in 587 when the armies of Babylon wipe out the last of royal Israel. But even here we are not at the end of God's faithfulness:

> Behold, the days are coming, says the Lord, when I will make a new covenant with the house of Israel and the house of Judah, not like the covenant which I made with their fathers when I took them by the hand to bring them out of the land of Egypt, my covenant which they broke, though I was their husband, says the Lord. But this is the covenant which I will make with the house of Israel after those days, says the Lord: I will put my law within them, and I will write it upon their hearts; and I will be their God and they shall be my people. And no longer shall each man teach his neighbour and each his brother, saying, 'Know the Lord,' for they shall all know me, from the least of them to the greatest, says the Lord, . . . and I will remember their sin no more (Jer. 31.31–4).

It is incredible to think that Jeremiah uttered these famous words almost as the walls of Jerusalem were being penetrated. An earlier prophetic word, uttered after the destruction of the Northern Kingdom and the subjugation of Jerusalem to a foreign ruler comes to us from Isaiah, who promises even more explicitly:

> There shall come forth a shoot from the stump of Jesse, and a branch shall grow out of his roots. And the spirit of the Lord shall rest upon him, the spirit of wisdom and understanding, the spirit of counsel and might, the spirit of knowledge and the fear of the Lord (Isa. 11.1–2).

Gone is the hope of a political power, and in its place has returned the fundamental openness to God that was demanded from them at Sinai, a God who would lead his people into a future which only *he* could determine.

A FUTURE HOPE

The great hopes and expectations of political and royal Israel had been dashed to the ground with the smashing down of the walls of Jerusalem. They had sought their answer to the call of a loving God in a show of arms and in princely splendour. They wanted to have all the answers to their problems in their hands by the use of a sword or sheckel – this was not to be. Jahweh calls to himself a remnant who will be faithful to his love, a remnant who will understand that through turning away from themselves and looking forward in hope and love, they will come to be a real people of God. Their saviour will not be a messianic king mounted upon a white charger, but a suffering servant:

> Behold, my servant shall prosper
> he shall be exalted and lifted up,
> and shall be very high.
> As many were astonished at him –
> his appearance was so marred,
> beyond human semblance,
> and his form beyond that of the sons of men –
> so shall he startle many nations;
> kings shall shut their mouths because of him;
> for that which has not been told them
> they shall see,
> and that which they have not heard
> they shall understand (Isa. 52.13–15).

We could have opened our Bibles and found many beautiful passages telling us how we should live together, and understood such a collection of passages as the biblical message on the Old Testament community. We have decided to be more faithful to the Old Testament itself. Israel, as a community, failed because it would not be faithful to a faithful God. But God still loved his community, and remained faithful in his love. He continued to call to himself a people, so that they would live in his love: 'Again and again you offered a covenant to man, and through the prophets taught him to hope for salvation' (Fourth eucharistic prayer). Instead, all too often, they lived in the love of themselves, refusing to face up to that risky future which is the destiny of any community which returns the love of a God who calls them forward – but that God still loves on and: 'In the fullness of time, God sent forth his Son, born of a woman' (Gal. 4.4), but that leads us into our next chapter on the communities of Jesus Christ.

5. *The Communities of Jesus Christ*[1]

This chapter, devoted to the communities which are created by faith in Jesus, must necessarily be divided into two major sections. In a first moment we must look at the community which was formed by Jesus – the disciples of Jesus, and secondly we must glance at the communities which sprang up as the earliest Church began its missionary task, especially around the person of St Paul. Again, all sorts of critical difficulties arise, particularly as regards our attempt to understand the disciples of Jesus, for while we are all very much aware that as far as the New Testament witness to communities is concerned, 'In the beginning was Jesus Christ', the Gospels are not a tape-recorded, day-by-day account of what he said and did.

The very first line of the very first Gospel tells us about the sort of literature we have before us: 'The beginning of the good news about Jesus who is the Christ, the Son of God' (Mark 1.1, A. T.). If we were to take up a modern book, and find that the opening paragraph read: 'The beginning of the good news about Idi Amin, the mightest warrior of all time and the saviour of Black Africa', we would know that we were about to read a very prejudiced book. The same has to be said of the Gospels. They are written by men who were so taken over by faith in Jesus as the Christ and the Son of God that they wrote their versions of what he said and did so that they might communicate that faith, and here the parallel with the book about Idi Amin must cease, because we *do* share that faith. Because of this the Gospels are not just prejudiced life-stories, but a word of life to those who share in the same faith, the same life of the Spirit which inspired those books.

THE COMMUNITY OF JESUS OF NAZARETH
There is not a phrase in the New Testament which does not come under the admission of the Gospel of John:[2] 'When therefore he was

61

raised from the dead, his disciples remembered that he had said this; and they believed the scripture and the word which Jesus had spoken' (John. 2.22. See also, 12.16). However, the question which must be asked, is: why did all this happen?[3] What caused these people to look back to the historical life of Jesus for their inspiration 'when he was raised from the dead'? To answer this query we must make a preliminary statement: 'While Jesus was alive, he gathered around himself a small band of followers . . . ', and that is the starting point for our discussion of the communities of Jesus Christ.

1. *The Call*

One cannot but be impressed by the way in which the various Evangelists, and indeed St Paul (see Gal. 1.12–17 and Acts 9.1–19) present that first impact which Jesus of Nazareth made upon those whom he chose to call to himself.[4] It appears that those men of first-century Galilee were deeply moved by the experience of being called by Jesus of Nazareth. This comes through very clearly in their various accounts: ' "Follow me and I will make you fishers of men." And they left their nets at once and followed him' (Matt. 4.19–20 J.B.), reports Matthew. Mark tells of Levi's call: 'As he was walking on he saw Levi, the son of Alphaeus, sitting by the customs house, and he said to him, "Follow me". And he got up and followed him' (Mark 2.14).

Luke sets the scene beside the lake (Luke 5.1–11) after a disastrous night's fishing and, after an initial obstinacy, Peter casts his nets for a miraculous draught of fishes and then: 'When Simon Peter saw this he fell at the knees of Jesus saying, "Leave me, Lord; I am a sinful man" ' (Luke 5.9). John also has a more gradual movement towards Jesus (John 1.35–51) as the disciples of the Baptist are directed towards 'the Lamb of God' (1.29–36) and 'the Son of God' (1.34) by their former master. Nathanael, again after a moment's hesitation, is eventually overpowered by the presence of Jesus and proclaims, 'Rabbi, you are the Son of God, you are the King of Israel' (John 1.49). It is most important to notice, however, that this last example is the only one among all the vocation stories where the newly called disciple makes a profession of faith in Jesus. Jesus, however, is not satisfied with this; the disciples still have a lot to learn and he promises them: 'You shall see greater things than these . . . You will see heaven opened and the angels of God ascending and descending upon the Son of Man' (John 1.50–1).[5]

2. *A 'formation' to the life-style of Jesus*

From the brief glance at these few texts it is clear that Jesus certainly made a great impression on people. He was undoubtedly a man who excited enthusiasm, but this spark of enthusiasm, kindled in the hearts of that small group of men and women who gathered around him, was in danger of running riot. This message of Jesus was in many ways a revolutionary message:

> You heard that it was said, 'You shall not commit adultery.' But I say to you that everyone who looks at a woman lustfully has already committed adultery with her in his heart (Matt. 5.27–8).

> It was also said, 'Whoever divorces his wife, let him give her a certificate of divorce.' But I say to you that everyone who divorces his wife . . . makes her an adultress; and whoever marries a divorced woman commits adultery' (Matt. 5.31–2).

> Again you have heard that it was said to the men of old, 'You shall not swear falsely, but shall perform to the Lord what you have sworn.' But I say to you, Do not swear at all (Matt. 5.33–4).

In these passages Jesus is daring to take the revealed law of the Old Testament (he is quoting here from Exod. 20.14; Deut. 24.1 and Exod. 20.7. See the whole of Matt. 5.20–48), only to stand it on its head! A Jewish listener was already waiting for a quotation from the Torah when he heard the phrase: 'You heard that it was said,' or other similar phrases. For the Jew that was the end of any further discussion, but Jesus then goes on to annouce, 'But I say to you'! This was a blasphemy for the legal purist, but the hint of a great new possibility to the group of simple people from Galilee who heard these words.

To appreciate fully this last point, one must understand that Galilee was rather looked down upon by the religious authorities and the purists from Jerusalem, the Temple city. Most of the Galileans worked the land, or fished in the lake in a way that put them somewhat on the fringe of the literal observance of the ordinances of the law. They were separated from Judea and the Temple by the alien land of Samaria and very few Galileans could make the long and dangerous journey to celebrate the Jewish feasts in the one and only centre of cult, the Jerusalem Temple. They even spoke a dialect which put them somewhat in a class of their own (see Matt. 26.73) and this general situation is reflected in Nathanael's contemptuous question: 'Can anything good come out of Nazareth?' (John 1.46).[6]

It is in this environment that the fanatical revolutionary groups (especially the Zealots, who eventually caused the destruction of Jerusalem in 70 AD) had most success. Distant from and rather despised by 'officialdom' they were ready for new possibilities, and what a marvellous new possibility the authority and overwhelming presence of this man Jesus seemed to offer. A great deal of the ministry of Jesus must be seen as an effort to 'form' his community, to teach them a basic law which was distant from any worldly revolution, but which was an almost impossible revolutionary teaching in the realm of the spirit: 'Love your enemies and pray for those who persecute you, so that you may be sons of your Father who is in heaven; for he makes the sun rise on the evil and on the good, and sends rain on the just and on the unjust' (Matt. 5.44–5). This 'formation process' comes out most clearly in Jesus' attempts to show and teach his disciples that he has not come to fulfill the role of the expected military, all-conquering Messiah, but to be a suffering Son of Man. This pattern is found throughout all four Gospels,[7] but I will give some simple examples to show the process at work.[8]

In Mark 8.27, Jesus asks his disciples: 'Who do men say that I am?'. They reply that he is understood by some as a John the Baptist *redivivus*, or Elijah or one of the Prophets. All of these personalities, in either the Christian or the Jewish tradition, are precursors to the Messiah. In v. 29 he asks his disciples: 'But who do you say that I am?' and Peter replies, 'You are the Christ.' In other words, Jesus is not a precursor, but the Christ himself. There is a sense, of course, in which this confession is correct, but in the light of first-century Jewish expectations there is a sense in which it is very wrong. Peter may have been merely confessing the belief of the disciples that Jesus was the expected political liberator, so Jesus 'charged them to tell no one about him. And he began to teach them that the Son of man must suffer many things . . . And he said this plainly' (vv. 30–2).[9] Peter is not at all prepared to accept such a Messiah, and he objects, only to be told: 'Get behind me, Satan! For you are not on the side of God, but of men' (v. 33). From here the discourse widens and Jesus explains what it means to follow a suffering Messiah: ' "If any man would come after me, let him deny himself and take up his cross and follow me" ' (v. 34). (See the whole passage from vv. 34–8, where the Son of Man title again occurs.) In chapter ten of the same Gospel, Jesus again tells his disciples, now 'on the road, going up to Jerusalem . . . amazed and full of fear' (10.32, A. T.), that the Son of Man must suffer and die before he comes to the glory of his resurrection.[10] However, this prediction of suffering is immediately followed by the request from the Sons of Zebedee to have positions of authority in the new political establishment which is about to be set up (10.35–7). Again he has 'caught them out' in their complete misunderstanding of the nature of his Kingdom. His words to them must be the blue-print for all communities which claim to be following the way of Jesus Christ:

'Are you able to drink the cup that I drink, to be baptised with the baptism with which I am baptised?' . . . 'You know that those who are supposed to rule over the Gentiles lord it over them, and their great men exercise authority over them. But it shall not be so among you; but whoever would be great among you must be your servant. For the Son of Man came not to be served but to serve, and to give his life as a ransom for many' (10.38, 42–5).[11]

The community of Jesus of Nazareth learnt – or rather, failed to learn – at the school of Jesus himself. As Jesus came closer to his 'hour' they seemed to understand less and less. The confession of Peter at Caesarea Philippi seemed to have been forgotten, or was still misunderstood, as even on the journey to Jerusalem they discussed who would be the greatest (Mark 10; Matt. 20; Luke 18). At the first Eucharistic meal one of them 'drops out', to betray his master and the last appearance of the disciples in Mark's Gospel is described as follows: 'And they all forsook him, and fled' (Mark 14.50).

3. *The Crucial Event – The Paschal Experience*

Must we conclude then, that there is no beautiful picture of Jesus and his community in the New Testament? In many ways, yes. The idyllic, artistic presentation of Jesus as a white-robed, quasi-angelic figure, gliding across the undulating hills of Palestine, followed by a devoted, open-mouthed and adoring group of disciples does not do justice to the New Testament.[12]

However, the message of the Gospels is far from negative. Even in what we have seen so far, there has always remained one saving, positive element – Jesus' presence in his community. As in the Old Testament, he now personalises the reality of God's continuing love for his community, despite its weaknesses, and failures. The patient presence of Jesus among his own now reaches its climax and its supreme moment in his 'passing over', in his Paschal Mystery – initiated by the first Eucharistic meal: ' "This is my blood of the covenant, which is poured out for many" ' (Mark 14.24). He has called them, instructed them and loved them even in their failure. Now he gathers them around a common table to set up the new covenant which will bind the community of Jesus to himself forever. This is what Luke is telling us when he gives us his version of the Eucharistic words:

> And when the hour came, he sat at the table, and the apostles with him. And he said to them, 'I have earnestly desired to eat this passover with you before I suffer; for I tell you I shall never eat it until it is fulfilled in the Kingdom of God' . . . and he took bread, and when he had given thanks he broke it and gave it to them saying, 'This is my body which is given for you. Do this in remembrance of me.' And likewise the cup after supper saying, 'This cup which is poured out for you is the new covenant in my blood' (Luke 22.14–16, 19–20 A.T.).

In terms of worldly success among men as the builder of a community, Jesus has not achieved a great deal. Brief moments have flashed through when it appeared that they understood, but they never really seemed to be able to go beyond what was human, what they could see and touch . . . but then came the events of Easter, and this is the basis of the community founded on Jesus.

The resurrection broke loose on this little community and finally made sense of all that Jesus had claimed to be and do. He had said that the Kingdom of God was breaking into history; he had spoken of his coming suffering and death as the Son of Man, but he had claimed that it would somehow make sense. Now his little group of followers could see that it had all really happened! He did suffer, but he is risen, and he has offered us a way of salvation! The Kingdom of God is here! And then they had the further experience of the Spirit of Christ living in them. In a scene that Luke obviously builds up to recall the first great covenant of God with his people at Sinai,[13] we have on the day of Pentecost, noise, wind and fire, as this little, fear-stricken community suddenly comes to the realisation that now, as at Sinai, God was with them. They are his people and he is their God. With strength, courage and even stupidity in the eyes of the world (they are accused of being drunk in Acts 2.12–15), they face the world with a message of Christ, the Son of God, the man who has brought salvation to the whole world.

4. *Conclusions*

Now, perhaps, we can see the role of Jesus as a community-builder. As in the Old Testament, the initiative is always on the side of God. However, this God is now a person in history. The mission and message of Jesus are the fulfilment of the will of God whom he called 'Father' (see especially Matt. 11.25–7), but this led him along the way of a suffering Son of Man. He called some to follow him along this way, and this was the risk and responsibility which the community of Jesus was not prepared to accept. But Jesus was aware of their difficulties. Indeed, he shared them, as the author of the Letter to the Hebrews tells us:

> We have not a high priest who is unable to sympathise with our weaknesses, but one who in every respect has been tempted as we are, yet without sinning (Heb. 4.15).

> In the days of his flesh, Jesus offered up prayers and supplications, with loud cries and tears, to him who was able to save him from death, and he was heard for his godly fear (Heb. 5.7).

In all of this, he stayed close to them, faithful in their failures, believing that he was preparing this community for some future encounter with the power of God, and when it came – Eucharist, Passion, Death and Resurrection and the life-giving presence of the Spirit – this community sprang into life. The parting words of the risen Jesus are reported in various ways by the four Evangelists, but they all send the community on its way with joy, courage and hope, for God is with them. We find no words of stodgy protectiveness, which would have been pointless to this Spirit-filled community, but:

> It is written that the Christ should suffer and on the third day rise from the dead, and that repentance and forgiveness of sins should be preached in his name to all nations . . . You are witnesses of these things. And behold, I send the promise of my Father upon you; (so that you may be) clothed with power from on high (Luke 24.46–9).

The earliest apostolic Church accepted the challenge of these words of Jesus, and this leads us to the second part of our chapter on the communities of Jesus Christ.

THE COMMUNITIES OF THE EARLY CHURCH

As this book is concerned only with the Biblical background to our lives in community, we must limit ourselves here to what the New Testament tells us about these communities. A great deal could be learnt from some of the earliest Fathers of the Church, but our clearest picture of the earliest Christian communities comes from the earliest of all Christian literature, the letters of St Paul.[14]

It is true that most discussions of the early community life in the Church centre their attention upon the Jerusalem Church as it is described in Acts 1–5. Two things must be said in defence of my decision to use the evidence which we can glean from Paul's letters, rather than the beautiful picture of the unified, praying, sharing community of Acts 1–5. First, the Acts of the Apostles were written after the Gospel of Luke, but by the same author, probably in the 80s of the first century. The author is looking back over 50 years. Paul's letters, written mostly in the 50s, are the letters of a shepherd and guide in continual contact with living communities. My second observation is closely linked to this first point. When Luke wrote his Gospel and the Acts of the Apostles, he deliberately looked back continually to Jerusalem (in the Gospel) and towards the first Christian Community in that city (in Acts 1–5) *as a model for his own Church in the 80s*. I am not saying that Acts 1–5 is all invented, but it is what one could call 'the ideal community'. One only has to read Acts 5.1–11 about Ananias and Sapphira, or Gal. 2.11–14 where Paul and Peter have a nasty encounter, to realise that all was not perfect. Not only is the Jerusalem community 'ideal', but it is also 'idealised' by Luke. Luke does this, not because he wishes to say that the past was perfect, but because he wants to say to his own Church, and to the Church of all time: this is how we *should* be![15] When we come to consider the *ideals* of our Christian and Religious communities, especially in our consideration of the Vow of Poverty, we will centre our attention on these beautiful passages from the Acts of the Apostles.[16]

1. *Saul of Tarsus to Paul the Community Builder*

A few years after the crucifixion of Jesus whom (as far as we can tell) he had not known, Saul of Tarsus experienced that same power of the risen Christ which, as we have just seen, transformed the lives and attitudes of Jesus' own disciples. Paul himself describes how he, a man who was 'perfect' as far as his Jewish credentials were concerned, suddenly saw that none of this was valid any longer, because of 'the power of his resurrection': 'Circumcised on the eighth day, of the people of Israel, of the tribe of Benjamin, a Hebrew born of Hebrews; as to the law a Pharisee, as to zeal a persecutor of the Church, as to righteousness under the law blameless.' Thus far, he has listed his Jewish credentials, but now he continues:

> But whatever gain I had, I counted as loss . . . because of the surpassing worth of knowing Christ Jesus my Lord. For his sake I have suffered the loss of all things, and count them as refuse, in order that I may gain Christ and be found in him, not having a righteousness of my own, based on law, but that which is through faith in Christ, the righteousness from God that depends on faith; that I may know him and the power of his resurrection, and may share his sufferings, becoming like him in his death,

that if possible, I may attain the resurrection from the dead (Phil. 3.7–11).

Whatever one makes of the story of the encounter which Paul had with the risen Jesus on the road to Damascus,[17] it is this encounter which overwhelmed, transformed and totally redirected the life of Saul of Tarsus. Out of this event, Paul the Apostle of the Gentiles reconstructed his life (see Acts. 9.1–19; 22.5–16; 26.10–18; Gal. 1.12–17; I Cor. 15.8–10). He saw his vocation as the conveying of the 'good news' of Jesus to those who were not Jews (see Rom. 1.1–6). He embarked on a prolonged missionary programme; partly preaching in new places, partly shepherding newly founded congregations, teaching them 'in season and out of season' (II Tim. 4.2) the news of the salvation which could now be ours because of the death and resurrection of Jesus of Nazareth.

It is from this latter activity, his shepherding of the young Churches of the Gentile world through his unforgettable letters, that we can catch our first glimpse of the Christian communities of the early Church. What we have here is no 'ideal situation', but the living experience of flesh-and-blood people in Christian communities.

2. *Paul and his Communities*

Perhaps one of the most important aspects of a Christian community which we can learn from Paul and his communities comes from the very fact that he even bothered to write letters to them. These letters were written by someone who cared! None of the letters is written merely to pass the time. They are all written because one or other of his communities needs help.[18] The opening and closing phrases of every letter tell us that for Paul these communities were made up of people, men and women, for whom Paul had a profound human feeling.

To Rome, a community which he himself did not found, and whom he had never personally met, he writes respectfully, but with expressions full of Christian hope: 'To all God's beloved in Rome, who are called to be saints: Grace to you and peace from God our Father and the Lord Jesus Christ' (Rom. 1.7).[19]

To Corinth, a community caught in the throes of so many difficulties, both internal and external, a community which caused Paul so much pain and even questioned his right to be an 'apostle'[20] he can still write: 'I give thanks to God always for you' (I Cor. 1.4), and in his second (and more angry) letter: 'If we are afflicted, it is for your comfort and salvation; and if we are comforted, it is for your comfort, which you experience when you patiently endure the same sufferings that we suffer' (II Cor 1.6).

The list could go on. The only letter which does not open with this sort of greeting is the letter to the Galations, where Paul is extremely concerned over that community's desire to return to the slavery of the law, but even here it is *human* concern which comes through: 'I am astonished that you are so quickly deserting him who called you in the grace of Christ and turning to a different Gospel' (Gal. 1.6. See also 4.20: 'I am perplexed about you').

Paul writes to groups of ordinary people, from a human point of view, and ordinary people in so far as their Christian faith did not lift them out of the situation in which they had to live their day-to-day lives. Sometimes (and especially at Corinth) the situation could be somewhat chaotic.[21] We cannot really appreciate the message of Paul or the difficulties of his communities unless we have some understanding of the situation of the Roman-Hellenistic world and its religions in the second half of the first century. It was a world where Romans governed, Greek was spoken and where the classical Greek religions were being modified by the introduction of Emperor worship and the mystery religions. Man then, as now, sought an answer to his deepest longings in some form of 'religion' that explained them. They were not, however, much interested in questions of morality and most of the cults were ordered to the satisfaction of man's question by some form of personal gratification. Into this world Paul writes asking them to follow the way of a crucified Christ, but he tells them – by the quality of his own life more than in his letters[23] – that their lives of foolishness for Christ must have roots in a warmly human, self-giving love for one another.

The warmest of all expressions of Paul's own feelings flows from his pen when he writes from Ephesus to the first community which he founded on European soil, at Philippi. The Christians at Philippi also had their problems (especially a lack of unity among themselves, see Phil. 2.1–11), but he can still write to them:

I thank God in all my remembrance of you, always in every

prayer of mine for you all making my prayer with joy, thankful for your partnership in the gospel from the first day until now. And I am sure that he who began a good work in you will bring it to completion at the day of Jesus Christ. It is right for me to feel thus about you all, because I hold you in my heart, for you are all partakers with me of grace, both in my imprisonment and in the defence and confirmation of the gospel. For God is my witness, how I yearn for you all with the affection of Christ Jesus. And it is my prayer that your love may abound more and more, with knowledge and all discernment, so that you may approve what is excellent, and may be pure and blameless for the day of Christ (Phil. 1.3–10).

3. *The Faith of Paul's Communities*

Paul's communities, therefore, were founded in love, supported by love and they had their life 'in Christ' only because they loved.[24] However, great and difficult things were demanded from them. These communities were asked to place all their faith in a salvation made possible by a man who died on a cross, and they were asked to believe that God had worked out man's salvation by raising him from the dead. This all sounds clear enough to us, but one should also understand how the Athenians reacted to Paul when he began to speak of the resurrection from the dead of a man crucified: 'Now when they heard of the resurrection of the dead, some mocked; but others said, "We will hear you again about this" ' (Acts 17.32). When looking at the communities in the early Church, we must never forget that Paul was asking them to take a leap into the darkness of human foolishness, in the belief that this foolishness could bring life:

> For Jews demand signs and Greeks seek wisdom, but we preach Christ crucified, a stumbling-block to the Jews and foolishness to the Gentiles, but to those who are called, both Jews and Greeks, Christ the power of God and the wisdom of God. For the foolishness of God is wiser than men, and the weakness of God is stronger than men (I Cor. 1.22–5).

How can this be? Is it humanly possible to take such a leap in the dark, to believe in a God who makes wisdom out of human foolishness? What was it that enabled these people to suffer the ridicule that their common belief in Christ brought upon them, and not only ridicule, but as early as 64 AD even organised violent persecution and death? The answer to this question is once again best found by listening to Paul speaking to a community: 'We rejoice in our sufferings, knowing that suffering produces endurance, and endurance produces character, and character produces hope, and hope does not disappoint us, because God's love has been poured into our hearts through the Holy Spirit who has been given to us' (Rom. 5.3–5). We are back to that essential open-mindedness to a future that God would establish. This was demanded of the Old Testament community, and formed the basis of Jesus' own community – 'a hope that does not disappoint us'.

However, now there is a difference, as this hope, like anything Christian, is rooted in Christ, whom Paul describes as 'the first born from the dead' (see I Cor. 15.20). He has already gone along the way to which a life of faith, hope and love will lead all Christians. We too can be born into the resurrection, but here the constant biblical message returns: only if we remain open to the demands of our mysterious but ever-present God as he leads us forward to *his* future.

4. *The Life of the Spirit*

How were these communities to know that this was the case? Was it all just a doctrine that Paul preached? No. The passage from Romans 5 has already told us that these communities did not survive merely because they believed and hoped in a preached doctrine. They had a very real *experience:* 'God's love has been poured into our hearts through the Holy Spirit who has been given to us' (Rom. 5.5). To use modern terms, that Paul and his communities probably would not recognise, the earliest communities were enthusiastic, charismatic communities. They were 'alive in the Spirit'.

The evidence for this aspect of the Pauline communities is found most clearly in I Cor. 12–14. I cannot give a detailed explanation of these very important chapters here but I will point out some of the more outstanding features of this 'experienced Christianity' of the Church's earliest communities.[25]

The most important thing to notice about these three chapters of

I Corinthians is that they are written by Paul the pastor *because the 'gifts' have become a problem.* Paul's whole purpose is to guide the Corinthian community towards a correct appreciation and use of the life of the Spirit among them. However, and this is important, he never for one moment questions either the presence of this exuberant life, nor its value. He lays down certain criteria.

1. Jesus is the Lord (12.3). Any charismatic experience which puts this question is no longer Christian.

2. The great and wonderful variety of charismatic gifts in the community must not create division, as they all form one body in Christ (12.4–31).[26]

3. There is a hierarchy to be observed in the evaluation: first apostles, second prophets, third teachers, then miracles, then the gift of healing, support, direction and various kinds of tongues (12.28). It is important to notice that Paul has no difficulty over the presence of such phenomena as miracles, healing and tongues. He takes it for granted that the Corinthian Church enjoys the presence of these signs of its life in the Spirit, but they are to be subordinated to the primary task of the Church: the administration of God's word and Sacrament through apostles, prophets and teachers.[27]

4. Supreme among all gifts of the Spirit in the community is the 'greater gift' of the love which unites them 'into Christ'. He concludes chapter 12 by saying: 'Strive for the greater gifts; and I am going to show you a better way' (v. 31) and then bursts into his unforgettably beautiful chapter on love (ch. 13). This message is crystal clear:

> If I speak in the tongues of men and of angels, but have not love, I am a noisy gong or a clanging cymbal. And if I have prophetic powers, and understand all mysteries and all knowledge, and if I have all faith, so as to remove mountains, but have not love, I am nothing (13.1–2).

5. The final section devoted to the question of the spiritual gifts (ch. 14) shows Paul the practical pastor seeing that his Spirit-filled enthusiastic community does not lose touch with the sense and purpose of their gifts, all of which are a wonderful proof of the fact that they are a community of Jesus Christ who has risen from the

dead, and who pours the gifts of God's love into the hearts of those who follow him. These gifts are wonderful (14.39–40) but the whole point of the superabundance of gifts is: 'for the building up of the Church' (v. 12).[28]

Thus, despite its risky nature, the community of Jesus Christ has a lived experience of the life of the Spirit of Jesus as a guarantee that their hope in the foolishness of God which is wiser than men somehow makes sense here and now. This led the community into a shared life of prayer, a prayer full of enthusiasm, joy and a convinced hope. Their faith had nothing to do with fleeing from the world into some sort of strange, un-worldly *Nirvana*, as they did not live by faith alone. They lived by faith, hope and love!

The early Church was firmly anchored in its first-century world, as the New Testament shows us in every verse. A Christian community did not soar above this vale of tears to some imagined heavenly bliss (and this was the danger that the Corinthian Church was running into by a misuse and a misunderstanding of the spiritual gifts). The community of the early Church, whose faith, hope and love sprang from the death and resurrection of Jesus saw that this way of life was not only to lead to the eternity of heaven, but could make sense of the earth upon which Christ's cross had stood, and this meant that the community went out from itself to all men. It was apostolic: 'To be a minister of Christ Jesus to the Gentiles in the priestly service of the gospel of God, so that the offering of the Gentiles may be acceptable, sanctified by the Holy Spirit' (Rom. 15.16).

5. *The Difficult Community*
This is all very moving, but it is the ideal. What we have seen up till now has always been what the master (Paul) is demanding from his communities. He is setting standards, but was it really like that? We know that it was not. As we have already mentioned, there was an Ananias and a Sapphira in the Jerusalem Church (Acts 5.1–11), there were harsh words and a serious difference of opinion between Peter and Paul over a meal at Antioch (Gal. 2.11–14), the preaching of Jesus' message to non-Jews almost split the Church (Acts 15.1–29) and we know that Paul's letters exist (with few exceptions) because things were not going as they should have been:

O foolish Galations! Who has bewitched you, before whose eyes Jesus Christ was publicly portrayed as crucified? (Gal. 3.1) But I, brethren, could not address you as spiritual men, but as men of the flesh, as babes in Christ. I fed you with milk, not solid food; for you were not ready for it; and even yet you are not ready, for you are still of the flesh (I Cor. 3.1–3).

Thank goodness for that! Thank goodness that the communities of the early Church were made up of normal, weak human beings who were not always faithful to the ideal which Paul placed before them. The idealistic picture of the early Church (especially as Luke describes it in Acts) could be a very disturbing thing, as it could cause us to wonder if the power of Christ's resurrection and the hope and love which it had provided had somehow lost its efficacy. Bogged down in the day-to-day life of a community we could ask if we are fired by the same Spirit. Yes, we are, but the nagging question that we so often brush aside is: are we fired by the same faith, hope and love?

A last word from Paul to his 'difficult' community at Corinth is all-important in this regard, because it is a word on discouragement. To this struggling community Paul himself confesses: 'For the sake of Christ, then, I am content with weaknesses, insults, hardships, persecutions and calamities; for when I am weak, then I am strong' (II Cor. 12.10). What does Paul mean when he says: 'When I am weak, then I am strong'? He means that his life of love is a two-sided affair where often his side of it is marked by failure to respond to the love of the other. However, it is not only Paul who is striving to live a life of love, but he knows (and this is not just 'knowledge' but an 'experienced' presence of the Spirit in his life) that Christ plays the major, more faithful role in this life of love. It is especially in his failures, in his calamities and in his sin that the power of the risen Christ is close at hand. That attitude of loving faithfulness, which has been a part of the biblical teaching on God right from the beginning, persists here. He will be faithful, despite our personal and community failures. We *must* be convinced of this.[29] It was because the early Church was convinced of this basic truth revealed in the person of Jesus and taught by Paul to his 'difficult' communities that we still exist today. They did not throw up their hands in despair in the face of the contradictions that existed among them. They well understood that there would be no true Christian life unless the Christian saw his life as lived within a mystery of a God who loves much more than the one who is seeking to love him.

6. *Conclusion*

The communities of the early Church paved the way and provided a model for all communities which call themselves Christian. Any community which claims that it is replying to the God of the Bible, made flesh in the Person and Word of Jesus of Nazareth must be prepared to take that leap into a future of darkness, lit up only by the light of the promised resurrection. In this situation we should be able to look to one another sincerely, knowing in the depths of our beings that beyond all our irrelevant differences of opinion and human difficulties there is something far greater that binds us intimately:

> Who shall separate us from the love of Christ? Shall tribulation, . . . or nakedness or peril or the sword? . . . No, in all these things we are more than conquerors through him who loved us. For I am sure that neither death nor life, nor angels, nor principalities, nor things present, nor things to come, nor powers, nor height, nor depth,[30] nor anything else in all creation, will be able to separate us from the love of God in Christ Jesus our Lord (Rom. 8.35–9).

To be able to say this to one another will not mean that we have arrived at the 'perfect community', just as the communities of the early Church never *arrived*, but it will mean that we are sincerely and honestly taking the risk of love to which we are called, following Christ, the first-born out of the death that sin has brought, through his 'passing over', through pain and suffering, to the glory which can and will also be ours.

6. *The Religious Community*

Thus far we have seen the biblical message of a God who calls and a community which answers. However, I insisted in the first chapter that this biblical message was not directed to Religious alone, but that all Christians 'of whatever rank or status are called to the fullness of the Christian life and the perfection of charity' (*Lumen Gentium* 40). As this is the case, then all that I have written about the biblical theology of community must apply to all Christians. Here I must briefly anticipate what I will say in a later chapter on the prophetic function of the Religious in the Church.[1]

While it remains true that all that has been said so far applies to all Christians, one does not have to be particularly alert to see that the community experience of Christian life is fast becoming a lost reality. This is a great tragedy, and our families, parishes and dioceses should be looking carefully at the reasons for the loss of one of the essential characteristics of the Christian vocation. Within this 'examination of conscience' the Religious community must play an all-important role. The preaching of the biblical message will rapidly decline into a serious 'double-talk', where we preach one thing and live another, unless somewhere the preached doctrine can be seen as a lived reality within the Church. The Religious community must see one of its essential apostolic functions as the resolving of that double-talk. Our communities must show the Church and the world that the biblical message is not just a 'pie in the sky' idealism, a non-lived preached doctrine, but that it is a *lived reality* within the Church. Paul VI put it beautifully when he spoke directly to Religious in his Apostolic Exhortation on Evangelisation:

> Religious for their part, find in their *consecrated life* a privileged means of effective evangelisation. At the deepest level of their being they are caught up in the dynamism of the Church's life, which is thirsty for the divine Absolute and called to holiness. It

is to this holiness that they bear witness. They embody the
Church in her desire to give herself completely to the radical
demands of the beatitudes. By their lives they are a sign of total
availability to God, the Church and the brethren (*Evangelii Nuntiandi* 69).

Convinced of this, I now wish to make six applications to the
Religious community which, I believe, flow directly from the analysis of the biblical material which I have just concluded. This book
is not primarily a full-scale theology of the Religious life. I am
attempting to find the biblical model against which we must
measure our lives as Christians and Religious. Because of this, I
will do nothing more than state these six theses. It would be the
task of a theologian to take them further.

1. A RELIGIOUS COMMUNITY IS THE RESULT OF THE INITIATIVE OF GOD

This fact is reflected in the very law of the Church, where Religious
Congregations are never merely the creations of a charismatic
individual. They must be approved by the Church.[2] Descending,
however, to the local level, we must ask: Why does this particular
community exist? Are we here as a work force, doing a job that any
other trained group could do? Or are we here because, in prayer
and trust, we have gathered together because God has called us
here to show, certainly through our work, that God exists, and that
our presence here depends entirely upon him? The words of Rabbi
Gamaliel I still ring true:

> 'Men of Israel, take care what you do with these men . . . In
> the present case I tell you, keep away from these men and let
> them alone; for if this plan or this undertaking is of men, it will
> fail; but if it is of God, you will not be able to overthrow them.
> You might even be found opposing God!' (Acts 5.35, 38–9).

2. A RELIGIOUS COMMUNITY CONTINUES BECAUSE OF THE CONTINUING PRESENCE OF GOD

Are our communities directed in a context of prayer and discernment, or are our community meetings and House Councils places

where the person who shouts loudest, longest or last wins through? Is it always the 'hierarchical heavy' who *must* have his way, no matter what other people feel or suffer because of a decision? What really is at the centre of our community life? We must not shilly-shally over this. It is too important. Is it *really* our shared life of prayer, our Eucharist, and the encounter with God which we should find in one another? Or rather, are these aspects of our life subordinated to the work in the hospital, the youth centre, the school, the social centre etc.?

3. A RELIGIOUS COMMUNITY IS NOT, ULTIMATELY, ABOUT 'SUCCESS' IN THE NORMAL SENSE OF THE WORD

At the centre of the biblical message on community stands the call to a radical reversal of ideas. Texts abound, and this is not the place to examine them.[3] The best way to explain what the Religious community is about would be simply to repeat two texts which we have already seen. One is from the life of Jesus: 'Whoever would be great among you must be your servant, and whoever would be first among you must be slave of all, for the Son of Man also came, not to be served, but to serve, and to give his life as a ransom for many' (Mark 10.43–5).

Another familiar passage comes from Paul:

In the wisdom of God, the world did not know God through wisdom, it pleased God through the folly of what we preach to save those who believe. For Jews demand signs and Greeks seek wisdom, but we preach Christ crucified, a stumbling-block to the Jews and folly to Gentiles, but to those who are called, both Jews and Greeks, Christ the power of God and the wisdom of God. For the foolishness of God is wiser than men, and the weakness of God is stronger than men (I Cor. 1.21–5).

Are we really committed to these criteria? How do we measure the success or failure of a Religious and of a Religious community? By the number of successful applications for university? By the new buildings completed? By the prosperous and successful Past Pupils society, or the Parents and Friends association? Or are we able to see through all that to the quality of a life of love and gift of self within the community? Is it a place where people simply like to be, irrespective of its successes or failures? Are we really questioning the usual cultural and historically conditioned value-system by the very presence of our community in this particular situation, or are we merely reinforcing these value-systems by flogging ourselves to death so that we may succeed according to their criteria?

4. A RELIGIOUS COMMUNITY IS PRIMARILY A FAITH COMMUNITY

None of my first three theses is true unless this one is true. We are *primarily* communities which have been called into existence by faith and which will continue to exist as Christian communities only if we are sustained by faith. One can have a hospital, a college, a youth club, a farm and a sports club *without* faith, but one can *never* be a Christian community as such. Is our life of faith, and the communication of that faith, not so much by words but by the quality of our lives, the *primary* reason for our existence?

5. WHAT THE RELIGIOUS COMMUNITY 'DOES' MUST FLOW FROM WHAT IT 'IS'

If our primary task is to show to the world what sort of God we believe in (and that was why this book started with an attempt to see just what sort of a God we do believe in), then we must naturally 'do' something in the world. We must not separate the two aspects of our lives, our 'being' and 'doing', but we must not put the cart before the horse, and I think that a great number of current Religious communities have been forced into a practice which has indeed placed the cart before the horse. How easily we hide behind structures. Candidates to Religious life are often judged and criticised on their ability to perform a task. How many of us, when asked how things are going, will be able to reel off a list of marvellous things that we are 'doing', but hesitate to say that we are lonely, that the prayer life and celebration of the Eucharist in the community mean nothing, that we are tortured by affective problems. Unfortunately, the quality of our community life, the quality of our shared life 'in Christ' is often very poor, and thus we rush to hide behind all the marvellous *things* that we have *done*, and dare

not consider the marvellous *persons* each one of us as individuals
and in community *could and should become.*

6. IT IS NOT OUR ACHIEVEMENTS THAT ULTIMATELY MATTER, BUT WHAT WE ARE

Coming closer to the biblical message, I should be more precise and
write, not so much what we *are*, but what we are *trying to be.*
Religious communities must reveal to the world the trust in God
and in our fellow-man which could bring relief to a tortured humanity. We show this, not so much by loving every man and woman in
the world, which is often a pietistic fantasy, but by doing all that
we can to live the concrete reality of a *loving and trusting community.*
Ultimately, it is the joy and the hope of our lives which will show
to the whole of mankind, grasping for control over all the mysteries
which surround it, that a: 'hope which is seen is not hope. For who
hopes for what he can see? We wait for it with patience and love'
(see Rom. 8.24–5).

IV

Through a Vowed Life ...

7. *Poverty*[1]

When organised Religious communities began to appear in the Church (in the 4th century) they immediately adopted a life-style which was called 'poor'. In doing this, however, the founders and members of these communities did not start a new fashion in the history of Christian life. Poverty had always been seen as a very important Christian ideal. The later books of the Old Testament (see Zeph. 3.12) and especially the Psalms (see Pss. 22.24; 40.17; 69.33; 86.1; 109.22 etc.) spoke of the blessedness of the *'anawim'*, the poor of Yahweh, and the New Testament, especially Luke's Gospel (see, for example, Luke 14.15–21; 16.19–31), appears to present 'poverty' as a virtue, contrary to the more ancient Old Testament idea that the wealthy man was the one blessed by God.[2]

Central to the Christian ideal of poverty stands the story of the rich young man (Mark 10.17–22; Matt. 19.16–22. Luke 18.18–23).[3] The tremendous ideal expressed in the words 'Go, sell what you have, and give to the poor, and you will have treasure in heaven; and come, follow me' (Mark 10.21) has, since the very first moment of the Church's history, fired the hearts of generous men and women. Ever since that time 'evangelical poverty' has remained one of the basic elements within the structure of Religious life. Even contemporary society, so critical of the supposed de-humanising effects of chastity and obedience, pays at least lip-service to the slavery which the search for material well-being can bring about. The younger generation often have little respect for chastity or for certain forms of obedience but how many of them are opting out of a system which is run by the financiers who ultimately decide what will happen in a capitalist society.

Despite all this, it must be recognised that the practice of poverty in Religious life today gives rise to an interminable number of practical problems and is the cause of an enormous amount of division and bickering! More serious, however, than these practical problems is the widely felt guilt expressed in the oft-heard words from sincere Religious: 'We are not really poor. We have plenty to eat, cars to move about in, a roof over our heads and a warm bed every night. Most of all, we do not experience that terrible insecurity about "tomorrow" that the truly poor experience.' As we continually laugh at the old joke aimed at us by non-Religious: 'You take the vow of poverty and we keep it!', we run the risk of thinking that, after all, they are correct. We do make a vow of poverty, but it would be better not to insist on this aspect of our lives. It seems to be a dangerous double-talk that lessens the effectiveness of our Christian presence in the Church and in the world.

In the period of renewal that has gone on since Vatican II, this problem has been very keenly felt. There seem to have been two major attempts to resolve this problem which, stated in their extremes could be formulated as follows:[1] (1) To speak today of a vow of poverty makes no sense. We should no longer refer to this vow as 'poverty' but simply give ourselves to our task, with all the material support that we need. This means that we make our contribution to the Church and the world, but we live, from a material point of view, like any ordinary person doing the task that we are doing. This point of view has become, in fact, the practice of many Religious individuals and communities in the more economically stable societies of the United States and Australia. (2) We must return to the radical command given to the rich young man: 'Go, sell what you have, and give to the poor' (Mark 10.21). This is interpreted as a continual effort on the part of Religious communities to strip themselves of all worldly possessions and trappings (large houses etc.) so that they may share the experience of those who are truly poor. Especially important is a sharing of their insecurity. This attitude has been adopted, in both theory and practice, by Religious individuals and communities living in the difficult situations of South America.

I am convinced that, judged in the light of the New Testament, both of these solutions (and the many other variations on the same themes) are wrong. They are not wrong because they are radical. As we have already seen, the Christian vocation is a call to radical living and the suggestions which I am about to make are also radical, in the true sense of the word – going back to the true 'roots' of evangelical poetry. This is where these suggestions fail; they are too much obsessed by the externals of 'haves' and 'have nots'. The first solution fails because it loses touch with an essential aspect of the Christian vocation, and an important aspect of the Religious' call to be an evangeliser through his 'consecrated life' (see *Evangelii Nuntiandi* 69). The second is also mistaken, but here the problem is more difficult. It is my conviction that it fails because of a faulty interpretation of the New Testament, particularly the Beatitudes (see Luke 6.20: 'Blessed are you poor, for yours is the kingdom of God') and the story of the rich young man.

THE BASIC PREMISE: A SHARED LIFE 'IN CHRIST'

A first reading of St Paul's letters suffices for us to notice that he speaks continually of our (and his) being 'in Christ'. This is one of his favourite expressions. From Romans alone, one can find almost every aspect of the Christian life described as 'in Christ'. The Christian is baptised 'in Christ' (Rom. 6.3), lives his everyday life, greets people, has his glory and the life of the Spirit 'in Christ' (6.11; 8.2; 9.1; 15.17; 16.3–10), forms 'one body' with other Christians 'in Christ' (12.5) and has redemption and eternal life 'in Christ' (3.24; 6.23). This may appear to be a roundabout way of speaking about poverty, but I hope to show that we must start here.

Scholars are well aware that the expression 'in Christ' is Paul's main way of describing what he means by Christian life. For Paul to exist as a Christian means to live 'in Christ': 'There is therefore now no condemnation for those who are in Christ Jesus' (Rom. 8.1). However, the expression is open to several quite different interpretations, as the preposition 'in' (in Greek *en*) has several possible translations. It can mean 'in', 'with', 'through', 'by' and several other nuances.[5] Precisely because it stands at the heart of Paul's message about what it means to exist as a Christian, scholars differ considerably in their interpretation of this expression.[6]

Rather than spending time on dictionaries it is best to go to some of Paul's texts, to see if we can find what is meant by the expression. The phrase is often associated with two other famous Pauline images: 'putting on Christ' and 'becoming a new man'. Unfortunately, these expressions are often used to speak of moral improvement, and understood as a call to behave as a better Christian but

Paul's meaning runs much deeper, as can be seen from the following passages:

> You have *put on the new man* . . . *where* there cannot be Greek and Jew, uncircumcised and circumcised, barbarian, Scythian, slave, freeman, *but Christ is all in all.* (Col. 3.10, A.T.)

> As many of you as were baptised *into Christ* have *put on Christ.* There is neither Jew nor Greek, there is neither slave nor free, neither male nor female; for *you are all one in Christ Jesus.* (Gal. 3.27–8).

Although these texts come from very different moments in Paul's activity, and they are written to different Churches, they are clearly very similar and reflect one of Paul's central ideas (see also Rom. 10.12–13; I Cor. 12.12–13; Eph. 2.11–22). They share the list of traditionally hostile and even naturally divided groups: Greek and Jew, circumcised and uncircumcised, slave and freeman, male and female. Both passages, however, claim that these accepted divisions are finished in the new situation which Paul describes as 'in Christ', 'in the new man'. In the passage from Colossians, 'the new man' is described as a place 'where there cannot be' division. The same idea of place is conveyed in Galatians when Paul describes this new situation as where Christians all constitute 'one man'. This cannot refer to a new set of moral habits. It is clearly a new *sphere of existence* which has been established by baptism into Christianity. It is a place, a spatial concept, where others form an integral part. This means, ultimately, that our very existence as Christians (called throughout Paul's letters to life 'in Christ') is not something which we personally possess. To be a Christian, therefore, is to participate in the life of others, to share, to break down all barriers which divide (see also Eph. 2.14: 'He is our peace, who has made us both one, and has broken down the dividing wall of hostility'). It would have been quite impossible for Paul to think of an *autonomous* Christian as the two words 'autonomous' and 'Christianity' are terms which contradict each other. We exist and have our life as Christians *only* in the union of other Christians. It is in this sphere of a shared existence, where all divisions are eliminated, that we can claim to be 'alive in Christ'.[7]

This profound vision touches all aspects of Christian life. No genuine Christian can live for himself because his very existence *as a Christian* is not his own to take. He has a Christian life only insofar as he depends upon others, insofar as he continually gives to others and receives from others. We exist as Christians, we *are* Christians in and through others. While the rest of the New Testament does not use the expression 'in Christ' in this way, or work out this theology of a life in Christ as fully as Paul, it is a basic presupposition for the continual insistence that there is only one law for Christians – the law of love. It simply must be so, as to *be*, to *exist* for others is the only way of human existence that is truly Christian. Behind all of this stands the New Testament understanding of God which we saw in an earlier chapter: God is love.[8] Because He is love, the evangelist John can report Jesus' new law: 'A new commandment I give to you, that you love one another; even as I have loved you, that you also love one another. By this all men will know that you are my disciples, if you have love for one another' (John 13.34–5). Only in this way can we express the heart and soul of our Christian existence: the mutual reciprocity and interdependence which is life 'in Christ'.

With this in mind, we can turn now to examine the texts used by Christian tradition as the biblical background for evangelical poverty.

THE 'POVERTY' OF THE JERUSALEM CHURCH

It has been traditional to look to the ideal community of the Jerusalem Church as described in the Acts of the Apostles in all our efforts to establish a biblical basis for Religious communities. Luke's purpose, however, was not to describe the ideal Religious community, but to describe the ideal Church. Only if we are convinced that the Religious community is a microcosm of the Church, that the Religious community is 'Church', may we turn to these texts. Basing ourselves on the insight which we have just gleaned from Paul: that the Christian is never a Christian on his own, but that our very life 'in Christ' depends upon our preparedness to share life, it is most significant that Luke recognises the same principle.

And all who believed were together and had all things in common;

and they sold their possessions and goods and distributed them
to all, *as any had need* (Acts 2.44–5).

Now the company of those who believed were of one heart and soul, and
no one said that any of the things which he possessed was his
own, but they had everything in common . . . *There was not a needy
person among them*, for as many as were possessors of lands or
houses sold them, and brought the proceeds of what was sold
and laid it at the apostles' feet; and distribution was made to
each *as any had need* (Acts 4.32–5).

Both of these passages begin by a simple statement of the fact
that a life of Christian faith means a life of oneness. Given that
basic premise, two further important points emerge.
1. The first Christians did not get rid of all their wealth and possessions. They shared them! There is no idea in these texts of
material things being intrinsically evil and therefore to be cast off
if one wished to become holy. The texts themselves make it clear
that what happened was a sharing of goods *to raise the standard of
living of the needy members of the community* (see 4.34: 'There was not
a needy person among them'). The handing in to the apostles of all
that one might possess was merely the means used to ensure the
material 'life' of *all* the members of the community. It was never an
end in itself. What Luke presents as the Christian ideal here is not
the ridding oneself of something corrupt and evil, but sharing all
that one has as a sign of your love for all, especially those who are
most in need.[9] What is described here, in fact, is a uniting love.
Because of this love, they all share in the material goods of the
community. This handing over of goods thus becomes the visible,
external, world-questioning sign of the deeper reality of the sustain-
ing love which is the element constituting the reality of a Christian
community – Paul's 'life in Christ'. In fact, it is not reported that
the non-Christians of the first centuries AD said of the Christians:
'See how these Christians hand in their goods.' No, what this
handing in of goods really signifies is seen and understood: 'See
how these Christians love one another!'
2. While the early Christians handed in their goods to make sure
that all the members of the community would be able to live on a
material level, this gesture would have a further practical conse-

quence. Given the fact that the goods were shared by all, everyone, including the wealthy, now depended upon the community for their physical well-being. No longer do we have a situation where some can dictate terms to others by giving to them. No, *all* is *shared* by *everyone*. Again, we find a situation that reflects, at a practical level, the mutual interdependence and sharing at the deeper level of a 'life in Christ' which stands at the basis of Christian existence. This common life witnessed to the world the reality of living 'in Christ Jesus'.

From these traditionally used texts, therefore, we can see that Christian poverty has two facets:
1. The handing in to the community of all that one has.
2. A shared responsibility for the material life of the community.
Each one of these aspects needs more detailed consideration.

THE HANDING IN OF ALL TO THE COMMUNITY

This aspect, the idea of giving away everything, is at the heart of some current suggestions for a return to Evangelical poverty.[10] Right from the outset one fact should be made clear. For the New Testament, complete personal deprivation, the lack of means of subsistence, is *not* a good thing. How is it possible to find in the Gospels praise for hunger and starvation, malnutrition, or death from exposure to the elements? All of this is a contradiction of the nature of the Kingdom of God, continually presented as a place of joy, peace, love, warmth, as a place where man is able to live with the dignity which is his because he is a creation of loving God.[11] The Bible speaks of freedom for the captives, health for the ill, and the images of wedding feasts and a superabundance of wine, food and all good things are used (see for example, Amos 9.13–14; Hos. 14.7; Jer. 31.12; Mark 2.22; Matt. 8.11; 22.1–14; Luke 22.16–18). How then have we come to the position, standing at the heart of that nagging feeling of guilt that disturbs many sincere Religious, that we are not evangelically poor? As I have already said, this comes from a mistaken interpretation of the New Testament, especially the Beatitudes and the story of the rich young man.

The Beatitudes

The Beatitudes have come down to us in two quite different versions, in Luke 6.20–3 and Matt. 5.3–10. Although both versions reflect the interest of the Evangelists, it is generally agreed that the form of these words of Jesus is much closer to the original in Luke than in Matthew.[12] The Lucan Beatitudes promise a fulfilment which the messianic era will bring for the underprivileged:

'Blessed are you poor, for yours is the kingdom of God. Blessed are you that hunger now, for you shall be satisfied. Blessed are you that weep now, for you shall laugh' (Luke 6.20–1).

This passage is often read as a beatification of the state of being poor and oppressed; only to these will the kingdom of God belong. This is a misreading of the text and a misplacing of the emphasis. The Messiah was not coming to establish a situation of poverty, but to free men from that situation. This is a common theme in the Old Testament, and in Luke's Gospel Jesus' first public act, in the Synagogue at Nazareth, is to proclaim that he has come to fulfill these Messianic expectations. Quoting from Isaiah 61.1–12 and Zeph. 2.3, he announces: "He has anointed me to preach good news to the poor. He has sent me to proclaim release to the captives and recovering of sight to the blind, to set at liberty those who are oppressed" (Luke 4.18). Jesus identifies himself as 'the anointed one', the Christos'[13] who has come not to bless poverty, hunger and tears, but to release people from these sufferings. What is needed, however, is an openness to Jesus and it is the poor, the hungry and the afflicted who will welcome him. These are the people who will gladly welcome the Kingdom announced by Jesus because they have no reason to defend the *status quo*. They will not react against the searing, questioning words of Jesus to defend their personal interests, because they have none! They are not happy with the *status quo* and thus they make ideal men and women of faith. They possess that basic discontent which is a necessary pre-requisite for faith, because without it there is no openness to a new future and, as we have seen from our consideration of the God who calls, we are summoned into a future which he will determine. Christian faith can never be a sitting down to be happy with what we have.

What is blessed in the Beatitudes is not material poverty, but the radical openness to a new future which is a characteristic of the poor.[14] It must be stressed that the material 'having nothing' is not a biblical virtue in itself. We should be warned against this sort of interpretation by looking to the third Beatitude:

'Blessed are you that weep now, for you shall laugh.' (Luke 6.21)

Those who weep are not only the poor, but they are also promised the joys of the kingdom, because they too are open to a new possibility. We are all aware that the materially wealthy, more often than not, can suffer tragedy and anguish. This sort of experience can also draw them to a realisation, in the midst of their tears, that they cannot control their ultimate hopes, plans and longings by their purse strings. *In itself* possession of wealth is not an obstacle to the possession of the kingdom, even though in many cases it does prove to be so. The important point, for our purposes, is to insist that there is *no universal law* which links material indigence to the following of Christ. How is it that the contrary is still maintained? Largely, because of the misinterpretation of the story of the rich young man.

The Story of the Rich Young Man[15]

I have already discussed Matthew's version of this story (Matt. 19.16–26), as it is often used to show that there is a qualitative distinction between a life lived according to the commandments (19.16–19), and the life of perfection involved in the evangelical counsel of poverty (19.20–2).[16] We have seen that this is to misunderstand the function of the passage within the context of the whole of Matthew's theology of 'perfection'. The rich young man was not called to Religious life, but to Christian life and Matthew calls that life, both in Matt. 5.48 and 19.21, a life of perfection.

We have already noticed that Matthew's version of the story has modified the original by adding this theology of 'perfection'. The original story is found in Mark 10.17–22 and this account is very closely followed by Luke 18.18–23 where the only significant difference is that he changes Mark's identification of the man in question from 'a certain man' to 'a ruler' (Mark 10.17; Luke 18.18).[17] No matter what the variations in the different traditions might be, the central point of the story remains the same.

All the Evangelists present him as a wealthy person who has administered this wealth with justice. This is the point of the list of commandments which Jesus asks him to observe (Mark 10.19; Matt. 19.18–19; Luke 18.20).[18] Only those commandments which a proud rich man would be most likely to break are put to him – those dealing with the treatment of his neighbour. On hearing from the man that he has always observed these commandments, 'Jesus looking upon him loved him' (Mark 10.21) and he calls him to be his disciple: ' "You lack one thing; go, sell what you have, and give to the poor, and you will have treasure in heaven; and come, follow me" ' (Mark 10.21). This is the radical demand which has inspired many courageous people to great things, but this should not block us from asking the most important question. Must this request be made of everyone who wishes to be a disciple of Jesus? Strangely enough, none of the other vocation stories in the New Testament has this request (see Mark 1.16–20; 2.14). The fishermen do abandon their boats and their father in Mark 1.16–20 and Levi does abandon his position in the taxhouse, but there is no command to poverty, nor is there the hint that all is sold up so that the proceeds could go to the poor. In fact, according to John 21.1–14[19] these same disciples return to the lake and their fishing after the death of Jesus.

As this is the case, then a further very important question must be asked: Why is this particular demand made of this particular man? The answer to the question is found in the self-confident request of the man himself, found in all three versions of this story (Mark 10.17; Matt. 19.16; Luke 18.18): 'What must *I do* to inherit eternal life?' Here we have a man who is used to deciding his own destiny, because he can pay for it. This is not the way of faith. Thus Jesus, in calling him to discipleship, must strip away all that stands between the man and a radical commitment to himself. *In the case of this man*, it is his wealth. He is blocked from a total commitment to Jesus because he wants to control his own future, as he always has. Thus, his wealth must go! The story is ultimately about the radical nature of true faith. All that stands between the believer and an unconditional surrender of self to Jesus must go. It is *not* a universal call to all who would wish to become disciples to reduce themselves to a state of financial indigence. That is to universalise a particular case.

There is a similar story, with the same call to radical faith in Matt. 8.21–2. In a context dealing with discipleship (vv. 18–27) we find the following: 'Another of the disciples said to him, "Lord, let me first go and bury my father." But Jesus said to him, "Follow me, and leave the dead to bury their own dead." ' Thank goodness that we have had the common sense not to universalise this story![20] As with the rich man, between this disciple and Jesus stands an obstacle, however, in this case it is not wealth, but an affective relationship. It has to go! Both stories are examples of the radical nature of faith. Wealth and affective relationships can block our commitment to Jesus, but these stories must not be taken as a Gospel message that *only* those who are economically underprivileged and people without attachment to their families, their fathers, mothers, wives and husbands can attain sanctity. That would be to make the Gospel call to sanctity quite irrelevant to the major part of humanity.

Yet, somehow, the stories do apply to our poverty, because our poverty does express our faith. Our vowed life announces to the world, not the evil of possessions, but the value of a shared life inspired by faith in Christ and a desire to live 'in Christ'. This shared life is outwardly reflected in the sharing of all that we are and all that we have and this leads us to a consideration of the second aspect of evangelical poverty which we gleaned from the Jerusalem community's attitude to its material wealth.

A SHARED RESPONSIBILITY FOR THE MATERIAL LIFE OF THE COMMUNITY

How does this New Testament notion of a shared life work itself out in the practice of the life of a vowed community in such a way that it proclaims to the world what 'life in Christ' can really mean?

It stands to reason that no community can survive unless each one of the members assumes an *active* responsibility for the other members. If our Christian existence depends upon our readiness to share, then all, in some way or another, must be productive. Primarily, each must generate the faith, hope and love that sustains others. There is little need to dwell here on the numerous examples of this which can be found in almost every Religious community: the smiling face of the infirm, elderly confrere who makes the struggling youngster see that, somehow, all this makes sense. The list could go on, but a similar productivity is also required from us at the level of material goods. This is where the notion of poverty as 'having nothing' falls short of the Christian ideal. None of us – no matter how aged, infirm or incompetent – has nothing. Each one of us is a unique creation of God, and this flows into what we do. Not all are gifted, in the sense that the world gives to this term, but what we are is reflected in what we do, however modest that may be.[21]

The idea that poverty is to have nothing and to wait for God to send bread from heaven has been seen as what the Gospels demand. I have insisted that this is to misunderstand the Gospels. In reality, it can often lead to a bone-lazy materialism, especially in some countries where the priests, brothers and 'the poor sisters' will never be left without, as they are surrounded by an adoring laity which considers itself as second class, and which subconsciously feels that some holiness will rub off if they associate with the Religious, the first-class citizens of the Kingdom. No Christian and therefore no Religious is called to live off his local community.

A look at the history of Religious life shows that right from the start communities have seen it as their responsibility to work for their own needs. Pachomius, the founder of the cenobitic life, hired himself and his monks out to work in the fields during the harvest season and Basil the Great demanded that all his monks have a trade. The name that comes to mind as an immediate objection is that of Francis of Assisi, so often romanticised in this connection. In fact, he was proud to earn his own living and ordered his followers to continue the trades which they practised before they came to him. It is important to know that he permitted them to beg only when there was no work, or when the salary was not enough to live on (*Regula Prima* 7; Test. 19–22).

The people among whom we live and for whom we work *see us* at work, and this is where we have to pose them questions. What I have written so far could be misunderstood; as if I were arguing that our poverty began and ended with work. We do *not* exist so that we may work. On the contrary! Our work points to *the reason why we exist as a consecrated Christian community*. We must question the values of the world by causing them to ask why talented, profes-sional, hard-working (or even not so talented) people, all work and exist together in and for a concrete, historical community. The witness value of our poverty does not lie in our parading through the streets with the soles flapping off our shoes or our elbows showing through our jackets. That sort of thing may raise eyebrows, but it does not command respect – much less imitation, and the most effective form of evangelisation is to live a life that causes people to want to follow it too. Our poverty calls us to a radical sharing of all that we are and all that we have, so that we may produce a quality of community life that makes people stop and wonder. When the world sees that all our efforts are directed, not to personal aggrandisement, but to the support and strengthening of our life in Christ, then we may be seen as 'world stoppers', questioning the futile values that the world creates when it makes a god of personal success and material values.

CONCLUSION

I would like to conclude with two concrete remarks:

1. We must drop once and for all, the notion that the vow of poverty dispenses the Religious from financial worries so that he or she may be free to work without any of the concerns which come from them. This view errs on two important issues:

i) It is not true. There are many Religious who are called to a service which is continually linked with financial questions. To present our life as free from such worries is a serious double-talk, and this stands at the basis of a lot of the misgivings which Religious have. Non-Religious smile as we speak in this way, as they see us working in fine schools, hospitals and worshipping in churches and living in comfortable houses. If we force people to look *through* these external signs to a genuine quality of shared life, this problem will be greatly reduced.

ii) The Religious who lives without the encumbrance of financial concerns can often be a person who abuses the material goods which do not really matter, but which are available to the community because they have been earned by the hard work of the members of that community.

Poverty is not about being free to serve. It is about showing the world, through the radical sharing of all that we have, that we also share all that we are, in our shared life of faith 'in Christ'. This must work itself out in the context of material things and can be formulated simply as: all that I have, I give *to* the community, all that I need, I receive *from* the community. Living in this way, each member of the community knows and experiences that the responsibility for the material well-being of the community lies with all the members and not just with the ones whose task it is to keep the books! However, this shared responsibility on a material level is nothing if not the external sign of the love which should unite a Christian community.

2. Given this first concluding point, it follows that we must try to avoid a hard and fast definition of the *things* which make for poverty. This will necessarily vary. It should be a matter of plain commonsense that the material context of no two communities (even in the same city) is the same. There can be no universal list of what we can have or not have. What matters is that our difference from the slavery of the world to personal achievements on the material plane be *visible*. This necessarily puts us within the context of material things, but they are not the ultimate measure of our poverty – our shared life 'in Christ' is. We cannot confine this to intellectual and practical criteria. Subtly, to allow these lists is to submit, like the rest of a society which we are trying to question, to the criterion of materialism itself. The roots of our poverty cannot and must not be intellectualised, because the reciprocal dependence and productivity, at all levels, which are the essence of the vow of poverty, cannot be intellectualised and made into a list of things. It acquires its value only if it is motivated by love of an exceptional quality.

Reasons can always be found for a list of do's and don'ts or may-haves and may-not-haves, but if we are honest, we must admit that the need for such lists in our community reflects a rather painful truth. The reality of our life together, the quality of our shared life in Christ, is often very poor, and thus we rush to create structures, to draw up lists which will convey (primarily to ourselves, because others are generally not fooled), an external sign that we are poor. The problem with this system, however, is that the self-centred, non-sharing member of a community can be 'perfect' in matters of poverty, while all sense of true biblically based poverty has been lost, and the community divided.

Genuine love, the self-sacrificing love of Christ, cannot be measured by laws and lists, as it goes beyond any sort of material measurement. Our vow of poverty is one of our major means of showing to the world that we are committed to this love and when we examine our consciences on poverty we must start at the level of our shared life of love, and only when we have come to grips with this basic motive for our very existence as a Christian community should we turn our attention to the material circumstances which are only the context within which our poverty, our shared life 'in Christ', must work itself out.[22]

8. *Chastity*

One of the great fathers of modern Religious life, St Ignatius, could limit his consideration of the vow of chastity to the following remarks: 'What pertains to the vow of chastity does not require explanation, since it is evident how perfectly it should be preserved through the endeavour in this matter to imitate angelic purity, by purity of body and mind' (*Constitutions,* Part VI, ch. 1. no. 1). The rest of Part VI is devoted to an examination and explanation of obedience, which stands at the heart of Jesuit spirituality. Ignatius' few words reflect the situation and the attitude of his own time, but today such a summary dismissal of this vow would not be tolerated. The very words of Ignatius would be questioned. Chastity does need a great deal of explanation, and it is not at all clear how one can preserve this virtue by an imitation of 'angelic' purity.[1] Perhaps even more important is the fact that all Christians, celibate or married, are called to 'purity of body and mind'. This is not the private concern of Religious.[2]

THE OBJECTIONS TO CHASTITY
We are all well aware of the series of objections that are put to a life of chastity from a secularised world which uses sex to add colour and interest to even the most innocent human interests and pastimes. A few hours in front of a television set will teach us all we need to know about these objections. However, I am not concerned with these problems, as it is precisely to this heavily sexualised world that our lives should speak. We will never convert that world by talking about chastity unless our lives continually make people wonder if, perhaps, they have not somehow gone wrong. My concern is to show that today there are serious objections to chastity which arise from within a Christian view of things.

The Second Vatican Council, for the first time in the history of the Church, made its own two very important new teachings which seriously question some of the traditional motives for chastity. I must stress here, however, that both of these teachings did not simply fall out of the heavens at the Council. They were merely the final magisterial articulation of theological reflection which had been widespread in the Church for the greater part of this century.

The first of these new teachings concerned the salvific value of created reality.[3] As a traditional spirituality attempted to show the value of chastity, there was a tendency to play down all that was natural, and man's being supernatural was seen as best expressed by his being chaste. This led to an under-valuation and at times, a rather negative view of all that was natural and physical. Against this tendency, Vatican II devoted a chapter of its decree on the Church in the Modern World to man's activity within the context of created reality (*Gaudium et Spes* 33–9). The role of created reality in the plan of God was beautifully expressed as the Church proclaimed:

> If by the autonomy of earthly affairs is meant the gradual discovery, exploitation and ordering of the laws and values of matter and society, then the demand for autonomy is perfectly in order: *it is at once the claim of modern man and the desire of the creator*. By the very nature of creation, material being is endowed with its own stability, truth and excellence, its own order and laws . . . Believers, no matter what their religion, have always recognised the voice and the revelation of God in the language of creatures (*Gaudium et Spes* 36).

Men and women are not saved *despite* their belonging to the world of material things, *despite* the fact that they are flesh and blood, and therefore sexual beings, but *because of it*, and in and through their being situated in God's creation.

A second very important teaching from Vatican II which is closely related to what we have just seen is a magnificent presentation of the sanctity of the married state, and the sanctification which comes to the married through a life of faithful gift of self in conjugal love. Here the teaching Church leans heavily on the Scriptures and especially on Eph. 5.21–3:

Just as of old God encountered his people with a covenant of love and fidelity, so our Saviour, the Spouse of the Church, now encounters Christian spouses through the Sacrament of marriage. He abides with them in order that by their mutual self-giving spouses will love each other with enduring fidelity, as he loved the Church and delivered himself for it. Authentic married love is caught up into divine love and is directed and enriched by the redemptive power of Christ and the salvific action of the Church (*Gaudium et Spes* 48).

There are two very important points to be noted here. There is a wonderful parallel drawn between the gift of Jesus in his sacrifice of self for the Church and the 'mutual self-giving' of married couples. That very aspect of marriage which is so abused and debased by contemporary culture, and which has been somewhat frowned upon in certain areas of Christian spirituality is paralleled (following Eph. 5.21–3) with the most wonderful moment in the history of God's relationship with man: Christ's gift of himself for us. Then there is that final statement that, in a situation of 'authentic married love'[4] we have the revelation of God's love reflected in the redemptive power of Christ at work in their lives. This is in no way a 'second-class' citizenship in the Kingdom. It is a wonderfully privileged place among men where a God who is love is revealed, and where men and women can find an exquisite means of sanctification.

If this is the case, what is the place of the vow of chastity and the practice of celibacy in Religious life?

THE TRADITIONAL CASE FOR CHASTITY

The Church has always seen virginity as having a special place among Christians. It appears that the saying about being 'eunuchs for the sake of the Kingdom of heaven' in Matt. 19.12 is a Gospel passage which shows the superiority of virginity and Paul certainly advises the Corinthians that if they are not married they would do well to remain so: 'to secure your undivided devotion to the Lord' (see I Cor. 7.32–5). The early centuries of the Church saw a great concentration on the state of virginity, and the writings of the Fathers of the Church certainly reflect an underlying feeling that baptism and marriage go together rather uncomfortably. Perhaps the greatest of the Fathers, St Augustine, is the best-known example. In trying to explain, in his struggle against Pelagius, that infants needed Grace, he had to solve the problem of how an innocent child could be 'of the world' and not 'of Christ'. He struggled for a long time with this problem, but his final solution is that essential to the conception of a child, even among Christian married couples, was concupiscence. All children are born within the context of a physical desire, concupiscence, and thus do not belong to God but to the world: 'Because of this concupiscence it comes to pass that even from just and rightful marriages of the children of God, not children of God but children of the world are born.'[5]

Augustine must be understood within his own historical context (he tended to react very strongly against his former way of life as a Manichean) and within the context of the overall argument which he is pursuing. His basic argument was extremely positive. He insisted upon a universal need for the grace of Christ, and the discussion about infants arose only within this context. Nevertheless, Augustine still reflects the negative stance already taken by some of the earlier Fathers,[6] and this generally felt view of marriage became rather fixed in tradition, although it never became a part of Church teaching.[7]

A certain interpretation of Matt. 19.12 and I Cor. 7.32–5, along with the consistent teaching of the Fathers of the Church have been very influential in the formation of a certain line of argument to defend the place of virginity in Christian tradition. Contemporary historical criticism is questioning the value of both of the sources for this longheld view. As we shall see, it is possible that Matt. 19.12 has nothing to do with the chastity of some who commit themselves to a vowed life of celibacy. St Paul's teaching in I Cor. 7 is very heavily influenced by his belief that the end time was to come very soon, a belief which proved to be wrong, and thus his argument loses its force. There is also a widespread insistence that we understand the Fathers of the Church within the context of their times. The early Church unconsciously reflected the decadent late Roman world in its over-reaction to the problems of sexual licence and it is also important to understand how their theology of virginity is closely linked to – and a continuation of – the theology of martyrdom. Thus, we have no right to *universalise* their teaching on virginity.[8] It appears, therefore, that we must look again to our sources and see if a helpful, guiding teaching on the sense and purpose of a vow of chastity can be discovered.

VATICAN II

Given the beautiful teaching which came from Vatican II on the holiness of conjugal love, we have every right to look to the teaching Church for guidance about a contemporary answer to the problems which a life of vowed chastity poses, from a Christian point of view. This question is dealt with explicitly in the document on the Renewal of Religious life:

> Chastity 'for the sake of the Kingdom of heaven' (Matt. 19.12) which religious profess, must be esteemed an exceptional gift of grace. It uniquely frees the heart of man (cf. I Cor. 7.32–5), so that he becomes more fervent in love for God and for all men. For this reason it is a special symbol of heavenly benefits, and for religious it is a most effective means of dedicating themselves wholeheartedly to the divine service and the works of apostolate. (*Perfectae Caritatis* 12)

The Religious, having read of the wonders of married love in *Gaudium et Spes* 48 has every right to feel a little disappointed with this treatment of his life of chastity. The number goes on with a series of warnings:

> Religious, at pains to be faithful
> They should not presume on their own strength
> They should practise mortification and custody of the senses
> Nor should they neglect the natural means which promote health of mind and body
> They should not be influenced by false doctrines
> Candidates ought not to go forward ... except after really adequate testing
> Warned against the dangers to chastity.

I am not saying that any of this is wrong, but we may have expected something a little more positive! This general atmosphere of danger, caution and fear does not help us a great deal in our attempt to formulate and live a positive and joyful theology of chastity.[9]

However, the reader who has followed me thus far is probably aware that I find this number of *Perfectae Caritatis* misleading on a far more important issue than its negative tone. Taking up the tradition, the Council has used Matt. 19.12 and I Cor. 7.32–5, interpreting these texts to mean that chastity 'frees the heart of man', and is thus 'a most effective means of dedicating themselves wholeheartedly to the divine service and the works of the apostolate'. The document goes on to speak very well of a chaste life being a wonderful eschatological 'sign', and this is very true, but the idea conveyed in the first part of the number is plainly that chastity is a means by which the Religious is freed from the encumbrance of a family so that he may be able to work and pray more effectively. I believe that this is to misinterpret the biblical evidence used (Matt. 19.12 and I Cor. 7.32–5), but it also poses a problem at a practical level. If the chaste celibate is able to come closer to God in work and prayer because of his celibacy, where does that put the married person? We must be logical and conclude that their being married takes them further away from God. That conclusion is, of course, ridiculous, and opposed to the teaching of Eph. 5.21–3 and *Gaudium et Spes* 48, which I discussed above. A careful analysis of the biblical material provides a different answer.

CONTEMPORARY BIBLICAL CRITICISM OF MATT. 19.12 AND I COR. 7.32–5

I mentioned above that there is some doubt among biblical scholars as to whether it is correct to use these passages as the biblical background for the vow of chastity. I wish to approach this biblical material in two steps. Firstly I wish to show how contemporary exegesis questions the traditional use of the texts, and secondly I would like to see if it is possible, after all, to find a more positive theology of chastity *from the same texts*.

Matthew 19.12[10]

As in all literary criticism, this famous passage on being a 'eunuch' must not be pulled out of its context and explained as if it was the only thing which Matthew reported from Jesus. It has a place in a whole Gospel, and within its own immediate context. It is precisely from the study of Matt. 19.12 within its context that scholars have come to doubt whether it is correctly used to speak of celibacy.

It comes as the final 'punch line' in the passage which runs from Matt. 19.3–12. The first part of the passage is taken up with a discussion between Jesus and the Pharisees (vv. 3–9). This passage is paralleled by Mark 10.1–12. The second part of the passage (vv. 10–12) is made up of a discussion with the disciples, and has no parallel in the rest of the New Testament. This should already put us on our guard. Matt. 19.10–12 is a passage which Matthew has added to his source, Mark 10.2–9, so he wants to say something special with this addition.

The encounter with the Pharisees follows the form of a Rabbinic discussion. In the first century there was a discussion over the causes of divorce. There were two schools of thought. A Rabbi Shammai insisted (interpreting Deut. 24.1) that one could only divorce one's wife when there was a serious cause, while Rabbi Hillel (interpreting the same text) said that a divorce was possible for any reason at all. In Matt. 19.3 Jesus' opinion is sought on this matter, as they ask him: ' "Is it lawful to divorce one's wife *for any cause?*" ', obviously wanting to see if he agreed with Hillel's position. Jesus' answer follows a good Rabbinic practice, as he quotes from the Law of Moses (Gen. 1.27 and 2.24), but he interprets these texts in a way which cuts across the question of divorce by saying that it is impossible: 'What therefore God has joined together, let no man put asunder' (Matt. 19.4–6). The Pharisees, not to be beaten, also go to the Law of Moses (Deut. 24.1) and ask why a bill of divorce was allowed by Moses himself, if there was to be no divorce (v. 7). Jesus tells them that it was because of the hardness of the heart of Israel that this happened, and then abandoning all reference to the Law of Moses he announces: ' "And I say to you:[11] whoever divorces his wife, except for unchastity, and marries another, commits adultery" ' (v. 9). Jesus lays down a prohibition of divorce, allowing only one exception. It is important to notice that Mark 10.11, which Matthew is using here, does not have 'except for unchastity'. In fact, the rest of the New Testament (see I Cor. 7.10–11; Luke 16.18; Mark 10.2–12) is absolute in its prohibition of divorce. Only Matthew, therefore, has added this exception, just as he has added vv. 10–12. We must ask why Matthew added these passages, but we must first take our analysis further.

We are now in the passage (vv. 10–12) which is found only in Matthew. The disciples are stunned by the severity of Jesus' teaching, and they exclaim: ' "If such is the case of a man with his wife, it is not expedient to marry" ' (v. 10). Translated into modern terms, the disciples are saying: ' "If I cannot get rid of her, I would be better off if I did not marry her in the first place!" ' Jesus' answer to this (v. 11) is to point out that it is no longer 'the case of a man with his wife'. What he had just announced is an entirely new situation which cannot be measured by merely human and social criteria. He is talking about the wonderful gift which is called *Christian* marriage: ' "Not all men can receive this precept, but only those to whom it is given" ' (v. 11). We are no longer dealing simply with the human, social and sexual situation of a man with a woman, but the 'graced' situation, the gift of Christian marriage. It is its specifically Christian character which makes it indissoluble. We then come to v. 12: ' "For there are eunuchs who have been so from birth, and there are eunuchs who have been made eunuchs by men, and there are eunuchs who have made themselves eunuchs for the sake of the Kingdom of heaven. He who is able to receive this, let him receive it." '

What are we to make of this passage in a context which is *entirely* made up of a discussion of divorce? If the passage is about consecrated celibacy, how does it relate to the rest of the context? This problem has led scholars to seek different solutions, but we must go back to the fact that Matthew, who is largely following Mark 10.2–12, has added two important further passages: 'except for unchastity' in v. 9 and the passage leading to and including the eunuch saying in vv. 11–12. If Matthew has added these passages, then we must suppose that he has added them for a purpose. There was some pastoral concern in the community for which he wrote his Gospel that he was trying to assist by these additions.

It is nowadays generally admitted that the Gospel of Matthew was written for a community largely composed of Jewish-Christians facing difficulties on two fronts:[12]
1. The expulsion from the ancient Torah-centred life-style as official Judaism gradually came to see that any sect which believed that Jesus was 'the Christ' could not remain in its ranks.

2. The Christian message, largely couched in Jewish terms and dependent upon Jewish tradition, was now being preached to the Gentiles, and they were joining the community without any Jewish background.

It seems that Matthew had to face two serious problems in questions of Christian marriage among those Gentiles who came into the community without any Jewish background or formation. In the first place, there were some who were married in a way which Jewish Law (Lev. 18.6–18) regarded as incestuous. We have a clear indication that this was happening from Paul's discussion of it in I Cor. 5.1–5. This is the situation where Matthew allows divorce. There is to be no divorce, except for these cases of incestuous relationships between people who had come to the Christian community from a culture where that same relationship was perfectly normal.[13] This was not the only problem that the ex-pagan converts caused. Some would have come into the community, married there, but then at a later stage, disenchanted, left, returning to their former culture and religion to marry and live on outside the Christian community. The problem to be faced here was that one partner of the marriage would have remained in the Christian community, still linked to his or her former partner by the bond of Christian marriage. How does Matthew solve this problem? He takes a very hard line and asks them to remain unmarried, to become 'Eunuchs for the sake of the kingdom of heaven' (19.12).

It appears to me that this is the best explanation of Matt. 19.12 because it solves three problems which 19.3–12 has always presented to interpreters:

1. To explain why Matthew inserted his exception clause to 19.9 and the passage from vv. 10–12.

2. What is more important is that it explains *both* insertions by relating them to the *same* pastoral problem: the difficulties faced by the irregular marital situation of the converted ex-pagans.

3. It explains v. 12 within the context of vv. 3–12. It is not left hanging limply on to the end of the passage as some sort of strange unconnected saying about consecrated celibacy.

The problem with this explanation, however, is that the traditional use of Matt. 19.12 can no longer be made. We must note carefully what we have seen so far. Up to this point I have examined what *Matthew* is saying in Matt. 19.3–12. I pointed out that vv. 3–9 come from Mark 10.2–12, but where did Matthew find v. 12? Did he invent it? There are very good reasons which indicate that he did not, but we will return to that after a consideration of I Cor. 7.32–5.

I Cor. 7.32–5[14]

A reading of this passage seems to show clearly that Paul advocates the state of celibacy as a superior state for a Christian:

> I want you to be free from anxieties. The unmarried man is anxious about the affairs of the Lord, how to please the Lord; but the married man is anxious about worldly affairs, how to please his wife, and his interests are divided. And the unmarried woman or girl is anxious about the affairs of the Lord, how to be holy in body and spirit; but the married woman is anxious about worldly affairs, how to please her husband. I say this for your own benefit, not to lay any restraint upon you, but to promote good order and to secure your undivided devotion to the Lord.

Once again, however, we must situate the passage in its context. In the passage which immediately precedes 7.32–5, Paul speaks about a series of worldly and human activities which must become relative.

> I think that *in view of the impending distress* it is well for a person to remain as he is . . . I mean, brethren, that *the appointed time has grown very short;* from now on let those who have wives live as though they had none, and those who mourn as though they were not mourning, and those who rejoice as though they were not rejoicing . . . *For the form of this world is passing away.* (7.26, 29–30, 31)

In this passage Paul gives his reasons why he believes that people must drop all attention to ordinary affairs:

'in view of the impending distress'

'the appointed time has grown very short'

'the form of this world is passing away'.

What does Paul mean by these expressions? It is clear that the early Paul was convinced and urged on in his preaching because he believed that the final end time, the return of the Lord, was only just around the corner. It is evident from his very first letters, the letters to the Thessalonians (written in the late 40s), that he had preached this message of the imminent return of the Lord with such conviction that the Christians had decided that all they had to do was sit and wait. There was no longer any need to apply themselves to their day-to-day tasks, if the Day of the Lord was about to arrive (see I Thess. 4.13–5.11, and the whole of II Thessalonians). The first letter to the Corinthians was probably written shortly after, in 54. Paul is still finding the urgency of his message in the conviction that all is about to end very shortly. It is because of this conviction that he can so strongly advocate that his Corinthian community devote all their time and attention, not to wives, husbands, mourning, rejoicing, buying, selling and dealing with the world (see I Cor. 7.29–31) but so that they might secure their undivided attention and devotion to the Lord who was about to come (see 7.35).

But he did not come – and he still has not come. If Paul's teaching on celibacy is so intimately linked to his presupposition that the end time is at hand, does this teaching not become somewhat relative when the end time does not come? In fact, Paul's own understanding of the end time develops. He was able to see, as the years passed by, that the Church was going to face a long history and thus several of his positions vary from those found in the Thessalonian correspondence and I Corinthians. If the end time is near at hand, there is no need for a theology of marriage, but if the Church is going to work its way through history, then such a theology is urgently needed – and it was provided by Eph. 5.21–3, the Pauline point of view that was used in *Gaudium et Spes* 48.[15]

Again we find that a study of the whole context of the passage used by the tradition as the biblical background for the vow of chastity rather lessens its significance. Are we, then, without support for this state of life within the Church? Here we must return to Matt. 19.12

THE EUNUCH SAYING ON THE LIPS OF JESUS

As I concluded my treatment of what the eunuch passage meant *within the context of Matt.* 19.3–12, I asked the question: Where did Matthew find v. 12? Did he invent it or did it come to him from some 'source'? It is widely accepted that Matthew did *not* invent 19.12, but that he found it among the remembered words of Jesus himself. Scholars have various criteria for determining whether or not certain passages were composed in the early Church, or whether they come from Jesus himself. The following are the main reasons which force us to conclude that Matt. 19.12 is something that Jesus actually said:

1. The word 'eunuch' is a very harsh word. It is a bad enough word today, but in the first century when these men were actually a rejected part of society, it was offensive and crude. There is no way that the early Church would have invented a saying which spoke of Jesus or his followers in such terms. If it is found in the Gospel, then it must have been said by Jesus. Despite the continual use of this very crude word, Matthew includes the passage because Jesus himself had said it.

2. The structure of the passage is typical of a semitic proverbial type passage, where the listener (or reader) is gradually led through a rhythmic play on a word, to the final point at the end of the passage.[17] This form is clear even in the English translation: 'There are eunuchs . . . and there are eunuchs . . . who have been made eunuchs . . . and there are eunuchs . . . who have made themselves eunuchs.' This means that it comes from an Aramaic-speaking background.

3. Although Luke and Mark (understandably) do not report this passage, it does turn up *in a slightly different form* in Justin Martyr and Epiphanius, two early Fathers of the Church. This suggests that they have also heard or seen this passage, but in a form slightly different from Matt. 19.12. They probably had it from an independent source, so Matthew did not invent it.

4. The most important factor, however, lies in the impossibility of seeing a situation in the life of the early Church which would have caused them to invent this passage. It must be there because Jesus said it.

If Jesus said it, then we must see if we can discover why he said it and what it meant to him. The attitude of people in first century

Judaism towards eunuchs was extremely negative,[18] yet the 'eunuch' theme is central to Matt. 19.12. Despite its crudeness and its offensive implications it is used in a noun and in a verbal form, no less than five times in this one verse. Why would Jesus use such an expression?

There is ample evidence in the Gospels that Jesus was the object of continual abuse from his opponents. He and his disciples did not fast (Mark 2.18), they violated the Sabbath (Mark 2.23) and they take their meals without the ritual lustrations (Mark 7.5). Jesus himself is called ' "a glutton and a drunkard, a friend of tax collectors and sinners" ' (Matt. 11.19). ' "You are a Samaritan and have a demon," ' accuse the Jews in John 8.48, and on another occasion we are told that ' "they have called the master of the household Beelzebul" ' (Matt. 10.25). It appears that this process of heaping abuse upon Jesus was a normal way of attack, and it seems more than probable that another term used to attack Jesus was 'Eunuch!'[19] Given the importance of marriage and the procreation of children, in obedience to Gen. 1.28, it appears more than probable that there was something about the life-style of Jesus of Nazareth which gave his opponents the chance to call him 'Eunuch!' in a derogatory and abusive sense. Matt 19.12 on the lips of Jesus was his calm reply to the attacks from his enemies who sought any excuse to hurl abuse at this troublesome character. Jesus was a celibate,[20] and was thus immediately open to such abuse, particularly as he was a public figure who troubled the establishment by the quality and authority of his life and preaching.[21] I would suggest that one of the reasons why this particular 'word of Jesus' remained alive in the tradition, despite the harshness of the word, 'eunuch', was because it was Jesus' regular answer to a regular form of abuse which was aimed at him.

It is not enough to establish, through our modern critical methods, the fact that a celibate Jesus replied to his enemies in the terms of Matt. 19.12. What is most important for us is to ask just what the saying meant for Jesus. Now we are right back into the heart of the subject of this chapter. We are now touching the reason why Jesus was a celibate. In Matt. 19.12, Matthew's context seems to be addressed to ex-pagan Christians who now find themselves alone and cannot remarry, but the passage had its origin on the *lips of*

Jesus, and there it meant something quite different: Why Jesus was celibate.

It has been traditional to understand the reason for being a eunuch as 'for the sake of the Kingdom of heaven' in a final sense. This means that one is celibate so that one may be free and able to give oneself for the construction of the Kingdom of heaven. This is the way *Perfectae Caritatis* 12 uses Matt. 19.12 and this is the source of my major difficulty with the passage from the Council. The original Greek text means more than that. The Greek uses a preposition (*dia* + accusative case) which indicates that Jesus announced that he was celibate 'because of' the Kingdom of heaven. He was not a celibate 'so that' he might construct the Kingdom, but 'because of' the overwhelming presence of the Kingdom. The Greek indicates that this is the primary meaning of the passage. It is the overwhelming power of the presence of the Kingdom in his life that led Jesus to celibacy. We must now explain Matt. 19.12 in this light. Jesus' opponents knew of two types of eunuch: the one born so and the one made so by man. Like Jesus, these people were 'unable' to accept a normal married situation. However, the motive for Jesus' inability was not physical. He was so taken over by the urgent presence of the Kingdom that he could do no other than give himself entirely to it. The celibacy of Jesus was not something which he made happen to himself by first deliberating whether or not it should happen, and then deciding in favour of it so that he would be free to dedicate himself entirely to the construction of the Kingdom to come. The causality ran in the opposite direction. In Jesus of Nazareth the guiding principle and the overwhelming experience of his life was the presence of the lordship of God whom he called 'Father' (see Matt. 11.27 par; Mark 13.32; 14.36; Luke 11.2 and the whole of the Fourth Gospel). It was this 'lordship' which led him to his state of celibacy, to his being a eunuch *because of* the overwhelming presence of the Kingdom in his life, and suddenly I Cor. 7.32–5 regains its sense.

We saw in our consideration of that passage that Paul claimed that marriage (and many other ordinary occupations) became relative in the light of the imminent return of the Lord. We also saw, however, that contemporary exegesis tends to take the sting out of Paul's claims as he was not correct in his ideas about the immediate return of the Lord. However, a celibacy lived under the urgent presence of the Kingdom of God again makes sense of Paul's argument. Contemporary exegesis is correct in claiming that we must not make this an important New Testament teaching on the relative value of marriage, but the celibacy of Jesus, lived because he could do no other as he was so overpowered by the presence of the Kingdom, renders Paul's mistaken idea about the sudden return of the Lord correct. The eschatological moment is *now*, because the Lord has taken me over *now*. Jesus was celibate because of an 'undivided attention to his Lord', God whom he called 'Father' (see I Cor. 7.35).

THE VOW OF CHASTITY TODAY

Thus far I have been speaking only about how Jesus saw and spoke about *his* celibacy. However, his reply to his opponents is not just a defence of himself and an explanation of why he was not married. It would have been then, and still remains today, an invitation to all those who hear this quiet reply to strident abuse to consider just what the Kingdom might hold if it has so determined the life of Jesus. Here is the authentically and radically evangelical basis for a life of celibacy. No longer are our lives based on an odd text which somehow was tacked on to the end of a discussion of divorce, but they are rooted in the life-style of Jesus himself.

Like Jesus, we are chaste because of the overwhelming presence of God's Kingdom which keeps crowding in on us. In other words, our ongoing decision for chastity is intelligible as a decision which comes about within the context of a major religious experience, just as the decision for marriage comes about within the context of a major religious experience.[22] Why does this particular man marry that particular girl? So many other combinations would have been possible, but something unique has happened between these two people. In an authentic situation, they 'fall in love'. They can do no other. There is a kingdom established between the two of them that renders them existentially incapable of doing anything else. All of this happens *before* any decision to marry. So must it be with the decision for chastity. A life of chastity is nothing else but the existential consequence which flows out of the prior experience of the urgent presence of the Kingdom of God. This is what it means to be 'a eunuch for the sake of the kingdom of heaven' (Matt. 19.12), drawn into a situation where all that matters is that we be 'anxious about the affairs of the Lord' (see I Cor. 7.32–5).[23]

A very important consequence of this re-reading of our traditional texts is that it gives the celibate every right to his place in society alongside all classes of men and women, married and unmarried. No longer can the celibate be regarded as deprived, deformed or in some way 'strange'. No longer is the life of chastity a 'stiff-upper lip' and a 'gritting your teeth' business. Where we stand as celibates flows out of exactly the same sort of experience which led that man to marry that woman: the overpowering presence of a Kingdom of love. Just as, in an authentic situation of sexual love, they can do no other than marry and consecrate themselves to each other and their families, so also the celibate, in an authentic situation of celibate love, can do no other than be a eunuch because of the Kingdom of love in his life. Seen in this *parallel* fashion, instead of the all-to-familiar *contrasting* fashion, these two different ways of living out the same overpowering experience can be mutually enriched. The celibate learns from married couples that God's love is revealed through the affective life of his creatures, while the married can see from the life of the celibate that the source of this love ultimately transcends what their limited human affection can demonstrate.[24]

CONCLUSIONS

I would like to make two more practical concluding remarks.

1. Behind this re-interpretation of our traditional biblical background for a life of chastity stands the conviction that our celibate lives have their source and strength from our stance *vis-à-vis* a God of love. However, this being taken over by this Kingdom must be reflected in and witnessed to the world by the *quality of our love*, that is, *the quality of our life together:* our community life. We are not *primarily* chaste so that we will be free to work, even though *Perfectae Caritatis* indicates that this is one of the major functions of a vow of chastity. J. Murphy-O'Connor stated the case well when he wrote:

It is an unfortunate paradox, but the idea that celibacy frees for universal love is one of the major reasons why religious communities have failed to fulfill their witness potential, because inevitably this gives rise to the view that the community is merely a base *from which* the real work is done. The result is that religious communities become loveless deserts. Not only does this make celibacy virtually impossible because man cannot live without love, but it means that the outsider who is shocked into asking 'What makes them different?' finds nothing but a verbal answer to his question. The real answer, the existential answer, is lacking. Not unnaturally, then, celibate life is judged to be meaningless.[25]

Again, when we come to examine our consciences about the significance of our chaste lives, we must start 'at home'.
2. Far too often, a difficulty in living the life of chastity is at the basis of both community and individual crises. I know that what follows is often said, but it bears repeating. All sorts of lack of love and sinfulness – back-biting conversations, deep divisions among confrères, carelessness about prayer and a lazy living off the hard work of the rest of the community – are tolerated and the Sacrament of Reconciliation is rightly judged as the place to start in an effort to overcome this sinfulness. However, a difficulty in the affective area all too often leads to a rapid decision that the person in question is 'out of place'. It is often difficult to find, in this situation, the same tolerance, love and understanding that are given to other problems. Yet, as far as the New Testament is concerned, discussions of moral questions centre their attention on the basic law of Christianity: the law of love. Among us, however, failures against the community, poverty and obedience are tolerated, but often the stern defence of the aspect of our lives which should show the quality of our love serves only to demonstrate its absence. In the Gospels, as far as affective problems are concerned, the sinners in question receive no condemnation, but pardon (see, for example, John 8.1–11).

In the light of this, we must learn to be patient with these difficulties, both our own and those of others. It is precisely here that the love and support of the people with whom we live are absolutely vital. Rollo May, the celebrated psychologist, has spoken of the sure sign of a mature and integrated personality as being 'the courage of imperfection'. We must allow ourselves the exhilaration, genuinely felt, and shown, and not just spoken about, which comes from loving and being loved. Only in this way and through this *experience* can we come closer to understanding a God who is defined as love (I John 4.8–16). Only then will we be able to see why we can and must be so swept off our feet by the urgent presence of the Lordship of that God.

All of us are made for intimacy. We must face this squarely, convinced that to live properly Christian lives is to live whole lives. Men and women usually resolve the crisis of intimacy when they choose one another. From that moment on all other options are existentially impossible because of the 'Kingdom' which has been established between them. So must the celibate also spend his or her life resolving the crisis of intimacy 'because of the Kingdom', and then it may be said at Vatican III of our lives, what Vatican II said about married love: 'Authentic celibate love is caught up into divine love and is directed and enriched by the redemptive power of Christ and the salvific action of the Church' (see *Gaudium et Spes* 48).

9. *Obedience*[1]

The reader may be somewhat overwhelmed by the idealistic nature of all that I have written so far, but a consideration of the biblical model for Christian obedience and authority will make this aspect of the Christian vocation seem an almost impossible ideal. Despite that fact, we must face the radical nature of the ideal to which we are called by our baptism and to which we daily commit ourselves in our continued decision to live in a Christian community.

Our task in this book is to ask the Scriptures, and especially the Gospels, to speak to us about the demands of God's Word in our call to poverty, chastity and obedience, in short, to a life of perfection. Traditionally we have used certain texts, and I have been looking again at these texts to see if modern biblical criticism can tell us something else, something new, something different, something perhaps even more difficult. I think that generally speaking we have found that a critical look at traditional texts does in fact put a whole new set of demands on us, demands which I believe are very liberating, despite the fact that they are very idealistic, in so far as they call us continually to a greater divinisation through a greater humanisation. So we come closer to God by being more fully human beings.

Turning to examine the vow of obedience, we find that there is not one single text which has been used continually in the tradition. For poverty, for example, there were the Beatitudes (Luke 6.20: 'Blessed are you poor . . . for yours is the kingdom of God') and especially the story of the rich young man (Mark 10.17–22 and parallels). These are texts which have always served both as the biblical background and the ideal model for an evangelical counsel of poverty. For chastity, there was particularly the eunuch passage (Matt. 19.12: 'There are eunuchs who made themselves eunuchs for the sake of the kingdom of heaven') and I Corinthians 7, which recommended that the Christian remained unmarried, 'to secure undivided attention to the Lord' (I Cor. 7.35). These passages were used by the documents of Vatican II. However, when we come to consider the vow of obedience we cannot refer to the tradition and say that we have a definite text from the Gospels on which a vow of obedience can be based. Yet, more than any of the vows this is the one that is most biblical. This is so because behind the call for obedience in the Christian life stands the call to follow the life-style of Jesus of Nazareth. His life is dominated by a profound openness and obedience to God, whom he called his Father.

VATICAN II

The attitude of Jesus is taken as fundamental to this vow and this is reflected in the Council document on Religious life (*Perfectae Caritatis* 14). Again, we find that the document uses very traditional language and in fact there is an expression here to which people nowadays react rather badly. Nevertheless, I believe that the traditional idea behind this number of the document still has a tremendous importance although perhaps it should have been expressed in different terms.

Even a first reading of the text shows that the Council Fathers have used an abundance of biblical references and thus have correctly founded this vow on the life-style of Jesus. 'Through the profession of obedience, religious offer to God a total dedication of their own wills as a sacrifice of themselves; they thereby unite themselves with greater steadiness and security to the saving will of God.' This introductory statement is already somewhat difficult for a generation of Religious who, quite correctly, do not see their lives of obedience as a loss of their unique individuality. However, the biblical section, which is very good, now follows: 'In this way they follow the pattern of Jesus Christ, who came to do the Father's will (cf. John 4.34; 5.30; Heb. 10.7; Ps.39.9). 'Taking the nature of a slave' (Phil. 2.7), He learned obedience from his sufferings (cf. Heb. 5.8). Under the influence of the Holy Spirit, religious submit themselves to their superiors, whom faith presents as God's representatives . . . ' This last expression, if understood in terms of the older idea that the superior more or less had a 'hot line' to God, is widely rejected in some circles today. The document goes on, still in rather traditional language: 'and through whom they are guided into the service of all their brothers in Christ. Thus did Christ himself out of submission to the Father minister to the brethren and surrender His life as a ransom for many (cf. Matt. 20.28; John 10.14–18). In this way, too, religious assume a firmer commitment to the ministry of the Church and labor to achieve the mature measure of the fullness of Christ' (cf. Eph. 4.13).

So we do find some of the older expression in this statement, but also present is an all-important biblical model, which I must examine, insisting that the Religious, in professing obedience, is called to follow the life-style of Jesus of Nazareth. This same point is made in the latter part of the document just quoted, which again draws the parallel between the service of the Religious and the service rendered by Christ 'in submission to the Father'. But once we have established that the imitation of Christ is where our obedience has its source, then we can see that my continual insistence throughout the whole of this book again comes to the fore: if a Religious must be obedient in imitation of Christ, *all* Christians must be obedient in imitation of Christ. The Religious is not the only one who is called to imitate Christ, all the baptised are. What then is the function of Religious obedience?

OBEDIENCE: THE IMITATION OF CHRIST

As I have been indicating throughout, the Religious community is a microcosm of the Church: the Church in action, a visible, tangible group which we can call 'Church', and it exists because the people who make up that community believe in the salvation which comes to us through Jesus of Nazareth. We are not an economic community, nor a football club, but a 'faith' community, and the goal of each one of us is to imitate the object of our faith as closely as possible – or to spend the rest of our lives working at it anyway! The fundamental need of a Religious committed to this life-style is to know Christ. How can one imitate a person if one does not know him? This I feel is one of the great problems of the Church and thus of Religious life. A recognition of the problem stands behind the Council's request that we return to the Scriptures (*Perfectae Caritatis* 2). We hear so often: 'Come closer to Jesus; know Jesus; pray to Jesus; imitate Jesus.' But who is he? What does he mean to me? Does he remain that image that appealed to me as a teenager?

Or have I grown in an understanding of the person and personality of this man? This is a very important question which is often never posed. We must *know* Christ Jesus and not just commit ourselves to some fantasy or some attractive, artistic presentation of him which strikes our fancy. A life based on this sort of commitment is destined for tragedy and the grim faces of many of our confrères in the light of modern biblical criticism is an indication that many have never come to grips with the unfathomable mystery of the person of Jesus into which our new methods are delving with greater insistence. The problem for many is that their image of Jesus is no longer quite so clear cut; they no longer have him 'in their pockets', and thus, in fear, many react negatively to new suggestions and possibilities coming from contemporary biblical research. This book is an attempt to show that their fears are groundless. We have to know this Christ Jesus and have him continually in front of us and we have to grow in this knowledge. The more we grow, the more we will be prepared to cast off *our* ideas and to lose ourselves in the mystery of him. This is faith and is also the reason why we exist as a Religious community. The challenge of faith, however, must become real and vital and this will happen only when it becomes a *personal* challenge. Only when we are called into action or into a quality of life because of the impact of a personality upon us will the challenge really transform us. Unless the challenge of faith is real and personal, it becomes a chasing after rainbows.

This fundamental need was recognised by Paul, as he wrote to the earliest communities of the Christian Church. He, or his successor,[2] could write to the Ephesians: 'Be imitators of God, as beloved children.' This comes from the Hebrew idea of imitating God as a child would imitate a father – the perfect Israelite being understood as the son of God in so far as he was an obedient follower of the Law of God. Then Paul adds: 'And walk in love, as Christ loved us and gave himself up for us, a fragrant offering and sacrifice to God' (Eph. 5.1–2). To be imitators of God sounds attractive to a person who believes, but how is this possible? What is the concrete modality of my imitation of God? The Ephesians are told that this is possible by 'walking in love'. Now, at least, we have something more concrete, but there are all sorts of 'love'. Is there any further indication how the Christian should love? A definite, concrete model is offered: 'As Christ loved us.' The Church is no longer faced with the challenge of a God who was always present, but never to be grasped, a God who revealed himself through battles, prophets and words, times of famine and times of plenty. Now he has become a personal encounter with a concrete, historical figure called Jesus of Nazareth, the Christ, and Paul asks that we imitate him. So Paul presents Christ as the concrete example; to imitate God, Christians have to love as Christ loved, that is, completely.

However, even a slight knowledge of the situation of this community reveals another problem. How many people in Ephesus knew Jesus? For how many Ephesians did that appeal to Jesus and his gift of self represent a personal calling? How many actually had experienced Jesus? Probably no one. So Paul must somehow render historical the Christ-Christian challenge. Paul was a realist; he was aware that one can talk endlessly about love but if the love that we believe in is the love that Christ showed us, then it must become a personal challenge, not merely something one talks about. Paul must solve this problem as very few of his communities had had this challenge. To do this, he takes the only step possible and in so doing lays the basis for all Christian authority: 'Be imitators of me, as I am of Christ' (I Cor. 11.1). Paul presents himself as an historical, concrete presence in the community who demands obedience from them on the basis of the fact that he is presenting the demand of Christ to them. This extraordinary statement in Paul: 'Be imitators of me as I am of Christ', has been explained as Paul in an 'off-moment', when he has become big-headed and wants to let everyone know how good he is. But all the letters of Paul, written to communities who knew him personally contained similar statements (e.g. I Thessalonians 1.6; I Corinthians 4.16–17; Galatians 4.12; Philippians 4.9). It would have been unrealistic of Paul to write to the Romans or the Colossians 'Be imitators of me ... ' because he was not known to them as a physical, historical imitator of Christ in their midst.

As a matter of fact, this idea is not restricted to Pauline writings; the first letter of Peter contains something similar. Writing to the authorities of the communities he says: 'Tend the flock of God that is in your charge not by constraint but willingly, not for shameful gain but eagerly, not as domineering over those in your charge but by being an example to the flock. An example that merits imitation'

(I Peter 5.2–3). As in Paul, the author is insisting that authority is only to be had and exercised by one who 'willingly' and 'eagerly' leads his community by his example.

Paul's awareness that it was useless merely preaching Christ, is shown in the fact that he keeps returning to this principle. He know that the only way he can claim to have any authority is by insisting that he represents the presence of Christ in their midst. Perhaps the clearest example of this comes at the end of the first chapter of Philippians:

> For me to live is Christ, and to die is gain. If it is to be life in the flesh, that means fruitful labour for me. Yet which I shall choose I cannot tell. I am hard pressed between the two. My desire is to depart and be with Christ, for that is far better. But to remain in the flesh is more necessary on your account. Convinced of this I know that I shall remain and continue with you all, for your progress and joy in the faith, so that in me you may have ample cause to glory in Christ Jesus, because of my coming to you again (Phil. 1.21–6).

Paul is nothing if not a great realist; the message of Paul is something that must go on through the ages. A little reflection shows that this is the only way we can have authority in a Christian community. We do not belong to economic communities, political communities, football clubs, social clubs, but we belong to a Christian community, a faith community. How often we are told: 'If you were working in a bank and you were told to do such and such, then you would do it.' The answer is: 'I am not working in a bank. I belong to a faith community that has its sense and its unity because of faith in Christ Jesus.' It is from this fact that I must work out my theology of obedience. Any other foundations would be false. Our Christian communities are based on the Incarnation. I cannot stress this enough because it is here that, despite the somewhat traditional expressions used by the Council, its teaching remains valid.

The traditional statement in the Council document spoke of the superior's taking the place of God. I would find that hard to accept if this meant that the superior was God on earth, with plenipotentiary powers over all men. It is not that the superior has a hot line to God, but that the authority-figure renders incarnational, in an historical, concrete person, the call to be imitators of Christ. The Christian authority-figure has authority only in so far as he can repeat with Paul: 'Be ye imitators of me, as I am of Christ!'[3] To the extent that the authority-figure re-incarnates Christ, he has authority in a Christian community. This sounds very idealistic and puts the stress on the authority-figure, so two points need to be made very clearly at this stage.

First, no authority-figure re-incarnates Christ, as all are sinners. However, the ideal is that all authority-figures see their primary task, within the context of their community, as a continual attempt, through a quality of life, to act as a central figure, continually reminding the people with whom they live of the values of Christ. The superior's task is to say to the community: 'Be ye imitators of me as I am trying to be an imitator of Christ.'

Secondly, any authority-figure who tries thus to exercise authority without a community which understands his role and function in the community in this way will soon come to grief. In other words, the ability for re-living the biblical model of Christian authority will be made possible only in a Christian community which shares that ideal. As we shall see later, this is ultimately where a great number of experiments to live such a form of authority and obedience have failed. The superiors appointed have done well, but the communities were not prepared to open themselves to the risk of the radical life-style of Jesus of Nazareth. However, it was generally the superior who was blamed for the failure.

I believe that the Pauline ideal of authority in the community acts as a force to draw the community together, in an attempt to constitute the whole Christ. As someone earnestly strives on a full-time basis to present the community with the realities of the call of Jesus to each one, that person becomes the head to whom all look in hope. This figure helps us to make sense of the everyday work in which we are involved, shows us that success at this level is not vital, and makes clear, not only in words but in his or her person and function within the community, what our life is really all about. Paul never speaks of obedience to the will of God and he never speaks of obedience to a 'law'. He speaks only of obedience to Christ (II Cor. 10.5–6) or to the Gospel (Rom. 10.16; Gal. 2.14; 5.7). These two, (Christ and the Gospel) are, in reality, one and the same, as the preaching of the Gospel continues the presence of Christ down through the centuries. Paul can thus speak of the obedience of faith, which means an obedience which is a total commitment of the believer to Christ.

We believe, along with St Irenaeus (who died about 180 AD), that those of us who are prepared to let everything go and commit ourselves totally to Christ will ultimately be those people most fully alive: 'The glory of God is man fully alive' (*Adversus Haereses* IV, 20.7).[4] We are convinced that we will be fully human only when we are fully Christian and that we will be fully Christian only when we are fully human. A fear-ridden individual who has to be protected from all decision-making by the strong superior, is not fully human and therefore not fully Christian. Another person who wants to do his or her 'own thing' all the time has lost the sense of the Cross, of being an imitator of Christ, who: 'though he was in the form of God, did not count equality with God a thing to be grasped, but emptied himself, taking the form of a servant' (Phil. 2.6–7). Such a person can hardly be called fully Christian and therefore not fully human either. Thus this vow of obedience becomes ultimately our means to the fullness of life, the fullness of Christianity, the fullness of humanity, and authority has the tremendously difficult task of creating a situation where this can happen: a situation in which a Religious can make a fully human and fully free decision to commit him or herself continually to the imitation of Christ. If this situation exists, by what right does a Religious refuse obedience? If it is lacking, by what right does the Religious superior ask for obedience?

THE PRACTICE OF OBEDIENCE

The biblical message is clear, but when we try to understand the working out of obedience in our daily lives then the difficulties arise. The message of an upward call into Christ (see Phil. 3.14) leaves totally free the individual's initiative or responsibility, but all of this has to be exercised in a context which calls the individual continually to be an imitator of Jesus Christ. This, of course, is very open to criticism and it would be foolish to assert that in this situation mistakes will be avoided. While this situation may produce many authentic decisions, it will not exclude the possibility of mistakes. As a rule we like to avoid mistakes; we like to have everything in order all the time, and obedience has often been used by superiors as a weapon to make sure this happens, by lopping off any initiative which may appear to be a threat to the established order. The Religious also used his obedience in the same way; he never ran the risk of making a mistake, as he could always claim to be acting under obedience. If anyone was at fault, it was the superior. Although this attitude to obedience has already been revised and much progress has been made, I still think we have to go on with a re-assessment of the subject and we need to work on renewal on two levels:

First, we need to review our attitude to the notion of a superior: who they are, how to choose them and what we expect from them. Behind this must stand the word of Jesus from the tenth chapter of Mark:

> You know that those who are supposed to rule over the Gentiles, lord it over them, and their great men exercise authority over them. *But it shall not be so among you;* but whoever would be great among you must be slave of all. For the Son of Man also came not to be served but to serve and to give his life as a ransom for many (Mark 10.42–5).[5]

Secondly, and perhaps more importantly, we need to undertake a renewal in ourselves, in our understanding of our life primarily as a life that makes sense because we belong to a faith community and at the centre of our lives should be a deep desire to be called further and further away from ourselves into the fullness of life that can be had only in Christ.

If we can work at these two tasks then I believe that obedience in our communities will become a sign in the world, a genuine instrument of evangelisation where members are seen to be maturely responsible but totally dedicated to life in Christ. The witness-value of our communities depends on their being a setting where members make decisions regarding their own lives. The usual objections will be made that this leads to chaos and we must admit that this has, to a certain extent, happened. Far too often, however, we merely criticise and never come to grips with the real reasons why certain things have happened. One of the most important reasons for some of the chaos is that so many of us were trained in a certain form and understanding of obedience that we were too immature to adapt to the new presentation of obedience offered us by the Church and our own Chapters. We either rejected it and withdrew from the risk of genuine obedience or abused our new-found 'freedom' by behaving like children just let out of school.

Any superior, even in this ideal situation, will, on occasion, have to act authoritatively. There will be times when they have to intervene as Paul did when things were not going well. We know that Paul gave a lot of specific directives; he was well aware that he needed sometimes to enter a discussion with severity and these interventions are known as Paul's moral imperatives. A very interesting phenomenon emerges from a close study of these imperatives which can be summed up in two conclusions:[6]

First, when Paul intervenes he does not do so on his own authority, but to call his converts back to the Lord. For example, he will continually indicate what comes from the Lord and what is merely his own (see I Thess. 4.1–12; I Cor. 7.25). This shows very well where Paul bases his authority. Paul is never issuing a call to life because of the great knowledge of Saul of Tarsus, but only in so far as he can call people to be imitators of him as he is of Christ. The rest becomes relative.

Secondly, Paul never makes a decision. He presents a teaching (the best example is the well-known case of incestuous relationships I Cor. 5), and states what is to be done in the light of their new life in Christ. He then leaves the matter to his community, and the person involved must decide for or against the word, person and teaching of Jesus. If he rejects Jesus, Paul has no hesitation in recommending his expulsion from the community but even this is to be a salvific punishment, 'that his spirit may be saved in the day of the Lord Jesus' (I Cor. 5.5).

Rules and Constitutions of Religious congregations and the directives of superiors have a value in so far as they attempt to re-incarnate and re-present in a contemporary situation, the words, message and demands of Jesus of Nazareth. Ultimately, this means that they are to call the Religious to live a life which is outstanding in the quality of its love. This was the way of Jesus of Nazareth, and it is the way his followers must go if they wish to show to the world that their obedience renders them authentically human.

To propose a love which reaches out to empower others as the criterion for authentic humanity could be as unrealistic as a suggestion to imitate the exploits of Asterix or Superman, if we did not know that one individual had once demonstrated this possibility. Because he was an historical figure, the mode of existence displayed by Jesus Christ remains a perpetual challenge to an attainable standard.[7]

The impression that the authorities decide every matter because of their own wisdom, insights and personal authority needs to be corrected. We have to reach decisions together,[8] but there will always be some situations where the superior will need to make the decisions, and these will cause anguish, pain, tears and real suffering. But if, behind these difficult situations, we have a community which is ultimately based on love, then the problems which arise are not insurmountable. In a context of loving obedience, no error on the part of subjects or the superiors will be irreparable, and this is another area where contemporary Religious life needs to examine its conscience. A lack of preparedness to accept error is a sign of a lack of love!

CONCLUSIONS

I believe that the so-called contemporary crisis of authority is a myth. The considerable amount of disarray we have experienced in the Religious life in recent years is not coming from a contempt for authority. I think that there is an innate feeling in people who read the Gospels that an authority that rules by law and rod is not Christian. What we want is real Christian leadership, and that is hard to find and even harder to put into practice. We will never succeed unless we are all convinced that we are called to the one task: to reproduce in history a quality of a life of love which will make the world ask, 'What do these people have which makes them what they are? Why do we not have it?' When we have this quality of a life of love in our communities then perhaps an authority will have a real chance to lead us continually towards Christ. In any other situation, free, open and joint prayer-filled decision-making is impossible, and the superior is swamped by bureaucratic requests and called upon to act as a referee in the many difficulties and disputes which will always arise among us, but which should be resolved by the shared commitment of ultimate values of the people involved, without having to call upon higher authority.

I believe that we live in an era of great opportunity and great light and not in a time of crisis, and that the responsibility for a return to an authority based on Gospel values, lies with everyone of us. The last Apostolic Exhortation made by Pope Paul VI, which I have already used, spoke about how Religious evangelise. In many ways the Holy Father's words sum up all I have been saying: 'Religious for their part, find in their consecrated lives a privileged means of effective evangelisation.' It is in our poverty, chastity and obedience, in our consecrated lives, that we find a privileged means of effective evangelisation – Why? The late Pope goes on to explain how this functions:

> At the deepest level of their being they are caught up in the dynamism of the Church's life, which is thirsty for the divine absolute and the call to holiness. It is to this universal holiness that they bear witness. They embody the Church in her desire to give herself completely to the radical demands of the Beatitudes. By the quality of their lives, they are a sign of total availability to God, the Church and the brethren. (*Evangelii Nuntiandi* 69)

This will happen only if the lives of each one of us command respect and ask questions of the world and of the people among whom we live. To do this we have to be fully mature Christians, and our communities should exist to give us this opportunity. This can only happen, however, if the ideal that calls this community, namely Christ, is re-incarnated in the person of the leader who is the symbolic centre without whom true community in the Christian sense is impossible. But the leader can be so only if the community governed is totally concerned with the values of Christ; committed to the task mapped out for us by the Word of God: 'It is no longer we who live, but Christ who lives in us; and the life we now live in the flesh we live by faith in the Son of God, who loved us and gave himself for us' (see Gal. 2.20).

V
To live as Disciples and Prophets

10. *Disciples of Jesus*

The risen Jesus is reported in Matthew's Gospel as issuing the command: 'Go therefore and make disciples of all nations' (Matt. 28.19). The Church exists today because that command was taken seriously, and we must consider in this chapter what it means to be a disciple of Jesus. Again we find that we are dealing with the vocation of the baptised, and not the unique preserve of the Religious. However, the Religious, precisely because he does belong to the baptised, is called to be a disciple of Jesus. His being a Religious does not make him any more a disciple, but it commits him to a public witnessing to the responsibility, the cost and the benefits of being a disciple of Jesus. We believe that Jesus of Nazareth has opened up an entirely new way to God, and that he himself trod that way. He did not, however, go alone. He called men and women to 'come after' him, to be his disciples. The Religious, precisely because he is baptised and because he has publicly announced the overpowering presence of God's Lordship in his life by a further commitment to a vowed community, *must* look to the Gospel message on discipleship as a biblical model for his life-style.

A further introductory point should be made. In recent years there has been a lot of discussion among Religious over the relationship between community and apostolate, and various positions have been taken in this debate.[1] In the light of the biblical tradition it seems to me that this is a false dilemma, and to force a wedge between the community as such, and what it does, is to create an intellectual problem which does not exist in real life.[2]

Already in the Old Testament the idea of belonging to Jahweh and the inherent obligation to love and serve him in life are seen as one and the same thing. When the sages of Israel eventually came to write down the Decalogue, they started with an expression of who they were – the people of Jahweh: '"I am the Lord your God"' (Exod. 20.2; Deut. 5.6). Once that fact was established, then the

133

various directions by which Israel had to live could follow logically. The Book of Deuteronomy has enshrined this same principle in the famous Jewish confession of faith: ' "Hear, O Israel: the Lord our God is one Lord; and you shall love the Lord your God with all your heart, and with all your soul, and with all your might" ' (Deut. 6.4). The Psalmist has proclaimed the same belief when he sang:

> Blessed is everyone who fears the Lord, who walks in his ways! You shall eat the fruit of the labour of your hands; you shall be happy, and it shall be well with you. (Ps. 128.1–2)

Israel was convinced that Jahweh had called her to be his people. She believed that she belonged to him in a very special way, but she was also conscious that this privilege brought with it the burden of doing his will. The individualisation of this principle is found dramatically presented in the Book of Job, and in the lives of the prophets. The story of Jeremiah's vocation is dominated by it: ' "To all to whom I send you you shall go, and whatever I command you you shall speak. Be not afraid of them, for I am with you to deliver you, says Jahweh" ' (Jer. 1.7–8). The belief that Israel and her saints belonged to God and had to be prepared to suffer the consequences, may well be the background for the more personally human bond that Jesus established between himself and those whom he called to be disciples. It seems to me that the Gospel presentation of the disciples of Jesus, as well as serving as a biblical model for Religious life, also resolves the so-called tension between community and apostolate. There should be no tension, as what the community *is* and what the members of the community *do* are inextricably bound together.[3]

The major part of this brief presentation of the disciples of Jesus will be devoted to the Gospel of Mark. This Evangelist is certainly not presenting a simple history of the relationship between Jesus and his disciples. He has a theology of discipleship which was influenced by the pastoral problems of his own particular community. However, I believe that through Mark we can come to a very good understanding of what it means to be a disciple, although we will have to call on Luke and Matthew occasionally to fill out the picture.[4]

THE VOCATION TO DISCIPLESHIP
In all the Gospels, Jesus opens his public ministry by calling disciples to himself. All the passages reflect the same idea of the call to be a disciple of Jesus.

Mark 1.16–20 and 2.13–14
In the first of these passages we have, in fact, two vocation stories:

(a) And passing along by the Sea of Galilee
> *he saw*
>> Simon and Andrew the brother of Simon
>> casting a net into the sea;
>> for they were fishermen.
> *And Jesus said* to them,
>> 'Follow me and *I will make you* become
>> fishers of men.' And immediately
>> *they left* their nets and *followed* him.

(b) And going on a little farther,
> *he saw*
>> James the Son of Zebedee and John his
>> brother, who were in their boat mending the nets
> And immediately *he called them;*
>> and *they left* their father Zebedee
>> in the boat with the hired servants,
>> and *followed* him.

From this structured presentation of the text, the reader can see immediately that both vocation stories make the same point. We must notice that Jesus is in motion. He is 'passing along' (v.16) and 'going on' (v. 19). Jesus is always moving onwards towards something. He is not like a Rabbi, who gathered his disciples around him in a school. He takes the initiative. This is of great importance as one can see from the story of the Gerasene demoniac (5.14–20). The ex-demoniac takes the initiative (5.18) but is not called to 'be with Jesus'. We will see that this 'being with' Jesus is a mark of those called to follow Jesus in 3.14. The ex-demoniac is given a task to do (5.19) and he succeeds in this task (5.20), but this happens only because it was Jesus who directed him to the task. This is where the initiative must lie.[5] In Mark 1.16–20, it is Jesus who 'saw' (vv. 16–19), he it is who 'said to them' (v.17) and 'called them' (v.20), and he says: 'I will make you fishers of men' (v.17). As we have seen throughout this book, everything in the realm of man's relationship with God has its initiative in God. The response of Simon, Andrew, James and John is immediate. There is not a word uttered by them. They simply leave and follow. The final point to notice in both these accounts is that they (like Abraham before them) leave all the things that would have been judged by their peers as necessary for their worldly success: nets, boats, hired servants and their father. Notice the growing importance of the things they left, from the tools of their trade to their family.

These seemingly simple passages are full of food for reflection. We have here the fascinating personality of Jesus, moving on to do his Father's will, calling simple men to associate themselves with him. In Greek, the word for 'follow' (akoloutheō) carries with it the idea of 'walking behind' someone. It is not only this, however, it also contains the idea of imitation. We have here the idea of an itinerant 'going along' behind someone which is both physical and spiritual.[6] The spontaneous and immediate abandoning of all that would be judged as necessary for success is simply the New Testament's repetition of the authentic response of man to the overpowering presence of the Lord.

It is not enough merely to look at these few verses pulled out from their context. It is important to see that these first vocation stories follow a most important summary from Mark about Jesus' breaking into his public mission: 'Now after John was arrested, Jesus came into Galilee, preaching the Gospel of God, and saying, "The time is fulfilled, and the kingdom of God is at hand; repent, and believe in the Gospel" ' (1.14–15). By placing the vocation of the first disciple immediately after this urgent announcement of the arrival of the Kingdom and the need for conversion, Mark wishes to show that the disciples, in being called to follow Jesus, are also called to share in his task of spreading the Gospel of the Kingdom. Jesus has a task; he calls others to follow him and together they go forth. 'The good news has come forth and is immediately accompanied by the call to follow.'[7]

A little later in the Gospel, there is an even briefer vocation story which repeats exactly the same structure and message, but which adds a further element:

> He *saw*
>> Levi, the son of Alphaeus
>> sitting at the tax office,
> and *he said* to him,
>> *'Follow me.'*
>> And he rose and *followed him.*
> (Mark 2.14)

It is obvious that the same model of the initiative of Jesus, the vocation and an immediate, wordless response in which the disciple, called to follow, rises, leaves all those things which ensured his worldly success and sets out to 'walk behind' Jesus. But here the man called is not a simple fisherman; he is a publican, a sinner, a Jew who had sold his soul to the hated foreign power which dominated God's land. Looking at the wider context of the passage we find that Jesus not only calls a sinner to follow him, but in 2.15–17, Jesus actually shares his table with such people, and he explains: 'I came not to call the righteous, but sinners' (2.17). By using the verb 'call' Mark shows that the discipleship of Jesus, which means the sharing of his life and even his table, cuts across all conventional barriers. No one is excluded, not even the ones whom the religious authorities condemned as sinners.

Luke 5.1–11

Matthew, with a few variations caused by his own special purpose and message, takes over these Marcan passages (Matt. 4.18–22; 9.9). Luke's version of the calling of the disciples beside the lake (5.1–11) is strikingly different, and adds further insight into the gospel presentation of the call to discipleship.

The scene at the opening of the passage is Jesus preaching, and the people are pressing about him, urgently desiring to hear his word (5.1). This is important, as in this situation we will find that Jesus now calls others to share in that task. Again Jesus takes the initiative: 'And he *saw* two boats by the lake; but the fishermen had gone out of them and were washing their nets' (v.2).[8] He takes over Simon's boat and continues to preach from the boat 'a little from the land' (v. 3). The call to discipleship now follows, but we do not find the technical call 'Follow me'. Taking the initiative again, Jesus commands Simon: ' "Put out into the deep, and let down your nets for a catch" ' (v. 4). At first, Simon is full of his own knowledge and experience. He should have known better, as, in the Lucan story, Jesus has just cured his mother-in-law (4.38–9).[9] However, he arrogantly replies: ' "Master, we toiled all night and took nothing!" ' (v. 5). But the fascination of the person of Jesus causes him to relent: ' "but *at your word* I will let down the nets" ' (v. 5). Luke continues to show that it is the authority and the initiative of Jesus which determine everything. The influence of Jesus is already having effect, but it grows as the account proceeds. At the miracle (vv. 6–7) Simon's self-assertiveness crumbles. Luke cunningly no longer calls him 'Simon', but 'Simon Peter', adding the Christian title 'Peter', as he crumbles completely before the one who confronts him. He repents and believes: 'He fell down at Jesus' knees, saying, "Depart from me for I am a sinful man" ' (v. 8). It is thus, as a believer, conscious of his own weakness and need before the person of Jesus, that Peter is made a disciple: '*And Jesus said* to Simon, "Do not be afraid; henceforth you will be catching men." And when they had brought their boats to land, *they left everything* and *followed him*' (vv. 10–11).[10]

By giving us this precious account, Luke has added a further dimension to our understanding of discipleship. The Marcan stories are all so immediate and sudden, but Luke shows us that there can be a growing inner effect of Jesus upon the disciple. Only gradually does he come to see the overwhelming need to be taken over by the person of Jesus. Once this need is seen, then the disciple is ready to be associated with the life and task of Jesus.

Mark 3.13–19

There is one final passage from Mark which in many ways simply repeats what we have already seen in the earlier Marcan passages. However, a few more important elements enter, and thus the passage merits our attention: 'And he went up into the hills, and *called* to him those whom *he desired;* And they came to him' (3.13). Thus far we have a repetition of the earlier vocation stories, although here no names are given. All the same elements are here: the initiative of Jesus and an immediate and uncompromising response.

However, following on from this general call there is a further, more specific, call: 'And he appointed twelve, *to be with him*, and to be sent out *to preach* and have authority *to cast out demons*' (3.14–15). Within the general call to discipleship Jesus 'appointed' a group of twelve.[11] Again the initiative of Jesus is present, but the group is now closely associated with Jesus. They are to be 'with him' and they will be sent out to preach and they will cast out demons. It is most important to notice that the only things which Jesus has *done* at this stage of the Gospel are preach, work miracles and cast out demons. The twelve are to be intimately associated with Jesus, not only by *being* with him, but also in *doing* what he himself does. The structure of the passage makes it clear that it is only in their being with him that they can do what he does. Although the text does not say so, it is implicit that, separated from him, they would be able to do nothing. As yet, this association with the work of Jesus is in the future tense. It is only a promise. It will be fulfilled in 6.6b–13.

The rest of this passage is made up of a list of names of the twelve,[12] and again the initiative of Jesus comes to the fore, as he gives names to Simon (v. 16) and to James and John (v. 17). One final point of importance in this list is the addition to the name of Judas Iscariot, 'who betrayed him'. For the first time we hear of the possible failure of a disciple. This is a theme which grows as Mark's Gospel develops. Some scholars have argued that, for Mark, the story of the disciples is a story of failure and that they, in fact, represent the elements in the Church of Mark against whom the Gospel was written.[13] This is wholly to ignore the wonderfully *positive* teaching on discipleship which can be gleaned from the texts which we have just analysed. Our considerations so far could lead us to say that the discipleship of Jesus involves the following factors:
1. Jesus sets up, through his initiative, a totally new situation of obedience and service.
2. These disciples are not rabbinic students, learning the law 'bookishly', they are to learn by 'walking after Jesus'. They gain their knowledge and sense of mission by being 'with Jesus' (3. 14). This is the importance of the physical connotation of the verbs 'to follow' or 'to come after'. The disciples, right from the first moment, as we can see from the close link between Mark 1.14–15 and 1.16–20, are not just 'with Jesus', they are closely associated with all that he has come to do.

3. They are called to move away from all standards usually judged by the world as necessary. This is particularly evident from 1.16–20. Jesus has set up a new 'family' which has its sense in being associated with Jesus in his task of bringing in the kingdom.

4. Discipleship cuts across all barriers. He has come to call sinners to share his life, his table and his ministry. This is the point of Levi's call in Mark 2.13–14, and is taken up again by Luke 5.1–11, where an arrogant Simon is gradually drawn by Jesus to become the humble disciple, Peter.

5. There is always the possibility of failure. One who was 'with the Lord' and constituted as 'one of the twelve' (see Mark 3.14) is also one 'who betrayed him' (3.19).

THE MISSION OF THE DISCIPLE

Although we have already seen that the disciples are associated with the task of Jesus in Mark 1.13–20, and that they are to be given authority to preach and to have power over evil because of their association with Jesus in 3.14–15, thus far it has been only a promise, and they merely seem to stand by until Mark 6.6b–13. Here what was promised becomes a fact: 'And he called to him the twelve, and began to send them out two by two, and gave them authority over the unclean spirits. . . So they went out and preached that men should repent. And they cast out many demons, and anointed with oil many that were sick and healed them' (6.7, 12–13). It is important to notice the *identity* between the mission of the disciples and the task of Jesus. In 1.15 Jesus burst onto the scene preaching repentance, and up to this stage in the Gospel, he has preached, healed and driven out demons. The disciples now are associated in everything which Jesus does. A glance at the wider context of our passage in Mark's Gospel shows that this is the case. After the promise in 3.14–15, the disciples stand by, hearing Jesus' words in 4.1–34, a section of the Gospel devoted entirely to the preaching of Jesus; seeing his mighty works in 4.35–6, 6a, where he calms the waters, heals a demoniac, cures the woman with a flow of blood and the final wonder of the raising of the daughter of Jairus. Despite all of this, his own people will not accept him (6.1–6a), questioning his wisdom (his preaching) and his works (see 6.2). In the light of this situation, he sends out his disciples.

It could be objected that it is only 'the twelve' who are associated in this task, and thus the message is not one which is to be linked with the general call to discipleship. Mark is certainly focusing his attention on the twelve, and this same story is repeated with variations by Matthew (9.35; 10.1, 9–11, 14) and Luke (9.1–6). However, it is again Luke who fills out the picture with yet another story of a mission. In this story, Luke makes it very clear that not only the twelve, but 'the others' are also called to this task: 'After this, the Lord appointed seventy others,[14] and he sent them on ahead of him, two by two, . . . "Heal the sick . . . and say to them 'The kingdom of God has come near to you . . .' nevertheless know this, that the kingdom of God has come near" ' (Luke 10. 1, 9, 11).

One of the surprising things, however, about these stories of the mission of the disciples, is that it seems to end here. As we have seen, the logic of the Gospel seems to be that Jesus calls his disciples, associates them with him as he presses relentlessly on, preaching God's Kingdom in word and deed, and then, when they are ready, he sends them on their way to carry out *his* task. What is amazing, therefore, is that they are never again involved in this task. One would have thought that after the wonderful start reported in Mark 6.6b–13, this activity would be a regular part of the life of the disciples, but we hear no more of it. From now on, one would expect a closer association and understanding of Jesus' person and message, and consequently a deeper understanding of their own mission. However, as we will see, the opposite seems to be the case. From now on they seem to go further and further away from Jesus until, in their last appearance in Mark's Gospel we read: 'And they all forsook him, and fled' (14.50).

Why did this happen? The answer to this puzzle is to be found in my stressing of the fact that the mission of the disciple only makes sense if it is seen and understood by the disciple as an involvement in the *task of Jesus*. All that they do is done because of their relationship with him (see 3.14–15). However, returning to the Marcan account of the mission, we find that they come back to Jesus after a series of successes, full of joy at all that they have accomplished, and Mark reports: 'The apostles[15] returned to Jesus, and told him *all that they had done and taught*' (6.30). As yet, this is only a hint of why the disciples ultimately seem to fail in their association with Jesus. They think that all that they have been able to do was because of their own authority, and they rush back to tell Jesus, the *real* source of that authority, just what *they* had been able to do! This leads directly into our next point – the cost of discipleship, and the failure of the disciples to understand and accept the sort of discipleship proposed by Jesus.

THE COST OF DISCIPLESHIP

We have just seen that the great danger for a disciple of Jesus is that he might think the wonders that the Lord works through him are his own. This, of course, is to fall into the trap of believing that the person and message of Jesus can be contained and exhausted by the criteria of human achievement. The whole of the New Testament sets out to show that Jesus and his message profoundly question the ways of men, their history and their culture, especially in the light of a cross and a resurrection. The second half of the Gospel of Mark is largely devoted to Jesus' attempt to educate his disciples to this truth.

The Cross (Mark 8.27–9.1)

We have already had a hint in 3.19 that a disciple can betray Jesus, and in 6.30, the disciples fall into the mistake of thinking that *they* have done and said wonderful things. The crucial moment for the disciples comes in 8.27–33 where Jesus asks them who it is they think they are following. We have considered this passage,[16] but we must mention it again here. After all that the disciples have seen, heard and even shared in, Jesus leads them, for the first time, to a correct understanding of just who he is. In 8.27, he asks his disciples, ' "Who do men say that I am?" ', and they answer in terms of great precursor figures: John the Baptist, Elijah or one of the prophets. This is a total blindness, as they have no understanding of just who Jesus is.[17] He then asks his disciples ' "But who do you say that I am?"' (v. 29), and Peter, in the name of all the disciples, replies '"You are the Christ" '. There is a sense, of course, in which this is correct, but there is also the possibility that the disciples are measuring Jesus' being the Messiah in terms of *their* expectations of what the Messiah should be: an all-conquering, powerful, political kingly figure. It is clear from the context that this is the faith that is expressed here.[18] Jesus: 'charged them to tell no one about him.

And he began to teach them that the Son of Man must suffer many things, and be rejected by the elders and the chief priests and the scribes, and be killed, and after three days rise again. And he said this plainly' (8.30–1). Here, for the first time in the Gospel, Jesus speaks clearly of who he is, and he describes his destiny. He is not a powerful kingly Messiah. His messiahship is to be found in his being a suffering Son of Man.[19]

This passage (v. 31) is the first of three passion predictions. Through each one of the predictions we find Jesus trying to lead his disciples first to a correct understanding of who he is and, flowing out of this, to a correct understanding of what it means to be his disciple. It is here that he spells out for them, by first presenting the way which he must tread, the price which they must pay if they wish 'to come after him'. In this first moment we find that Peter is in no way prepared to accept Jesus as a suffering Messiah. It is important to notice that Jesus: 'Turning and *seeing his disciples,* he rebuked Peter, and said, "Get behind me, Satan! For you are not on the side of God, but *of men*"' (8. 33). The correction of Peter is not for Peter alone, but for all the disciples.[20] The issue is that the disciples are seeing Jesus from the point of view of their human expectations. They are on the side 'of men'. God does not work within these categories. Jesus is to be a suffering Messiah, and anyone who wishes to follow him must follow him along his way of suffering.

The discourse which follows hardly needs comment. It clearly tells the disciples of all ages that the cost of following Jesus is nothing less than the Cross: ' "If any man would *come after me,* let him deny himself and take up his cross and *follow me*" ' (8.34). Notice the deliberate use of discipleship language, which we met in our very first vocation story in 1.16–20: 'come after me' and 'follow me'. The rest of the discourse (8.34–9.1) makes crystal clear what Jesus demands from his disciples. However, as Jesus saw himself as ultimately coming through to his glory and vindication through suffering (v. 31: 'and after three days rise again'), so it will be with any disciple who is prepared to lose himself for Jesus and the Gospel, which is the continuing presence of Jesus among men. They will ' "see the kingdom of God come with power" ' (9.1).[21]

There is a very important feature about the instruction of the disciples which we will see repeated in each instance. Jesus speaks of his own as a way of suffering and death, but the disciples do not and will not understand his teaching. This we have already seen, but the important factor is that *Jesus does not abandon them in their ignorance and failure*.[22] Here we find again a repetition of one of the most outstanding features of God's dealing with men which we traced throughout the earlier part of this book: the God of Israel who loved so much that he would never abandon his recalcitrant, sinful people.[23] Now, in the Gospels, we find this feature of God's way with men repeated in the person of Jesus of Nazareth.

Service (Mark 9.30–7)

The second passion prediction is found in 9.31. Notice again the insistence that Jesus is teaching his disciples: 'For he was teaching his disciples, saying to them, "The Son of Man will be delivered into the hands of men, and they will kill him; and when he is killed, after three days he will rise."' The reaction of the disciples, as usual, is marked by fear and lack of understanding: 'But they did not understand the saying, and they were afraid to ask' (9.32). Not only do they not understand, but again they show that they are not prepared to accept the sort of messiahship, the sort of kingdom and the sort of discipleship which these words of Jesus demand. They are on their way to Capernaum, and when they arrive there and are settled for the night, Jesus asks them what they were discussing along the way. Their reaction shows that they have not gone beyond the hopes expressed in Peter's confession (8.27–35). They are still blocked in their categories of human achievement: 'They were silent; for on the way they had discussed with one another who was the greatest' (9.34). Their interest is in who will have most authority in the newly established power structure which they still think Jesus has come to build. Again Jesus does not leave them in their ignorance. He takes the matter up with them, and tells them that to follow him means to abandon all human aspirations of power and authority: ' "If anyone would be first, he must be last of all and servant of all" ' (9.35). He then goes on to explain what this means in practice by actually taking a child and putting this child in the midst of them. He takes the child in his arms. This gesture, coming through the pages of the Gospel as a precious memory of the sort of man Jesus was, is not, however, simply that. Jesus is using the child to show just what it means to be 'with him' (3.14) as his true disciple. The disciple of Jesus is not one who dictates terms in the Kingdom, but one who is *receptive*. Openness, the mark of the humble servant and the innocent child, is reflected in the disciple's openness to all that Jesus asks of him. Ultimately, this means that the disciple will be open to God. Only with such an approach to others is one a disciple of Jesus: ' "Whoever receives one such child in my name receives me; and whoever receives me, receives not me, but him who sent me" ' (9.37). The four-fold repetition of the same verb, 'to receive' clearly indicates the main point of the passage. Also important is the last phrase, where Jesus points out that he himself is not a man who acts through his own authority and power. He too is 'receiving'. He is merely serving the one who sent him. As always in the Gospel teaching on discipleship, Jesus does not demand something from his disciples as a distant legislator. He always asks them to 'follow' him, to go along the way which he himself must walk.

The Cross and Servanthood (10.32–45)
In our consideration of the section of Mark's Gospel which is devoted especially to Jesus' teaching his disciples the cost of their discipleship, we have seen that he has made it clear to them that they are called to share his vocation to a Cross (8.27–9.1) and to service (9.30–7). In the context of the third and final passion prediction (10.32–4), we find that there is no new teaching, but that there is a continuation and a further deepening of the two aspects of discipleship which we have already seen. Like Jesus, the Son of Man, the disciple is called to the Cross and to service.[24]

The third and final passion prediction is full of all the details of what actually happened to Jesus, and thus his destiny is made crystal clear.[25] However, Mark introduces this prediction by centring his attention, not on Jesus, but on the disciples: 'And they were on the road, going up to Jerusalem, and Jesus was walking ahead of them; and they were amazed, and those who followed were afraid' (10.32). Again Mark has set the scene by showing that the passage is for Jesus' disciples. They are 'on the road'. The relentless journey to death goes on, and 'Jesus was walking ahead of them', as he strides on to do the will of the one who sent him (9.37). Then we are told of the sentiments of the disciples: they were 'amazed' and 'afraid'. The two Greek words used express a profound emotional experience. They are deeply moved as Jesus strides on ahead of them, but despite all of this, they are still called 'those who followed'. A gap is widening as Jesus strides on, and they struggle along behind full of commotion and fear, but they are still there, 'with him'. In this situation, Jesus confirms them in their fears:

> 'Behold, we are going up to Jerusalem; and the Son of Man will be delivered to the chief priests and the scribes, and they will condemn him to death, and deliver him to the Gentiles; and they will mock him, and spit upon him, and scourge him, and kill him; and after three days he will rise' (10.33–4).

Mark has already shown us, in v. 32, that they were still not prepared for this teaching about a suffering Son of Man, but the passage which *immediately* follows shows that the disciples are still at the level of the messianic expectations of 8.27–33. The sons of Zebedee step forward and ask: ' "Grant us to sit, one at your right and one at your left, in your glory" '(10.37). Again, complete misunderstanding! Translated into modern terms, one might say that James and John, who were among the very first to respond spontaneously to the call to discipleship (1.16–20), are asking that one might be Prime Minister and the other the Minister of Finance in the powerful kingdom which they believe Jesus is about to set up on his arrival in Jerusalem! Jesus does not abandon them, but tells them that they must share in the cup of his suffering and the baptism of his death (10.38–9). As in 8.34–9.1 Jesus tells them, in the face of their failure, that they are called to follow him along the way of the Cross, but this is not accepted, and is met with further misunderstanding. 'And when the ten heard it, they began to be indignant at James and John' (10.41). Their sentiments are understandable, as they are angry with these two 'pushy' characters who are trying to jockey themselves into powerful positions by requesting special favours of the Lord (see vv. 35–6). In the face of Jesus' continual call to suffering and service, they are still limited to seeing things 'in the ways of men' (8.33). Even now Jesus does not abandon them, but taking them to himself instructs them once more on the price of discipleship. This preaching, like all Jesus' teaching on discipleship, is not a laying down of laws, but an invitation to 'follow' the way of the suffering and serving Son of Man (see especially v. 45), a way which reverses and calls into question all human patterns of authority and service:

> 'You know that those who are supposed to rule over the Gentiles lord it over them, and their great men exercise authority over them. *But it shall not be so among you*; but whoever would be great among you must be your servant, and whoever would be first among you must be slave of all. For the Son of Man also came not to be served but to serve, and to give his life as a ransom for many' (10.42–5).

In this way, Jesus' three moments of intensive preparation of his disciples comes to a conclusion. As we have seen twice before, the passion prediction, here even clearer than either of the other two, is simply ignored by his disciples, as the sons of Zebedee request positions of earthly power and honour. Jesus' answer to them is the promise of suffering and the Cross. He then has to turn to all of the *disciples* (the other ten) and call them to service. The disciples of Jesus are called to a gift of self in service and Cross because they are following him, who leads those who 'are following behind him' (see 10.32) into service and suffering. Thus the series of instructions concludes with the christological motivation for all discipleship: ' "For the Son of Man also came not to be served, but to serve, and to give his life as a ransom for many" '(10.45).

THE LAST ENCOUNTER

One of the outstanding features of all that we have seen so far has been the never-faltering, leading, instructing and faithful presence of Jesus in the midst of failure. Even though the disciples have not been able to grasp all that was being demanded of them, Jesus has never left them, and his message on discipleship has gradually become very clear. The last appearances of Jesus and his disciples together in the Gospel of Mark bring out the contrast between the loving faithfulness of Jesus and the failure of the disciples to grasp all the implications of what it meant to 'follow' Jesus.

Two scenes are to be found in Mark 14.17–52: the last supper (vv. 17–31) and the agony of Jesus in Gethsemani (vv. 32–52). In the first of these scenes, Jesus sets up a loving bond between himself and his disciples, and in the second, they abandon him.

The Marcan version of the last supper is also devoted to the theme of betrayal. It opens with Jesus' referring to the betrayal of Judas: '"One of you will betray me, one who is eating with me"' (14.18). Here the contrast is made particularly clear. Even one of those who share his life and his table as disciples is about to betray him. However, as we shall see, it is not only Judas who breaks the union which Jesus has been attempting to build, as the last supper account closes with a journey to the Mount of Olives, during which Jesus prophesies the betrayal of Peter (14.26–31). To think in merely human terms would lead us to conclude that Jesus' attempt to form disciples who were prepared not only to share his life and his table but also his mission and destiny has been a failure, but this would be to approach the question with the wrong categories. In the context of the prophecies of betrayal, Jesus announces: ' "For the Son of Man goes as it is written of him" '(14.21). To the minds of men all this may appear to be failure, but it is nothing more than the fulfilment of God's purpose, as it was written in the Scriptures. This is the normal way for the New Testament to indicate that what is happening is in fulfilment of God's plan (see, for example, Matt. 1.22; 2.5; 3.3; John 19.24, 36 etc.).

Jesus then takes the bread, blesses it, breaks it and gives it to them, saying: ' "Take; this is my body" ' (14.22). He then takes a cup and after giving thanks, he passes it to them all, announcing: 'This is the blood of the covenant, which is poured out for many' (14.24). With these words, Jesus, despite the prophecies of betrayal which frame the account itself, and despite the repeated failure of the disciples to understand the significance of his death, binds these very same disciples into a covenant with himself by calling them to share in the saving benefits of his sacrificial death. He then adds a promise which almost seems out of place in the context: ' "Truly, I say to you, I shall not drink again of the fruit of the vine until that day when I drink it new in the kingdom of God" '(14.25). The word 'until' is the word which rings of confidence and hope (see also Matt. 26.29; Luke 22.16; I Cor. 11.26). This is not the end, although to worldly judges it may appear to be. It contains a joyous expression of hope that the Kingdom of God is about to be established, and the joyous hope transforms that moment of the last supper, full of risks, dangers and the threat of betrayal and death. The covenant which Jesus has established in the first Eucharistic meal is not just a once-and-for-all happening. It is to endure into an indefinite future. There is no shadow of failure here. Jesus promises his continuing presence, even if this promise is set between two failure stories.

The meal closes with the account of the future betrayal of Peter (14.26–31). Notice how the theme of covenant presence and joy to be had through participation in the Eucharist is framed by stories of failure. However, betrayal and failure are not limited to Judas and Peter. In 14.32–53 the story of Gethsemani is reported. The atmosphere is heavy as Jesus, full of sorrow, prays in endearing terms[26] to his Father, but shows that right to the end he is open to his will. In this Jesus is alone, as his disciples, as yet, were not prepared to make such a risky commitment. He has attempted to bring Peter, James and John (see 1.16–20) with him into this most intimate moment, but they fall asleep and leave him in his solitude. The gap widens still further when Judas, explicitly named as 'one of the twelve', along with a crowd from the chief priests, scribes and elders, comes to arrest him. Judas betrays him. Jesus is arrested and the disciples make their last appearance in the Gospel of Mark: 'And they all forsook him, and fled' (14.50).

This passage is followed by a strange incident which only Mark records: 'And a young man followed him, with nothing but a linen cloth about his body; and they seized him, but he left the linen cloth and ran away naked' (14.51–2). It has often been suggested that the young man in question was the Evangelist Mark, and thus the historical value of the Gospel was assured. This would be the strangest autograph in the history of literature! The meaning of the message runs much deeper than that. It is a symbolic commentary on what has just happened to the disciples. They too 'followed him', but at the threat of danger ran away naked. All that they have had and all that they have been from the moment of their call to this moment, they have been because they were 'with Jesus' (3.14). Now, having fled, they are naked in their nothingness. The failure of the disciples has been a failure to appreciate that all that they had and were came to them from Jesus. As long as discipleship is built on *human* achievement and *human* aspirations, it is destined to failure.

This message has come to us very clearly from our systematic reading of all the discipleship texts. However, the story does not finish there. Does the faithful, loving presence of Jesus with his disciples finish with the Cross? The fact that we exist as 'followers' of Jesus today, as Mark's community existed as 'followers' of Jesus in the 60s of the first century, is clear enough proof that, although the attempts of the disciples failed, the purpose of God to form disciples did not. In the midst of prophecies about the failure of Judas, Peter and the rest of the disciples, Jesus announced: '"You will all fall away; for it is written, 'I will strike the shepherd, and the sheep will be scattered.' But after I am raised up, I will go before you into Galilee" '(14.27–8). It is the risen Christ who will reconstitute his disciples, and then they will be ready to follow him along his way of service and death, convinced that through a courageous discipleship, they will also share in his glory.

THE RECONSTITUTION OF DISCIPLESHIP

Strangely enough, Mark's Gospel has no stories of the risen Christ.[27] Mark concludes his Gospel with the finding of an empty tomb (16.1–5) and a promise which takes up what Jesus had said to his disciples in the midst of their failure (see 14.27-8): ' "But go, tell his disciples and Peter that he is going before you to Galilee; there you will see him, as he told you" '(16.7). The initiative once more stands entirely on the side of God. The disciples had failed because they were not prepared to pay the price of being a disciple of Jesus, but now, in the midst of even further failure, they are assured that they will see the risen Jesus in Galilee, just as he had promised in 14.27–8. Mark is relentless in his criticism of men and women who attempt to subordinate Jesus and his plan for his disciples to the criteria of men. I said just now that the final promise of Mark 16.7 is made in the midst of further failure, as the very last verse of this Gospel runs: 'And they went out and fled from the tomb; for trembling and astonishment had come upon them; and they said nothing to anyone, for they were afraid' (16.8). The reaction of the women repeats what we have already seen in the reactions of the disciples as they moved further and further away from the plans which Jesus had for them: they fled (see 14.50) and they were afraid (see 10.32). In writing of the women's flight and fear, Mark uses the same verbs as he had used of the frightened and fleeing disciples. Even though the verbs which refer to the other emotional experiences of the women are different, their trembling and astonishment are a repetition of the disciples' reactions. They too were amazed and afraid (see 10.32). A complete lack of trust and belief in the saving initiative of God in Jesus is again found, and the result is that 'They said nothing to anyone' (16.8).

Throughout Mark's Gospel we have seen the same pattern repeated: Jesus calls to a very special life-style, a failure to accept this life-style within Jesus' categories on the part of the disciples, met by the never-failing, continuing presence of Jesus, despite his failure. How did Mark resolve this last failure? As he spoke to his community, and wrote a Gospel for them in the 60s of the first century, he was able to point to the very fact of their existence as a Christian community, to their celebration of the Eucharist, just as Jesus had promised. *Men* had failed, but somewhere, somehow, *God* had won through in the risen Christ, and he had reconstituted his discipleship. They had met the risen Christ, and *he* had reconstituted *his* discipleship.

Although we have largely been following Mark, the message of Matthew and Luke repeats what Mark had already given us. However, they do not end their Gospels with a promise. They show that it is, in fact, the risen Jesus who returns to his disciples. Luke does this most poignantly by a short episode, the walk to Emmaus (Luke 24.13–35), which shows how deep depression marked the period between the crucifixion and the proclamation of the risen Christ. The reason for this depression is to be found in the fate which had befallen the person of Jesus. All their hopes of a political messiah have come to nothing: ' "Are you the only visitor to Jerusalem who does not know these things that have happened there in these days . . . Concerning Jesus of Nazareth, who was a prophet mighty in deed and word before God and all the people? . . . We had hoped that he was the one to redeem Israel" ' (Luke 24.18–19,21). As in Mark, Jesus walks with them, instructs them by showing them from the Scriptures that all of this had to happen, and finally he celebrates 'the breaking of the bread' with them, and suddenly they come to life: ' "Did not our hearts burn within us while he talked to us on the road . . . ?" ' (Luke 24.32).

The risen Christ reconstitutes his discipleship. Once again he calls his own to a discipleship and a personal union and fellowship with him. The Fourth Gospel has caught this well when the risen Jesus first restores what they have lost by forgiving them their sins. Once this has been done, he gives them the authority to go out and forgive the sins of others (see John 20.22–3). The same message is found behind the story of the doubting Thomas who will only believe what *he* can control, and he *knows* that Jesus was pierced by nails and by a spear. It is only through an encounter with the risen Christ that he is led to abandon all his criteria, and to fall down (as Peter did in Luke 5.1–11) to confess: ' "My Lord and my God!" ' (John 20.28).

Because of the resurrection something radically new happened. The disciples were called by Jesus and linked to him in a profound way both during his ministry and after the resurrection. The difference is that after the resurrection they are prepared to abandon all *their* hopes and to live as disciples of *Jesus*. Under the influence of the Spirit, they became witnesses to the revelation disclosed in the person of Jesus: '"You are witnesses of these things. And behold, I send the promise of my Father upon you"' (Luke 24.48–9). In the Acts of the Apostles the same promise is made by the risen Jesus, before he leaves his disciples: ' "But you shall receive power when the Holy Spirit has come upon you; and you shall be my witnesses in Jerusalem . . . and Samaria and to the end of the earth" ' (Acts 1.8). The rest of the Acts of the Apostles tells the story of how this happened. The disciples began in a unity of love and with a Spirit-inspired courage in Jerusalem (Acts 1–5). Through all their trials they finally arrive in Rome, the centre of the world, and the book ends with Paul's: 'preaching the kingdom of God and teaching about the Lord Jesus Christ quite openly and unhindered' (Acts 28.31).[28]

CONCLUSION: THE RELIGIOUS AS A DISCIPLE OF JESUS

Once again I must anticipate the major thesis of the chapter which follows. It is clear that all who are baptised are called to discipleship, and that the Religious can claim to be 'following Jesus' only because he is baptised. Discipleship is not the special preserve of Religious.[29] Nevertheless, there is an urgent need in the Church and in the world that true discipleship be *seen*, and this is why we have *publicly* committed ourselves to a *public* life of 'following Jesus' in our commitment to Religious life.

Our analysis of the Gospel picture of the disciples of Jesus is full of challenge and consolation. Most of all, our lives must show to the world that what we are stems from God's initiative and our 'being with him' (Mark 3.14). This has been the outstanding feature of all the passages which we have examined. To lose touch by measuring ourselves, our Church and God's way in the world by human criteria, is to fail as a disciple of Jesus. We are called to 'be with him' and to follow him along *his* way of abandoning all the absolutes of worldly criteria (Mark 1.16–20; 2.13–14) into suffering and service (Mark 8.22–10.45) convinced, in faith, that *only* this way leads to the ultimate answer to the deepest longings of man's heart: resurrection (Mark 8.35; 16; Luke 24; Matt. 28; John 20). The risen life, however, is not something we grimly push on towards, in the midst of tight-lipped suffering and service, it must be seen as already present among us as we celebrate his life, death and re-surrection in our Eucharist 'until he comes'. (I Cor. 11.26; See Mark 14.25; Matt. 26.29; Luke 22.16) and in our shared lives of love and service.[30] It is here that I find the intellectual distinction between community and apostolate false. Certainly, it is the shared life of a genuine Christian community which gives us the 'possibility of discipleship'. Unless there is a shared life of love, there will be no genuinely Christian service. The disciples were able to do what Jesus did because they were 'with him' (Mark 3.14). There is no place for the Religious in the Church and in the world who is simply a member of the work force. Our consecrated life is, as Pope Paul VI insisted, 'A privileged means of evangelisation' (*Evangelii Nuntiandi* 69), but it must be *seen*. This will happen only when we courageously accept the challenge of the call to serve the Church and the world publicly as disciples of Jesus.[31] There will always be a tension between what we are, and what we are doing, but this must be courageously accepted as a fact of life, knowing that we cannot really work it out, but that the overwhelming presence of the risen Lord in our lives will somehow make sense out of it. Cost what it may, suffering and service, we are called to take the risk of associating ourselves intimately with Christ in his task of spreading the kingdom.

How difficult that task is! We are all human, we fail, and often our lives seem to be more marked by failure than by success. How often, like the disciples, as Jesus leads on 'we are amazed, and we who follow are afraid' (see Mark 10.32). But even here the Gospel message on discipleship rings true. We have seen that the story of discipleship is not a success story; it is deeply marked by failure. Throughout all the Gospels, and indeed throughout the whole of the Bible, we have found that we do not commit ourselves to a God who relentlessly demands: 'Success or nothing!' To create a God like that is to submit to human patterns of behaviour and judgement, to 'become like the other nations'. But our God is not like the gods of the other nations: '"I will not give rein to my fierce anger, I will not destroy Ephraim again, *for I am God, not man*: I am the Holy One in your midst and have no wish to destroy"' (Hosea 11.8–9, J. B.). This God has become flesh and dwelt among us in the person of Jesus of Nazareth, and the Fourth Evangelist takes up Hosea's message when he has Jesus proclaim: 'For God so loved the world that he gave his only Son, that whoever believes in him should not perish but have eternal life. For God sent the Son into the world, not to condemn the world, but that the world might be saved through him' (John 3.16–17).

Our study of discipleship should lead us to a deeper understanding of what our God has said to his prophets and to his disciples of all ages, when they shook with fear at the immensity of the task, in the light of their human limitations: 'If I thought *you* could do it, I would not have asked you. It is *my* work, not yours. You can only manifest what I have accomplished in you.'

11. *Prophets of the Lord*[1]

The opening chapter of this book was an attempt to show from the Scriptures and the teaching of the Church that the call to sanctity, to the 'perfection of charity' (*Lumen Gentium* 40) is a universal call. This raised the inevitable question: why Religious? If the call to perfection is a call to all the baptised, is there any specific function within the context of the universal call which the Religious fulfills? It is a pity that the Gospels leave so many 'loose ends'. Even Jesus was a bit of a disappointment to us in this. He has left so many 'loose ends' that the whole of the history of the Church, with its interaction between the revelation of Scripture and Tradition and the practical living and preaching of that revelation, still has not been (nor will it ever be) sorted out.

Even in the New Testament, we see some striking 'loose ends' causing problems to the earliest Church. For example, the early Church was not sure whether the *identity* of a Christian had to be found within Judaism, or whether non-Jews could become Christians without submitting to the structures of Judaism. This problem stands behind a great deal of Paul's life and work (see especially Galatians), and the so-called Council of Jerusalem reported in Acts 15, is Luke's description of how the problem was solved.[2]

The Second Vatican Council has left behind some similar 'loose ends' and one of these is, in my opinion, the specific role of Religious life within the Church. *Lumen Gentium* buried the idea that Religious life was a qualitatively superior life-style but, in doing so, created an identity crisis which has been very evident over the last 15 years. I claimed above,[3] that community, vows and especially the apostolate, should not be seen as the place where Religious find their *identity*. They must be seen as the all-important *means to an end*. What, then, is the *specific identity* of the Religious in the Church?

A BIBLICAL MODEL?

It is well known that the Church looked seriously at her own identity at Vatican II and that she repeatedly went back to biblical models to speak of that identity. She spoke of herself as a people of God, a pilgrim people, the body of Christ and she stressed the 'mystery' of the Church. Is it possible for Religious life also to look to the Scriptures for a model? A problem arises, because the Church is a concept and a reality which already exists in the New Testament,[4] while this cannot be said for Religious life, which had its organised origins in the fourth century.[5] Must we therefore abandon all attempts to find a biblical model for Religious life? It was the intuition of a famous Protestant scholar, W. F. Albright, to suggest an analogy between the beginnings of the prophetic movement in the Old Testament and the growth of the Religious life within the Church.[6]

As long as Israel was a pilgrim people in the desert, or a charismatic group under the early leadership of the Judges, she was a 'people' only because of her consciousness of the covenant which God made with her. In other words, central to the people of God's very existence as such was the lived consciousness of the covenant. With the gradual settling down of this people in Canaan, the all-pervading consciousness that held them together as God's people was threatened. The passage from the charismatic leadership into the dangers of an established worldly kingdom, 'like the other nations' has been very well caught in I Samuel 8.4–7:[7]

> Then all the elders of Israel gathered together and came to Samuel at Ramah, and said to him, 'Behold, you are old and your sons do not walk in your ways; now appoint for us a king to govern us *like all the nations*.' But the thing displeased Samuel when they said, 'Give us a king to govern us.' And Samuel prayed to the Lord. And the Lord said to Samuel, 'Hearken to the voice of the people in all that they say to you; for they have not rejected you, but *they have rejected me from being king over them*.'

Although Samuel lists all the evils that a king would bring upon them, (vv. 11–18), the people nevertheless cry out: ' "No! but we will have a king over us, that we also may be like all the nations" '

(vv. 19–20), and thus they surrender their uniqueness, in a desire to be 'like all the nations'.

As the history books of the Bible show, Samuel's worst fears are fulfilled. Israel becomes a powerful nation especially under David, but with strength comes the kingly court, the international glitter of the royal capital, Jerusalem, the royal army using conscripted soldiers and foreign mercenaries, and this leads to the tragedy of Solomon and the division of the nation.[8] It is within this historical context that the prophets emerge in Israel. The first of the classical prophets are Elijah and Elisha whose activities are reported in the midst of a series of unfaithful kings, in I Kings 17 – II Kings 13.[9] From then on the presence of a prophetic element was something permanent in Israel. We must not be misled by finding only a few books of the Prophets in the Old Testament. These are only what are called 'the writing prophets'. It is clear that there were many other forms of prophecy, and we read of the sons of the prophets, the disciples of the prophets, the Nazirites, the Rechabites, the remnant and the *anawim*. All of these groups formed a continual stream of prophetic presence among the people of Israel.

The function of the prophetic movement in Israel was not primarily to speak about future events. This is an unfortunate misunderstanding, and the common application of the word 'prophet' in contemporary society to one who utters dire threats about the future focuses its attention on a secondary aspect of the function of the prophet in Israel.[10] Above all, the prophets were men who were entirely taken up with their loyalty to the covenant. As we have already seen in our brief consideration of Jeremiah's confessions, the presence of Jahweh and his command were like a fire burning within them. Ultimately, they are best described as lovers, men who are so entirely taken up with the overpowering presence of the Lordship of Jahweh that they are deeply hurt when they see Jahweh's people living in division, adoring false gods, behaving 'like all the nations', alienated from one another, and from their unique God. In this situation they can do no other than burst forth into criticism of this situation, both by the quality of their lives (and this is the significance of the many prophetic gestures. See, for example, Jer. 16.1–9; Ezek. 4.1–5.12) and by their fierce and courageous preaching. In the light of criticism and rebuke, Amos can only reply that he is not his own master. He has been 'taken' by the Lord, and so must announce his word, cost what it may: ' "I am no prophet, nor a prophet's son; but I am a herdsman, and a dresser of sycamore trees, and Yahweh took me from following the flock, and Yahweh said to me, 'Go prophesy to my people Israel" ' (Amos 7.14–15).

Their function is to call Israel back to the original covenant love which was established between Jahweh and his people at Sinai. Thus, the prophet looks back to the period of original faithfulness. He looks back to the laws that were set up for the keeping of the covenant, and he criticises the unfaithfulness of his present situation in the light of that law, and in the light of that original faithfulness.[11] The oracles telling of future blessings or of future punishments are merely the final guarantee that this prophet is, in fact, announcing God's word, and not his own:

> And if you say in your heart, 'How may we know the word which the Lord has not spoken? – when a prophet speaks in the name of the Lord, if the word does not come to pass or come true, that is a word which the Lord has not spoken; the prophet has spoken it presumptuously, you need not be afraid of him (Deut. 18.21–2).

Thus, the function of the biblical prophet was to act as a continual thorn in the side of the established Israel, to remind the establishment of Israel continually why she was established originally: to live in covenant love with her unique God, Jahweh, and at peace with one another (see, for example, Amos 2.6–16, where the prophet speaks out against the division and avarice of Israel).

There is a unique parallel between the origin and purpose of Old Testament prophecy and the origin and purpose of Religious life in the Christian Church. The parallel was seen at the very beginning of organised Religious life by the fourth-century monk, John Cassian, who wrote that the first Religious went apart 'to practise those things which they had learned to have been ordered by the apostles throughout the body of the Church in general' (*Collationes* XVIII, ch. 5).[12] Cassian describes a situation in the fourth-century Church where the ideals which had been 'ordered by the apostles throughout the body of the Church in general' were not being lived. Thus, he says, monks formed communities to see that these ideals be not just spoken about but lived.

A little reflection shows how close this 'movement' in the fourth century AD is to the beginnings of prophetic movement in the ninth century BC. For the first three centuries of the Church's existence, it lived, closely knit together, in small communities, which professed their faith as the odd men out. They were a unique group of people, attempting to live a unique life-style, following the commandment of Jesus: ' " A new commandment I give to you, that you love one another; even as I have loved you, that you also love one another. By this all men will know that you are my disciples, if you have love for one another" ' (John 13.34–5). The Johannine community is reflecting its own situation here. It is called to a unity of love which will announce to 'all men' that they are the followers of Jesus. This is the Johannine version of what Paul described as 'life in Christ' and which Luke sets up as an ideal as he describes the Jerusalem community: 'Now the company of those who believed were of one heart and soul' (Acts 4.32). This was the covenant of love which had been established by Jesus when he founded his Church.

However, with the gradual growth and final liberation of Christianity in 313 by Constantine, a completely new situation was established. To be a Christian no longer meant to belong to a peripheral, persecuted or at best tolerated, despised sect. On the contrary! There were now definite advantages to be had in belonging to the faith which had become the Imperial religion. In fact, before long heads would roll if they were not prepared to accept the religion of Jesus Christ. In this situation whole cities and countries became Christian. Little wonder! However, this change of situation brought with it the same danger that faced Israel in her movement from a charismatic covenant-centred people, to a royal, temple-centred people. Also with the Christian Church in the fourth century there is a move towards becoming the institutional Church. The Christian Church was now a definite social institution and with this came the bureaucracy of such an institution, the court, the ritual and the ceremony which threatened to push the basic oneness of love 'ordered by the apostles' into the background. It is in this situation that Religious life springs into existence, in an attempt to make sure that those values which stood at the heart of the Church founded by Jesus Christ be not lost. In fact, these groups deliberately attempted to live the ideals described in the Acts of the Apostles.[13]

The parallel with the rise of the prophetic movement in Israel is striking. As God's people move into a situation which threatens an original pact of love made between God and his people, God calls forth a 'prophetic movement', in both the Old Testament era and in the era of the Church, continually to remind the Institution (royal Israel or the institutional Church) why it was instituted!

The Church was founded to carry on in history the saving work of Christ. As we have seen, Paul announces this salvation as a new life in Christ, where man finds himself in his radical union with others, cutting through all barriers, even natural barriers: 'For as many of you as were baptised into Christ have put on Christ. There is neither Jew nor Greek, there is neither slave nor free, there is neither male nor female; for you are all one in Christ Jesus' (Gal. 3.27–8). The Church, therefore, must carry on that task of bringing men into communion with one another and with their God whom they can now call ' "Abba! Father!" ' (see Gal. 4.6–7). Religious belong to this Church. They are in no way a group apart, but from the heart of the Church they act out their lives as prophets. They are there to show that the unity among men with God, preached by the Church is not an unachievable, preached doctrine, some 'pie in the sky' impossible dream, but a lived reality. By the quality of their lives in community, responding to a unique God who calls, through their lives publicly committed to poverty, chastity and obedience, they show that the prayer of Christ has not been frustrated: ' "That they may all be one; even as thou, Father, art in me, and I in thee, that they also may be in us, so that the world may believe that thou hast sent me" ' (John 17.21).

The parallel with the Old Testament prophets does not cease here. Vatican II laid down three criteria to be used in the renewal of Religious life: a return to the Scriptures, a return to the charism of the founder, and a reading of the signs of the times. Again we find the Religious called to repeat in the heart of the Church what the prophets did in Israel.

A RETURN TO THE SCRIPTURES
It hardly bears repeating that the Old Testament prophets did not invent the message which they announced to wayward Israel. They went back continually to the law, to the desert experience, and to

the God who had revealed himself to Israel in 'many and varied ways' (Heb. 1.1). A prophet who preached his own word was no prophet of Jahweh. A true prophet looked at the present with his eyes on the past interventions of God among his people, and praised or condemned the present in the light of the past. Only in this way could God's future be established. So must it be with a Religious in the Christian Church. The whole renewal process must look to the Word of God as its model and ideal if it is to be a renewal that follows God's ways. Sociology, psychology, history, literature and modern scientific research and methods will all play their part in the formation of an authentically Christian community, but if the dominating criterion is not the Word of God, it will be the product of the hands and minds of men. As such, it will ultimately outlive its usefulness.

Thus, like the prophets, the Religious looks at the present in the light of that once and for all Word of God, Jesus Christ, and opens himself to a future which only God can determine. In doing so his function is not one of a superior Christian living out his special privileges, but a Christian among Christians, showing them that this is what God called all men to live.

A RETURN TO THE CHARISM OF THE FOUNDER

As we have just indicated, the prophets looked back to the great Fathers of Israel to find their message for the contemporary situation in Israel which they were facing. Most of all they looked back to Moses who was the model of all prophets: ' "I will raise up for them a prophet like you from among their brethren; and I will put my words in his mouth, and he shall speak to them all that I command him" '(Deut. 18.18). This promise of Jahweh to Moses in the Book of Deuteronomy makes Moses the model of the perfect prophet in Israel.[14] Abraham is presented as the father of the faith of Israel, and all David's sins are forgotten as he too becomes the model of the perfect King of Israel and the promise of a kingly messiah. Thus the prophets did not merely look back to the past, but they fastened their attention on the great charismatic figures of the past, and used them time and again to call Israel back to her God.

When each Religious family looks back to the charism of its

founder, it finds men and women who were authentic prophets in their own times. One only has to name Benedict, Francis, Dominic, Ignatius, Vincent de Paul, Louise de Marillac, John Bosco, Elizabeth Seton or Mother Teresa, to see the validity of that statement. 'They loved the Church so much, and saw its unrealized potential in certain areas, that the spirit moved them to establish communities through which God's covenant love would be manifested in life and service.'[15] Here, of course, one of our major difficulties is found. We must not go back to these figures and absolutise their times, the problems they faced and the solutions they offered. We must *rediscover* the prophetic element in their lives and repeat that same phenomenon in our own times and in the light of our own problems.

Once more the Religious is repeating in his own life what the prophets of the Old Testament did in theirs.

A READING OF THE SIGNS OF THE TIMES
I wish to dwell at greater length on this subject, as it is here that I feel that our whole treatment reaches some sort of conclusion. I have been insisting that the function of the Religious within the Church is that of a prophet, that the biblical model for Religious life is the model of the prophet. This book has argued that it is our task to be communities responding to God through lives of poverty, chastity and obedience. The tradition of the Church assures us that this is what we are called to do. How does our vocation to community, poverty, chastity and obedience correspond to the prophetic model? In what ways are our community and our vowed lives 'prophetic'? First we must again look quickly at the critical function of the prophetic charism in the Old Testament and also in Jesus. None of the prophets spoke into a situation where their oracles were irrelevant. They were men who were tightly bound up in the situation of God's people, and precisely because they felt themselves part of what they saw, they cried out their protest in the name of Jahweh. The signs of the times that the prophets saw varied greatly through the history of Israel. Isaiah, Amos and Hosea faced a very different situation from Jeremiah and Ezekiel, but always there were the problems of a people divided, a lack of any deep-felt religious attachment to Jahweh. Religion was often reduced to the externals of mere legalism, where those who imposed the law lived as 'white-

washed tombs' (Matt. 23.27). A careful reading of Jesus' attack on
the scribes and Pharisees in Matthew 23 will show that prophetism
did not stop with the Old Testament. Jesus, like all the prophets
before him, was revolted by a religious practice which paraded as
faith. The work of the prophet is to comfort the afflicted and afflict
the comfortable and this was done relentlessly by the prophets of
the Old Testament and by Jesus himself, cost what it might.

At the end of Matthew 23 (vv. 37–9), Jesus laments over Jerusalem which has killed the prophets and rejected his own call to
life, but the task of the prophet must go on, and Jesus himself
reassures the prophets of a new age with the words: ' "Blessed is he
comes in the name of the Lord" ' (Matt. 23.39). With this blessing
in mind, we can now look to the prophetic role of the Religious in
the Church and world of today, coming 'in the name of the Lord'
to live in communion the vows of poverty, chastity and obedience.

THE PROPHETIC FUNCTION OF PUBLIC COMMUNITY LIVING

One of the most extraordinary 'signs of the times' of our own era
is a strange contradiction. There is a growth of philosophical schools
(exemplified by Martin Heidegger and the later existentialists or,
more recently, by the Marxist philosophers), theological schools
(exemplified by men like Dietrich Bonhoeffer, Harvey Cox and Karl
Rahner) and psychological schools (exemplified by Viktor Frankl
and Rollo May) which are all converging to point out that man will
become fully all that he has the potential to be only when he opens
himself up to become 'a man for others'. We also have a society
which is more and more geared to a sense of community. Fewer
and fewer people own their own houses, but share buildings. Many
western societies are moving towards a welfare situation where man
depends greatly upon others, and the increase and perfection of the
means of communication should be bringing all of us closer and
closer together.

Instead, man seems to be getting more and more lonely. 'A phil-
osopher can write 'hell is other people' and a popular song calls out
that 'hell is in "hello"'. So many people are talking about 'getting
out of the rat race' and many of the young have simply 'opted out'
so as not to be caught up in some of the wonders which 20th-

century man thought would lead to his liberation. All of this shows that somewhere, somehow, something has gone wrong. Tension is deeply felt, and two World Wars with numerous other smaller (or not so small!) wars have filled the intervals showing that man, called by the intellectuals to realise himself by being 'a man for others', has decided that the only way to survive is to do it all on his own.[16]

Yet contemporary philosophy, theology, psychology and technology, which are merely catching up with an age-old biblical message, are correct in their evaluation of the deepest needs of man being resolved only when he looks to others in love. However, the writers and preachers seem to go on proclaiming their truths into the nothingness of their gilded cages, while modern man finds no *existential* answer to the terrible divisions which are a sign of our times.

As Christian men and women, we believe that life 'in Christ' is the vocation of all God's creatures. We point out that the Church, the continuing, saving and uniting presence of Christ in the world, has the answer. The Church offers to the world true community, where: 'love . . . binds everything together in perfect harmony' (Col. 3.14), and in which man can find that deep harmony which only faith in Christ can bring. Yet the Church seems to be having very little success in communicating this message of life-giving harmony. Why is this so?[17] I believe that the reasons given for the Church's failure are often superficially analysed. There are two possible culprits: either the world will not listen, or the Church is not communicating her message with conviction. Far too often we glibly point out that the world has become too hardened in its wicked ways and will not listen. While this may be part of the answer, it is to undervalue the genuine searching that is going on in the world. Perhaps we would do well to be more Christian in our analysis, and start with some self-examination.

One of the main reasons why the Church is having so little success in her proclamation of herself as a community of love, reflecting the God who called her into existence, through the loving gift of his Son (see John 3.16), is because this proclamation is not on the same level as the world's question. The question so anxiously posed comes at the level of 'life', and the answer comes back at the level of 'words'. The world is *told* that the Church offers the possibility of a true union of love, but it asks to be *shown*. We live in a world which has been deceived too often by empty promises. They have little credibility if the promise is not backed up with a lived, convincing sign that the promise can be a reality. This means that the Christian answer to the world's deeply felt desire to live in a unity of love and peace will convince only if the world can see that it works in practice.

This is the prophetic function of a publicly lived commitment to a Religious community within the Church. We Religious are not qualitatively superior, but we publicly accept a task of a *public living* of a quality of life 'in Christ' to which all are called. For a variety of reasons, the unity of love which all the baptised are called to live is either not achieved or not seen. This should be a matter of great concern for each and every member of the Church, but too little attention is paid to it at all levels. This is another 'sign of the times'. The fact that the Church at large seemingly finds it impossible to show forth to the world its vocation to 'perfect harmony', makes the Religious community the prophet of our age. We must:

1. Show to the world that the call of life 'in Christ' is not just a preached doctrine but an achievable reality, and thus give both Christians and non-Christians hope[18]

2. Point our finger at the institution of the Christian Church which lays claim to be an institution of love, faith and hope, asking: 'Are you, the institution, really living what you were instituted for?'[19] Our most effective means of performing this two-fold task is the quality of our lives together. We must not *tell* the world and the Church that we share life. This would be to fall back into the errors that we are called to criticise. We must *show* them by *living* it.

THE PROPHETIC FUNCTION OF A PUBLICLY LIVED VOW OF POVERTY

All Christians are called by the Gospels to a radical sharing of all that they have. I hope that my analysis of the material from the New Testament has shown this. The message of the Gospel is clear: all men should have the possibility of becoming all that God made them to be. To make this possible, all are called to a radical sharing, if they profess the faith of the Gospels. This, ultimately, was the sense of the sharing that went on in the apostolic community: 'There was not a needy person among them.' (Acts 4.34).

The signs of our times show that the world, and possibly the Christian Church, seem to have lost touch with this radical call to evangelical poverty. We see a Christian Europe and a Christian North America living with an easy conscience beside Africa and South America, but these are the immediately obvious examples of the scandal of contemporary Christian society. Closer to home, in each village and hamlet, society is clearly divided between those who have, and those who do not have. As management locks itself in bitter struggle against a protesting, striking work force no one seems to recognise that all this strife is nothing more than a sub-conscious screaming out that man was not made to live this way.[20] These divisions are also found within the confines of the confessing Christian Churches, where wealth of possessions and culture in one community can live side by side with terrible poverty in another. This sort of division makes a lie out of the same Gospel which *both* the communities *preach*. They are called to *live* that Gospel.

In this situation the challenge of Religious poverty, which is a radical sharing of all that we have and all that we are, takes on a prophetic function. Again, the Religious community has publicly committed itself to showing, by the quality of its shared life, that true humanity, and thus true Christianity, is not just a *preached* message, but a lived reality *within the Church*, and fired by the same ideals which fire the whole Church.[21] Again we find that the vow of poverty is not an end in itself. It is a major aspect of our prophetic function within the Church.

THE PROPHETIC FUNCTION OF A PUBLICLY LIVED VOW OF CHASTITY

All Christians are called to a chaste love, because this is the only sort of love which creates. The exhilarating and joyful *total* gift of self can take place only in the context of a profound loyalty and trust. The Scriptures parallel it with the gift of Christ for the Church and the Church says of it that it is 'caught up into divine love and is directed and enriched by the redemptive power of Christ and the salvific action of the Church' (*Gaudium et Spes* 48). Why is this so? What is so special about this 'gift' of authentic married love? It is the unique place among men and women where the affective nature of a God who is love is revealed to the world. The Gospels tell us that God loved so much that the Incarnation had to burst forth from the immensity of that love (see John 3.16). Love is not love unless it is felt – and this is the love which is revealed by authentic married love – the call to chastity of the major part of Christianity.

Need I list the signs of the times? – the use of sex to sell all sorts of innocent wares, and to add spice to an already drugged society; the education of the young to a life-style where to give and receive oneself totally is like sharing a cup of coffee – as long as both parties think that it may be a useful experience; the breakdown of marriage and the family. It is pointless to go on, as we all live – and often wonder at ourselves – in the context of this new dogma of: 'If you like it, do it!'

Religious, vowed to their particular form of chastity, are not superior in this department. The pain which a chaste life can often cause tells us that. However, we are calling out to a topsy-turvy world that they may have abundant pleasure, but they have lost love. Swept off our feet by the Lordship of a God who is love, we show the world that genuine affection is not found in a predatory man or woman hunt, but in the loss of self, as we are taken over by the presence of so great a love that we can do no other than give ourselves uniquely to this love. As I have already said, this does not make it any easier, but from here we can speak to all Christians; we can prophesy again as did the prophets of old, that the exquisite experience of loving and belonging to the loved one is not something which we can determine, but is a reflection of the loving gift of a caring, creating, fruitful and loving God: 'But God shows his love for us in that while we were yet sinners, Christ died for us' (Rom. 5.8). Again the function of our chaste love is not to make us something different or 'odd' within the context of the universal call to sanctity, but to call all Christians back to the authentic, faithful, loving and joyful gift of self which is the mark of all Christians, celibate or married.

THE PROPHETIC FUNCTION OF A PUBLICLY LIVED VOW OF OBEDIENCE

Here we are at the heart of the Christian vocation, as we all attempt to follow the life-style of Jesus of Nazareth who was totally directed by the will of God whom he called his Father. All Christians are called to this form of life and since the Incarnation the Church has rendered 'incarnational' the call to obedience as she attempts to present the person and the word of Jesus to men and women of all ages in all their concerns.

Turning from the ideal to the signs of the times, there are two problems that I would like simply to point out:

1. The immediately obvious one that man (from the earliest times) tends to tear himself away from God and has a profound drive to be the absolute master of his own destiny. How well this tragedy is described already in the ninth century BC in Genesis 1–11. Again there is little need for me to make a list of the continued arrogance and egoism which is so much a part of our contemporary situation. The signs of the times mentioned while discussing poverty and chastity could simply be repeated here as they all reflect a basic movement away from the creating, calling Exodus God to whom man cannot dictate terms.

2. Closer to home, we find a terrible danger within our own Church. As the historical, human institution of the Church is made up of men and structures, she will always be exposed to the risk of losing sight of the fact that she exists to call all men to 'life in Christ' through the ministry of Christ's word and sacrament. When this happens, the very sense of our existence as the Church founded by Christ is put into jeopardy. Little wonder that the Council spoke of the need for a Church which is: 'at the same time holy and always in need of being purified' (*Lumen Gentium* 8).[22]

Religious obedience is again the obedience of a prophet. We must be seen as living under the divine urgency to go away from ourselves and to lose ourselves in the mysterious plan of a mysterious God. In this way we will continue to proclaim to the people among whom we live, the freedom which a radical openness to God can create, but above all, we will act as a thorn in the side of an over-confident, over-organised, over-institutionalised Church, as the quality of our free but obedient lives will keep posing the question – Just why were you instituted in the first place?

CONCLUSION: THE RELIGIOUS AS A PROPHET

The tradition of the Church makes it clear that the Religious families in her midst are to live poverty, chastity and obedience within a community. However, I hope that this book has shown that the Religious does not find his or her *identity* in community, poverty, chastity or obedience.[23] Nevertheless, these traditional marks of Religious life are the essential *means by which* a Religious lives out his unique function within the context of the universal call to sanctity: his function as a prophet. It is here that we find the *identity* of the Religious.

Most prophetic communities will be called to prophesy by quietly showing to the Church and the world a quality of life that calls them back to the design of God in Christ Jesus. Occasionally, a speaking prophet will certainly arise, where great love for the potential of mankind and the Christian Church will cause him to speak out: ' "to pluck up and to break down, to destroy and to overthrow, to build and to plant" ' (Jer. 1.10). Many of our founders were such men and women. As is evident from the lives of those prophets, such a vocation is a painful one for, as with Jeremiah and Jesus himself, more often than not ' "a prophet is not without honour, except in his own country, and among his own kin, and in his own house" ' (Mark 6.4).

We are living in an era when many people are 'turned off' by the structure and organisation of the Christian Church and they 'throw out the baby with the bath water', as they turn to the oriental cults and other more 'free-wheeling' groups and sects, or decide that they are happy to go along with any sort of religion. How often we hear it said: 'I have my own kind of religion, and we are all ultimately the same, aren't we!' While one respects the positions of these good people, and knows that God loves all men, no matter what their faith and practice, we are what we are because we believe that Jesus Christ has made a difference. We must start talking less about that difference, and showing by the quality of our poor, chaste and obedient lives together that it has made us into 'new men and women in Christ', to paraphrase some Pauline expressions (see Col. 3.10 and Gal. 3.27–8). It is my conviction and experience that people are 'turned-on' to the deeper reality and mystery of the Church when they see and touch that reality in genuine communities bound together by the love that is generated by a profound life in Christ. There is no great need to *speak* about that sort of love, but there is an urgent need to *live* it.

As this is the case, Religious life is not a thing of the past. It is the urgent need of our times, but Religious must courageously accept the frightening mission which the Lord has entrusted to them: to live as prophets. In the face of this tremendous task we will often, like Jeremiah, feel helpless: ' "Ah Lord God! Behold, I do not know how to speak, for I am only a youth" '(Jer. 1.6). In this situation we must recall again the lesson which we learnt from our study of discipleship. Not only to his disciples, but also to his prophets, the Lord announces: 'If I thought that *you* could do it, I would not have asked you. It is *my* work, not yours. You can only manifest what I have accomplished in you.'

Notes

Superior numerals, appearing with a publication date,
e.g. 1978[2], indicate edition number.

PREFACE

1. One thinks immediately of such men as Rudolf Schnackenburg, Raymond Brown, Anton Vögtle and Joseph Fitzmyer, who are the outstanding world authorities in their respective fields. All are Catholic priests.
2. It has often been pointed out that Vatican II gave us wonderful documents on the Church (*Lumen Gentium*), Revelation (*Dei Verbum*) and the Church in the Modern World (*Gaudium et Spes*), but that the document on the Religious Life (*Perfectae Caritatis*) still leaves a lot to be desired. One of the reasons for this is that previous to the Council there was already a flourishing theology of the Church and Revelation, and this is reflected in the documents. The same cannot be said of Religious life. It is only since the Council that we have seen this need. As yet we have no comprehensive work in this field in English. There is a wonderful book in French: J. M. R. Tillard, *Devant Dieu et pour le monde*, Cogitatio Fidei 75, Paris (Editions du Cerf, 1975), which certainly merits translation. Although aimed at Benedictine monasticism, a great deal of valuable theological reflection applicable to all forms of Religious life can be found in D. Rees and Others, *Consider your Call: A Theology of Monastic Life Today*, London (SPCK, 1978).
3. The work of Fr Tillard, just mentioned, has been a constant source of ideas and information. English readers should also see his *The Gospel Path: The Religious Life* and *There are Charisms and Charisms: The Religious Life* (Bruxelles, Lumen Vitae, 1977). Fr Murphy-O'Connor's well-known contribution is: 'What is Religious Life? – Ask the Scriptures', *Supplement to Doctrine and Life* 45 (1973). The whole issue was devoted to his study. This work caused a discussion which was carried on for some time in the same journal. The original contribution and the discussion which followed have now been published as a book: *What is Religious Life? A Critical Reappraisal* (Dublin, Dominican Publications, 1977). I will refer to the page numbers of the original study through this book. Fr Murphy-O'Connor gives the biblical underpinning for much of his work on Religious life in *Becoming*

Human Together (Dublin, Veritas, 1977).

4. The reader will find that I refer continually to B. W. Anderson, *The Living World of the Old Testament* (London, Longmans, 1978³) for a summary of Old Testament criticism, and R. A. Spivey and D. M. Smith, *Anatomy of the New Testament: A Guide to its Structure and Meaning* (London, Macmillan, 1974²) for the New Testament.

CHAPTER 1: *The Universal Call to Sanctity*

1. This document had a rather unfortunate history which can briefly be summarised as follows: there was an original *schema* prepared by a pre-Conciliar commission published in early 1962. It was quickly seen that this long document did not reflect what was expected by John XXIII, and it was scrapped. The Conciliar discussion of the Church eventually led to a complete section on Religious (*Lumen Gentium* 43–7), and thus a document specifically directed to the renewal of Religious life was taken up by a new commission. This document went through no less that five *schemas* before it was finally approved. Many specialists felt that this troubled passage was unfortunate, as in places the earlier documents, which had been rejected, were better. We shall see in the course of our study, that at least from a biblical point of view, there are several lacunae in the Conciliar document as we now have it. On the history of the document, see J. M. R. Tillard and Y. Congar (eds.), *L'adaptation et la rénovation de la vie religieuse. Decret 'Perfectae Caritatis'*, Unam Sanctam 62 (Paris, Editions du Cerf, 1967) pp. 51–72. The article is by Bishop Armand Le Bourgeois.

2. See the criticism of this number by J. M. R. Tillard, *op. cit.*, pp. 90–100. The problem arises from the juridical, rather than theological, nature of the document.

3. Stress mine.

4. W. Abbott, *The Documents of Vatican II*, (London, Geoffrey Chapman, 1965), p. 66, note 184. Stress mine.

5. *ibid.*, p. 73, note 207. Stress mine. See also, Sacred Congregation for Religious and for Secular Institutes – Sacred Congregation of Bishops, *Directives for the Mutual Relations between Bishops and Religious in the Church*, Issued at Rome on 14th May, 1978. Hereafter referred to as *Mutuae Relationes*. Sections 1–4 and 10–14 treat explicitly of the *function* of the Religious within the universal call to sanctity. On this important document, see the fine article of J. Snijders, 'Bishops and Religious: A Vatican Document on the Mutual Relations between Bishops and Religious in the Church', *The Australasian Catholic Record* 56 (1979) 192–203. Also useful is J. Jukes, 'A commentary on the "*Notae Directivae*" for the Mutual Relations between Bishops and Religious in the Church', *The Clergy Review* 63 (1978) 472–7.

Unfortunately, not all Roman documents follow *Lumen Gentium* in the way of *Mutuae Relationes*. See *Schema of Canons on Institutes of Life Consecrated by Profession of the Evangelical Counsels*, A draft issued at Rome on 2 February, 1977. Canons 1–3 still indicate that Religious are called to a superior form of Christian life. See, on this, J. Murphy-O'Connor, 'The New Canon Law versus the Gospel: a critique', *Supplement to Doctrine and Life* 63 (1976) 38–57.

6. There are still some who hold this, despite *Lumen Gentium* and *Mutuae Relationes*. One very recent example will suffice. In the letters to the Editor of *Zealandia* on Sunday 4 February, 1979 (p. 2) a correspondent (an ex-seminary professor and a Religious) writes: 'Many will interpret what you report as meaning that there is no real difference between the vocation of the religious and that of the lay person. Which is contrary to the teaching of the Church.' He then quotes from Pius XII's *Sacra Virginitas* and adds: 'I know of no statement by a later pope or of the Vatican Council that would make a "pre-Vatican II ghost" of that teaching.' As the correspondent was a professor of scholastic philosophy, I am taking his use of the term 'real difference' as indicating what I have called a 'qualitative distinction'. He shows no knowledge of *Lumen Gentium* and *Mutuae Relationes*.

7. See especially John XXIII's address to the Council, *Gaudet Mater Ecclesia*, 45–55.

8. This is the sense of Abbott's phrase: 'It would be an error', cited above. In more traditional language, Vatican I would have stated: 'If anyone says (*si quis dixerit*) that the Religious life is a qualitatively superior life-style among the baptised, let him be anathema (*anathema sit*)!'

9. See, for example, J. Aubry, *Teologia della vita religiosa alla luce del Vaticano II*, pp. 11–25; J. Cambier, 'Realtà carismatica ed ecclesiale della vita religiosa', in A. Favale (ed.), *Per una presenza viva dei religiosi nella Chiesa e nel mondo*, pp. 229–82; J. M. R. Tillard, *Les religieux au coeur de l'Eglise*, Problèmes de vie religieuse 30 (Paris, Editions du Cerf, 1969) pp. 9–21; T. Matura, *Célibat et communauté. Les fondements évangéliques de la vie religieuse* (Paris, Editions du Cerf, 1967) pp. 11–38.

10. The Council spoke of the Gospel as the ultimate norm for the renewal of Religious life. See *Perfectae Caritatis* 2.

11. See also the Council's statement on this ongoing revelation down through history, in the document on Revelation: *Dei Verbum* 7–10.

12. This point may be strangely new to many readers, but it would take another small book to explain it in detail. The Pentateuch (Genesis, Exodus, Numbers, Leviticus and Deuteronomy) did not come into existence overnight through some wonderful act of inspired writing, as if an angel guided the hand of Moses. On the contrary, many ancient oral and written traditions were collected, remembered, passed on etc., until they were finally assembled into the books as we know them. Scholars are able to identify

these various traditions, their history in the developing thought of Israel, their particular use of words and concepts, and their particular theological viewpoint. These traditions are called: Jahwistic, Elohistic, Priestly and Deuteronomic. The Priestly tradition was responsible for assembling the book of Genesis as we have it now. See, for a further explanation of this, B. W. Anderson, *The Living World of the Old Testament*, pp. 17–23; 420–36, or the more scholarly but still very readable work of J. A. Soggin, *Introduction to the Old Testament* (London, SCM Press, 1976) pp. 79–146.

13. A careful reader of Genesis will notice how chapter one summarises in a magnificent synthesis all the creating activity of God. This is the work of the Priestly author. In 2.4b the story starts again, and we are told in a narrative form of the creation, especially of man and woman. This is the work of the Jahwist. Occasionally I have changed the Revised Standard Version's use of 'the Lord' in Old Testament passages to 'Jahweh' where the original Hebrew permitted this. I have consistently written 'the Son of Man' for 'the Son of man'.

14. For a good summary of these discussions, and some valuable suggestions of his own, see C. K. Barrett, *The Epistle to the Romans*, Black's New Testament Commentaries (London, A. and C. Black, 1957) pp. 165–7.

15. Again the reader may be surprised to find that Ephesians may have been written by a later follower of Paul. There are many reasons for this commonly held view. See W. G. Kümmel, *Introduction to the New Testament* (London, SCM Press, 1976) pp. 350–66. What is important is that Paul's follower in no way betrays his teacher. Ephesians is a later but authentically 'Pauline' development of Paul's letter to the Colossians. The Greek for 'all things' *(ta panta)* is a neuter plural word, and clearly refers to the whole of creation. Stress mine in this and all biblical quotations.

16. Notice that this point is made *only* in Matthew's account. Matthew is most probably using Mark 10.17–22. In Mark he is not a 'young man', but he has kept the commandments 'from his youth' (v. 20). In Mark there is no mention of 'perfection'. The Lucan version of this passage (Luke 18.19–24) largely follows Mark. Again there is no theology of 'perfection'. See, on this, T. Matura, *Le radicalisme évangélique: Aux sources de la vie chrétienne,* Lectio Divina 97 (Paris, Editions du Cerf, 1978) pp. 69–75.

17. This passage became the proof text from Scripture for both a life of perfection and the vow of poverty. See A. Tanquerey, *The Spiritual Life: A Treatise on Ascetical and Mystical Theology* (Desclée, Tournai, 1930) pp. 169–70, 426–7. The older apologetic biblical exegesis came to the same conclusions. See J. -A. van Steenkiste, *Sanctum Jesu Christi Evangelium secundum Matthaeum* (Bruges C. Begaert, 1903[4]) vol. II, p. 616: 'Distinctio inter praecepta et consilia evangelica contra protestantes istis verbis certissime demonstratur'.

It has been recently defended by J. Galot, 'Le fondement évangélique du voeu religieux de pauvreté', *Gregorianum* 56 (1975) 441–67, but see the reply of J. M. R. Tillard, 'Le propos de pauvreté et l'exigence évangélique', *Nouvelle Revue Théologique* 100 (1978). 207–32, especially 207–16. A most recent, but typical, example of its uncritical use is found in V. J. Genovesi, 'The Faith of Christ: Source of the Virtues of the Vows', *Review for Religious* 38 (1979) 187. Genovesi writes of a poverty 'which is a matter of godly conviction and choice', and describes it as 'the poverty of those who voluntarily accede to Christ's admonition: "If you wish to be perfect, go and sell what you own and give the money to the poor, and you will have treasure in heaven; then come follow me"' (Matt. 19.21). It is difficult to eradicate this uncritical use of traditional 'proof texts', even among trained theologians.

18. The most important work on the Sermon on the Mount is W. D. Davies, *The Setting of the Sermon on the Mount* (Cambridge, University Press, 1963). There is a more popular version of the book, *The Sermon on the Mount* (Cambridge, University Press, 1966).

19. This expression comes from K. Stendhal. *The School of St. Matthew* (Philadelphia, Fortress Press, 1966) p. xi.

20. The radical nature of this demand, a call to 'perfection', was already seen as too idealistic by Luke, who wrote: 'Be *merciful*, even as your Father is merciful' (Luke 6.36). Most commentators, following G. Dalman, *The Words of Jesus* (Edinburgh, T. and T. Clark, 1902) pp. 66 and 204 argue that it is Matthew who changed the saying, as 'merciful' is often used of God in the Old Testament, but he is never spoken of as 'perfect'. However, one should see the use of 'perfect' in Pss. 18.30 and 19.7. Matthew's phrase is very Aramaic in structure while Luke has a better Greek sentence. Matthew may have the original version of the saying. This discussion, of course, in no way touches our consideration, as we are interested in what *Matthew* has to say to his community.

21. See the fine analysis of Matt. 19.16–22 by J. P. Burchill, 'Biblical Basis of Religious Life', *Review for Religious* 36 (1977) 900–17. Our brief look at Matthew's texts has been a simple example of the modern method of studying the Gospels. Firstly one must discover the situation in the life of Matthew's Church which made him use his source (Mark in this particular case) in his own special way. This is called 'Form Criticism'. Then one must understand the passage within the developing theological argument of the whole Gospel. This is called 'Redaction Criticism'. On Matthew's (and Jesus') 'radicalisation of the Law', see T. Matura, *Le radicalisme évangélique*, pp. 111–38. On the six antitheses, see pp. 116–26.

22. This is one of the outstanding characteristics of the Priestly section of the Pentateuch. There is no great show of story-telling imagination, but a

well-organised, systematic statement of facts or interpretation of those facts. See B. W. Anderson, *The Living World of the Old Testament*, pp. 422–5.

23. I say 'perhaps' because some scholars would also place Ephesians in the 80s (or even later).

24. J. D. G. Dunn, in a recent book, *Unity and Diversity in the New Testament: An Enquiry into the Character of Earliest Christianity* (London, SCM Press, 1977), has warned us against any attempt to find '*the* New Testament message' of any particular theme, as there is so much diversity within the New Testament itself. Dunn himself shows, however, that a basic unity of idea can still be traced, despite the all-important diversity. This co-existence of 'unity' and 'diversity', already present in the New Testament, also has important consequences for a biblical understanding of Religious life. On the question of following Jesus, see the closely related discussion of ministry in J. D. G. Dunn, *Unity and Diversity*, pp. 103–23.

25. We have already seen that Matt. 19.16–22 should not be used as the biblical foundation for the evangelical counsel of poverty.

26. See especially J. M. R. Tillard, 'Le fondement évangélique de la vie religieuse', *Nouvelle Revue Théologique* 91 (1969) 916–55 and J. M. van Cangh, 'Fondement évangélique de la vie religieuse', *Nouvelle Revue Théologique* 95 (1973) 635–47.

27. It is not my task to discuss these two thorny questions here. However, as the reader will discover, I will eventually be making a case for a radical commitment which will show that habits and rules *must* be seen as peripheral questions, despite their centrality in a great deal of current discussion. For a magnificent historical survey, and an evaluation of the (relative) role which the religious habit has played throughout the history of Religious life, see M. Auge, 'L'abito religioso', *Claretianum* 16 (1976) 33–95; 17(1977) 5–106. A valuable bibliography can be found on pp. 102–6.

CHAPTER 2: The God of the Old Testament

1. Particularly helpful for this presentation of the God of the Old Testament is the little book of R. A. F. Mackenzie, *Faith and History in the Old Testament* (New York, Macmillan, 1963) pp. 26–39. Mackenzie shows how Israel's God is a uniquely *personal* God within the context of the other gods and goddesses of the Middle East in the Old Testament period. I will be drawing heavily from this book in the pages that follow. The more interested reader may like to consult some of the scholarly theologies of the Old Testament. See W. Eichrodt, *Theology of the Old Testament* (London, SCM Press, 1961) Vol. I, pp. 178–88; G. von Rad, *Old Testament Theology* (Edinburgh, Oliver and Boyd, 1962) Vol. I, pp. 165–231; E. Jacob, *Theology of the Old Testament* (London, Hodder and Stoughton, 1958) pp. 37–120; H.

H. Rowley, *The Faith of Israel: Aspects of Old Testament Thought* (London, SCM Press, 1956) pp. 48–73.

2. Particularly an outstanding German Old Testament scholar, Martin Noth, and his many followers.

3. The Jahwistic tradition always uses the name 'Jahweh' to speak of God. The Elohistic tradition always calls God 'Elohim'.

4. Especially important are such famous Old Testament scholars as G. von Rad, W. F. Albright and J. Bright.

5. For an excellent, up-to-date study of the whole of Genesis, see B. Vawter, *On Genesis: A New Reading* (London, Geoffrey Chapman, 1977). On Gen. 1–11, see pp. 37–163. Another very important work is G. von Rad, *Genesis* (London, SCM Press, 1976[2].)

6. This is well presented in *A New Catechism: Catholic Faith for Adults* (London, Burns and Oates, 1970) pp. 261–2.

7. The reader will notice that these lively and powerful stories are interspersed with orderly and mathematically calculated genealogies (see 4.17–22; 5.1–32) and other precise details which could prove very upsetting if we were to maintain that all this is history 'as it really happened'. For example, where did Cain's wife come from? These questions, of course, need not be posed. The genealogies are typical of the Priestly sections of the text.

8. It is important to notice the universalism of this earliest concept of the God of Israel. It shows no trace of the later idea that Jahweh belonged to Israel alone.

9. This is again a passage from the Jahwist.

10. The Patriarchs, in fact, would still have had several 'gods', but slowly the superiority of their chief God (El Shaddai) would have been forged into what later became the monotheistic faith of Israel. A very good presentation of this is found in the classical German article of O. Eissfeldt, 'Jahwe, der Gott der Väter', *Theologische Literaturzeitung* 88 (1963) 481–90. It can also be found in the works mentioned above, in note 1.

11. Again the reader can refer to the theologies of the Old Testament mentioned in note 1. Particularly helpful is the study of H. Renckens, *The Religion of Israel* (London, Sheed and Ward, 1967) pp. 97–139. The following depends heavily upon the work of Renckens.

12. As this is such a vital question for the understanding of Israel's God, there are many opinions about the etymology and the precise significance of the verbal form 'jahweh'. Naturally, we cannot enter this discussion here. H. Renckens, *op. cit.*, pp. 107–10 gives a good summary of the discussion.

13. H. Renckens, *op. cit.*, p. 122.

14. *Ibid.*, p. 139.

15. As God defines himself in terms of the verb 'to be', traditional theological manuals have used Exod. 3.14–15 as a proof text to show that the Bible speaks of God as 'subsistent being' (*Ipsum esse subsistens*). This notion, of course, was never a part of Israel's faith, however well it may provide a philosophical definition of God.

16. J. Ratzinger, *Introduction to Christianity* (London, Burns and Oates, 1969) p. 92.

17. The majority of the 'historical' books belong to the same school of thought, thus this theme is very strong in I–II Samuel and I–II Kings. Jeremiah is also very closely linked with the theology of the Deuteronomist.

18. There are many good commentaries on Jeremiah. The best is, as yet, only in German: K. Rudolph, *Jeremia* (Tübingen, J. C. B. Mohr, 1958). In English, see J. Bright, *Jeremiah*, The Anchor Bible 21 (New York, Doubleday, 1965). Also very useful is E. A . Leslie, *Jeremiah. Chronologically arranged, translated and interpreted* (New York, Abingdon, 1954). For the experience of Jeremiah, still valuable is J. Skinner, *Prophecy and Religion: Studies in the Life of Jeremiah* (Cambridge, University Press, 1922). See especially pp. 201–30 on 'The Inner Life of Jeremiah'. I have deliberately chosen Jeremiah as our example because of my conviction that the function of the Religious in the Church is also prophetic. See below, the final chapter of this book.

19. This expression, particularly applicable to consecrated Christian life, comes from P. Volz, *Der Prophet Jeremia* (Leipzig, A. Deichert, 1922) p. 207.

20. I have not included v. 12, as it has been inserted into the text at this point from 11.20, where it was original. The writings of all the prophets have had a long history before they finally received their present form, and there are frequent secondary insertions into the texts.

21. See R. E. Brown, *The Birth of the Messiah. A Commentary on the Infancy Narratives in Matthew and Luke* (London, Geoffrey Chapman, 1977) pp. 350–65. Brown argues that all the canticles in Luke's infancy narrative are deeply rooted in Old Testament faith, especially as it was expressed by the *anawim*: 'those who could not trust in their own strength' (p. 351).

CHAPTER 3: The New Testament: God is Love

1. See AA. VV., *The God of Israel, The God of Christians: The Great Themes of Scripture* (New York, Desclée, 1961) and W. Marchel, *Abba Vater! Die Vaterbotschaft des Neuen Testaments* (Düsseldorf, Patmos Verlag, 1964).

2. The relationship between these various elements, the historical Jesus to the Gospels and the various Gospels to one another, ranks among the most debated questions of New Testament scholarship. I do not want the reader to believe that one flowed neatly into the other. On the contrary, each Evangelist has his own very special theological point of view and was

strongly conditioned by the pastoral needs of his own community. Nevertheless, behind all this stands a very singular idea of God which was faithfully transmitted. This, of course, reflects one of the most important Jewish aspects of the earliest Christian Church.

3. Again the question of relationships arises. John's Gospel is unique in the way it presents the 'relation' of the Father to the Son and vice-versa. John has a clear teaching on the pre-existence of the Word (1.1–5) and Jesus has been 'sent' by the Father, and will eventually return to him (see 4.34; 5.23, 24, 30, 37; 6.38, 39, 44, 62; 7.16; 13.1; 17.5 etc.). However, this does not ultimately change the concept of 'God' which stands behind all the teaching of the New Testament. What is special to John is his particular vision of how that God has been revealed among men, i.e. his unique *christology*.

4. See on this, F. J. Moloney, 'The Johannine Son of God', *Salesianum* 38 (1976) 71–86, especially pp. 83–5 where the earlier Christian tradition is shown to be the background for John's idea of Jesus as 'the Son of God'.

5. It is very important to understand that the Fourth Gospel's use of the term 'the Jews' does not refer to a nation, as it does today. It refers to those people from Judaism who refused to accept Jesus and who had 'cast out' the Johannine Church from the Synagogue. See, on this, R. E. Brown, *The Gospel According to John (i–xii)*, The Anchor Bible 29 (New York, Doubleday, 1966) pp. lxx–lxxiii and F. J. Moloney, 'From Cana to Cana' (John 2.1–4,54) and the Fourth Evangelist's Concept of Correct (and Incorrect) Faith', *Salesianum* 40 (1978) 830–5; 840–1. The article runs from pp. 817–43.

6. This is the only story in the Gospels where a man *born* blind is cured. John's point is that Jesus does not merely restore a light which the man had once lost. It is an entirely new creation. On John 9, see F. J. Moloney, *The Johannine Son of Man*, Biblioteca di Scienza Religiose 14 (Rome, LAS, 1978²) pp. 142–59.

7. The Gospel and the first letter of John certainly came from the same community. There are differences, especially in their varying understanding of eschatology and ecclesiology, but these are to be explained by the changing situation of the community. See J. L. Houlden, *A Commentary on the Johannine Epistles*, Black's New Testament Commentaries (London, A. and C. Black, 1975) pp. 1–42, and especially, R. E. Brown, *The Community of the Beloved Disciple* (London, Geoffrey Chapman, 1979).

8. It is also possible that God is 'defined' as 'light' in I John 1.5, but this is not necessarily the case. See J. L. Houlden, *op. cit.*, pp. 57–60.

9. I am, of course, simplifying matters here. I refer continually to 'John', but we cannot be certain of the name of the man who stood behind this tradition. Nor can we be certain that the development of the theology of

the Johannine literature was due to the direct influence of this personality. However, it appears to me that the line of development which I have just indicated reflects what happened. For a discussion of the growth of the Johannine community, and my suggestions regarding the role of the apostolic figure behind the community, see F. J. Moloney, *The Word Became Flesh: A Study of Jesus in the Fourth Gospel* (Cork, Mercier Press, 1979) pp. 15–18 and Idem, *The Johannine Son of Man*, pp. 247–56.

10. See, for example, B. Lindars, *The Gospel of John*, New Century Bible (London, Oliphants, 1972) pp. 24–5.

11. It is important to notice that the Fourth Gospel has a very positive idea of the world. Unfortunately, John uses the same Greek word (*kosmos*) to speak of 'the world' in three different ways:

(i) the created universe, in a neutral sense (see, for example, 11.9; 17.5; 17.24)

(ii) humanity, created by God and loved by God. This aspect of 'the world' will come to life only if it finds in Jesus the revelation of a God of love (see, for example, 1.29; 3.16–19; 4.42; 6.14; 9.5; 16.28; 18.20, 37)

(iii) that part of humanity which has closed itself off from the light of God's revelation in Jesus and which has thus submitted to the power of darkness (see, for example, 7.7; 12.31; 14.17, 22, 27, 30; 15.18, 19; 16.8, 11, 20, 33).

See, on this, N. H. Cassem, 'A Grammatical and Contextual Inventory of the Use of *kosmos* in the Johannine Corpus with some Implications for a Johannine Cosmic Theology', *New Testament Studies* 19 (1972–3) 81–90.

12. In fact, the Greek word for 'he gave' (*edōken*) immediately suggests to what extent God was prepared to hand over his Son, as various forms of the same word are used throughout the New Testament to speak of the 'giving over' of Jesus to death.

13. I am giving the Greek here as I wish to point out the close connection that John sees between Jesus' accomplishment of his task and the Cross. To show the relationship he continually uses Greek words which come from *telos*.

14. For this translation of John 1.18, see my argument in F. J. Moloney, *The Word Became Flesh*, pp. 50–2.

15. Again the translation differs from the Revised Standard Version. Here I am following the majority of commentators. See F. J. Moloney, *The Johannine Son of Man*, p. 64, note 113.

16. Some recent scholars accuse the Johannine Church of being such a ghetto. See, for example, the extreme position of J. T. Sanders, *Ethics in the New Testament: Change and Development* (London, SCM Press, 1975). Sanders writes: 'If you believe you will have eternal life, promises the Johannine Christian, while the dying man's blood stains the ground' (p. 100). This

is, in my opinion, a gross misunderstanding of the Fourth Gospel.

17. I am limiting myself to a selection of texts from the Gospel so that the reader may follow John's thought more easily. However, there are several other passages where Jesus calls his disciples to a new and radical law of love. See, for example, 14.23–4; 15.9–13,17. On the whole question, see V. P. Furnish, *The Love Command in the New Testament* (London, SCM Press, 1973).

18. This is the significance of the insistence of the Church, even from a legal point of view, that a Religious should make *public* vows, as opposed to the private vows of many private individuals who remain outside Religious life. See the *Code of Canon Law*, Canon 572. The draft *schema* for *Institutes of Consecrated Life* only mentions the public nature of the vows passingly in Canon 58, para. 2. More satisfactory is *Mutuae Relationes* 10.

19. I stress these words because, as we will see as the book progresses, poverty, chastity and obedience, much less community and apostolate, must *never* be taken as ends in themselves. As we all know from experience, the absolutisation of any one of these 'means' generally results in a warped vision of life, and often produces strange human beings. As such, it cannot even be considered Christian.

20. I do not wish to be misunderstood. I heartily support (and work in) many of these activities as there is a great need among Christians and Religious to come to grips with the *content* of their faith. This sort of 'knowledge' has to be learnt, and thus teaching and study should be an important feature of the renewal process. Again, however, I insist that the frequenting of 'courses' must never become the symbol of the 'open-minded' or 'renewed' Religious!

21. For a moving presentation of what this means, see Y. Raguin, *La Profondeur de Dieu*, Collection Christus 33 (Bruges, Desclée de Brouwer, 1973) and Idem, *L'Esprit sur le monde*, Collection Christus 40 (Bruges, Desclée de Brouwer, 1975). It does *not* mean to escape from the world, creation and our role within that context by somehow losing ourselves in a transcendent God. As we shall see, the contrary is the case, as it must be for those who are loved and who reply to the love of an 'ever-present' God.

CHAPTER 4: The Old Testament 'Community'

1. Some of what follows was originally published in an article, 'Why Community?', *Supplement to Doctrine and Life* 49 (1974) 19–31. See especially 19–25.

2. There are all sorts of historical questions which scholars ask about the events which are described in Deuteronomy: the exodus and the theophany at Sinai being two of the thorniest of these questions. We must trace the

meaning of both the events, and Israel's understanding of them, so that we can see how she spoke about her own consciousness of being the people of God. Whatever one makes of the 'facts' behind the interpretations (and we will be dealing largely with interpretations), one 'fact' remains firm (and still remains firm in the belief of contemporary Judaism): Israel was called to be God's chosen people. We must see what that meant, and how Israel responded to that vocation.

3. Moses, of course, is presented throughout the book of Deuteronomy as speaking directly to the people of Israel, telling them what is required of them if they wish to be God's people. As we will see, the book itself is much later than Moses and he is used as a literary figure. However, the traditions and the faith expressed in Deuteronomy are not new. They go back to Israel's earliest experiences. In this way one can speak of these words as 'words of Moses', the original mediator between God and his people for the revelation of God's Law.

4. See, on Deuteronomy, the commentaries of G. von Rad, *Deuteronomy* (London, SCM Press, 1966) and J. Blenkinsopp, 'Deuteronomy', in *The Jerome Biblical Commentary* (London, Geoffrey Chapman, 1969) pp. 101–22. Again, most helpful is B. W. Anderson, *The Living World of the Old Testament*, pp. 348–66.

5. Previous to Sinai, God already 'reveals' himself to men: Abraham and the Patriarchs, down to the presence of Israel in Egypt. All of this is a promise. Only with Moses, the desert and the encounter with God at Sinai is God's people, under God's Law, finally founded. Israel is now 'convenanted' with God.

6. The idea of God's 'presence' is very important in the book of Exodus. It is called 'the glory of Jahweh', and it is something that can be seen, touched and even eaten, as with the manna. All of these experiences of the loving presence of God among his people are called 'the glory of Jahweh'. Jahweh is no distant God, but a God who cares, and who is to be found among his people. See, for example, Exod. 16.6–10; 24.16–17; 33.17–23. See also Lev. 9.6, 23; Num. 14.21.

7. The notion of Jahweh as a 'jealous' God is strange to us, as we tend to understand jealousy as a warped and possibly psychopathic human emotion. However, when God *is* love, then 'jealousy' is the only word which we can use to express his dealings with a people who always have an inclination to abandon him. For a beautiful and important reflection on this, see A. Sicari, *Matrimonio e verginità nella rivelazione. L'uomo di fronte alla 'Gelosia di Dio'*, Già e non ancora 31 (Milano, Jaca Book, 1978) pp. 69–151.

8. Scholars point out that the story of the finding of the book of the Law in the repairs of the Temple is probably a literary trick, or perhaps the result of the book's being placed there. Josiah was already committed to

his reform when the book was found. These details need not delay us. See B. W. Anderson, *The Living World of the Old Testament*, pp. 348–66.

9. These history books are called 'deuteronomist' because of their obvious dependence upon the theology of the authors of the book of Deuteronomy. Even in English it is clear that the judgements (negative or positive) are always couched in the same words. All are judged by the same consistent criteria. See B. W. Anderson, *The Living World of the Old Testament*, pp. 232–4.

10. See the considerations of J. P. Milton, *Prophecy Interpreted* (London, Geoffrey Chapman, 1974) pp. 77–108 regarding the interplay between past, present and future in the role of prophecy is Israel.

11. Most of the history books of Israel were written by the deuteronomic school, and they are behind the theological scheme whch I am about to outline. Only the books of Chronicles, which stem from priestly circles, reflect a different point of view. See B. W. Anderson, *The Living World of the Old Testament*, pp. 426–33.

CHAPTER 5: The Communities of Jesus Christ

1. Some of what follows was originally published in 'Why Community?', *Supplement to Doctrine and Life* 49 (1974) 25–31 and 'The Communities of the Early Church', *Supplement to Doctrine and Life* 50 (1974) 24–30.

2. The Johannine admission that the Gospels are the result of the reflection of the disciples upon the words and deeds of Jesus 'when he was raised from the dead' has been restated by the Council Fathers at Vatican II: 'For, after the ascension of the Lord, the apostles handed on to their hearers what he had said and done, but with that fuller understanding which they, instructed by the glorious events of Christ and enlightened by the Spirit of truth, now enjoyed' (*Dei Verbum* 19). For a succinct presentation of this question, see R. A. Spivey and D. M. Smith, *Anatomy of the New Testament*, pp. 183–7.

3. It is a question which is not asked seriously enough by some scholars, who rush into an 'existential', non-historical understanding of the Gospels. For the classical statement of this position, see R. Bultman, *Jesus Christ and Mythology* (London, SCM Press, 1960) or his book on Jesus, *Jesus and the Word*, Fontana (London, Collins, 1958).

4. The four different ways in which the four different Evangelists report these 'vocation stories' are already an indication that each Evangelist wishes to communicate his own particular point of view. However, despite these differences, there is a certain common experience which probably goes back to the historical experience of the men and women who first formed community with Jesus of Nazareth. See R. A. Spivey and D. M. Smith, *Anatomy*

of the New Testament, pp. 222–3.

5. See, on this, F. J. Moloney, *The Johannine Son of Man*, pp. 23–41. I have entitled this chapter on John 1.51: 'The Promise of the Son of Man'.

6. It appears probable that there was a peripheral, second-class group in first-century Judaism which was almost a sect on its own. They were called the *'ham ha-aretz'*, the people of the land. The Galileans (and perhaps the majority of the members of the earliest Church) would have been classified as 'people of the land' by the Jewish authorities – Jews, but only just! See R. A. Spivey and D. M. Smith, *The Anatomy of the New Testament*, p. 27.

7. It is surprising that it is still found in the Fourth Gospel, which was written towards the end of the first century. The example already given, of Nathanael's messianic confession of Jesus as 'Rabbi, Son of God and King of Israel', corrected by Jesus' promise of something quite different, in terms of 'the Son of Man' (John 1.49–51) is one of several cases in this Gospel (see also 3.13–14; 6.27; 8.28; 9.35; 12.23).

8. We will see this process again towards the end of this book when we consider what it means to be a disciple of Jesus.

9. Most English translations of the New Testament put a full stop after v. 30 and begin a new paragraph with v. 31. The original Greek manuscripts have no punctuation, and I believe that we should join these two verses with a comma.

10. Here we meet the difficult question of the detailed passion predictions, uttered by Jesus before it all happened. Mark 10.33–4 goes into all the lurid details, right down to the spitting and mocking. Jesus almost certainly spoke about his coming death, but as the Gospels were written *after* it all happened, the predictions are 'filled out' by the Evangelists' describing what, in fact, did happen. Mark 9.31 is probably very close to what Jesus actually said: ' "The Son of Man will be delivered into the hands of men and they will kill him" ' (see also Lk. 9.44: ' "Let these words sink into your ears: for the Son of Man is to be delivered into the hands of men" ').

11. The Evangelist has certainly placed all these pieces of Gospel tradition: passion prediction, request from the sons of Zebedee, the questioning of the sons of Zebedee, the general teaching in service and the final saying on the Son of Man, in this order. Much of it would have been independent material in the earlier oral or written traditions. However, even though the present order of events is an indication of Mark's theological ability, I believe it also reflects a genuine reminiscence of Jesus' formation of his first disciples. Not all scholars would agree.

12. One thinks immediately of the immensely successful (from a box-office point of view) *Jesus of Nazareth* by Zeferelli. The photography is superb and the film is often moving, but it does not present the community of Jesus as the New Testament gives it (and this is not the only lack of faithfulness to

the Gospel picture!). In this respect, the theatrical production (not so much the filmed version) *Jesus Christ Superstar*, despite its flaws, is nearer to the truth. It is important to read a contemporary 'Jesus book'. The best and most available are G. Bornkamm, *Jesus of Nazareth* (London, Hodder and Stoughton, 1960) and C. H. Dodd, *The Founder of Christianity* (London, Collins, 1971). Another most useful little book is D. Senior, *Jesus: A Gospel Portrait* (Dayton, Pflaum, 1975). Excellent suggestions for further reading, and a critically assessed bibliography on Jesus, can be found in R. A. Spivey and D. M. Smith, *Anatomy of the New Testament*, pp. 245–8. The synthesis offered by this book on pp. 182–245 is again very well done.

13. Only Luke places this experience within the context of the Jewish feast of Pentecost, the feast in which the Jews celebrated the giving of the Law to Moses on Sinai.

14. For a well-organised and illuminating presentation of Paul, his Churches and his letters, see R. A. Spivey and D. M. Smith, *Anatomy of the New Testament*, pp. 288–333. Also very useful are G. Bornkamm, *Paul* (London, Hodder and Stoughton, 1971) and F. F. Bruce, *Paul: Apostle of the Free Spirit* (Exeter, Paternoster Press, 1977).

15. Notice that it is *the Church* which is idealised as a loving, united and praying community. Acts 1–5 is not primarily about Religious communities. However, if Religious are prepared to admit that they are not a class apart (see *Lumen Gentium* 40), then a Religious community becomes a microcosm of the Church, and Acts 1–5 does become the ideal of the Religious community. More will be made of this below. See pp. 158–60. On the idealisation of the Jerusalem community, see R. A. Spivey and D. M. Smith, *Anatomy of the New Testament*, pp. 253–66.

16. See below, pp. 89–91.

17. The precise nature of this encounter is difficult to determine. It is reported three times in Acts (9.1–19; 22.5–16; 26.10–18) but these accounts differ in detail. It is reported again by Paul himself in Gal. 1.12–17 and I Cor 15.8–10. Several times he seems to allude to it (see, for example, I Cor. 9.16–17; Eph. 3.2–3). Whatever one makes of the details of the encounter, it is fundamental to Paul's understanding of himself as an apostle of Jesus Christ (see I Cor. 15.3–11).

18.   This fact stands behind one of our biggest difficulties in interpreting Paul. It is as if we are listening to only one end of a telephone conversation. We are often not too sure of the exact nature of the problems that Paul is dealing with. However, that every letter deals with a Church in need is obvious from only a passing acquaintance with the texts.

19. Scholars correctly point out that the terms 'grace and peace' were regularly used in secular letter-writing of this period. However, all the rest of the salutation comes from quite a different background!

20. There are two very fine commentaries on the Corinthian letters by C. K. Barrett, *The First Epistle to the Corinthians*, Black's New Testament Commentaries (London, A. and C. Black, 1971) and *The Second Epistle to the Corinthians*, Black's New Testament Commentaries (London, A. and C. Black, 1973).

21. See C. K. Barrett, *The First Epistle to the Corinthians*, pp. 1–11.

22. For an excellent synthesis, see R. A. Spivey and D. M. Smith, *Anatomy of the New Testament*, pp. 27–48.

23. We shall see how important this is for Paul when we come to consider the vow of obedience. See below, pp. 120–3.

24. I will devote more space to the Pauline notion of life 'in Christ' as a life lived in the unity which only love can establish when I consider the vow of poverty. See below, pp. 87–9.

25. The reader would do well to see some serious analysis of these passages, as they are often misread and misused. See especially C. K. Barrett, The *First Epistle to the Corinthians*, pp. 277–34 and A. Bittlinger, *Gifts and Graces: A Commentary on I Corinthians 12–14* (London, Hodder and Stoughton, 1973). The latter book is useful because it is written by a biblical specialist who is, at the same time, involved in the Charismatic renewal. More scientific, but certainly the best book currently available on the whole question of the life of the Spirit in the early Church is J. D. G. Dunn, *Jesus and the Spirit* (London, SCM Press, 1975). Again, Dunn is a fine exegete who is much involved in Charismatic renewal. On Paul, see pp. 199–342.

26. This is a warning that Charismatics are not the only 'real' Christians, while the non-Charismatic is an 'also ran'.

27. Again Paul warns us that a seeking for the external phenomena is not the *primary* function of a Charismatic community.

28. It is a great pity that some Religious find a life of prayer and a community outside their Religious families, and thus the communities (the Church) are not 'built up', but are 'torn apart'. It is not always the fault of the Religious who goes out to pray. Before being critical of such a Religious, his or her community should examine their prayer life as a community, and the quality of the love that is *supposed* to unite them.

29. In the fifth and sixth centuries the Church struggled with a heresy called Pelagianism and a similar heresy called Semi-Pelagianism. These people taught that man saved himself by his good deeds. Central to the Bible and thus to the teaching of the Church is the belief that we are saved by a 'free gift', the Grace of God. All that pertains to our salvation begins and ends in him. While this has been the *constant* teaching of the Church, a great deal of spirituality has been somewhat Pelagian. We have been led to think that it is our success or failure in prayer and good works that ultimately counts. This, to put it bluntly, is quite wrong. Let us first find

and attempt to understand a faithful, loving God, and then place our prayer and good works within the context of the gifts which he gives us. See, on this, the most helpful little book of J. Laplace, *Prayer according to the Scriptures* (Brighton, Mass., Religious of the Cenacle, no date). Only in this way will we come to have more patience with our own failures and the failures of others, as our faithful God will come to meet us where we fall short. Do we really take seriously enough the implications of Rom. 5.8: 'God shows his love for us in that while we were yet sinners, Christ died for us' (see also I John 4.10)?

30. Paul is here listing a variety of real problems that did, in fact, threaten to divide his communities from their source of unity, the love of Christ. We could add more of our own problems to the list: religious habits, structures of government, different forms of apostolate. Put within this context, the relative nature of these questions should become apparent.

CHAPTER 6: The Religious Community

1. See below, pp. 163–70.
2. See the *Code of Canon Law*, Canons 492–8, and, more recently, *Mutuae Relationes* 8.
3. Strangely enough there is only one book, to my knowledge, which systematically studies this aspect of the Gospels. See T. Matura, *Le radicalisme évangélique*. There are, of course, many studies on various aspects of this reversal of values. Matura gives a good introductory bibliography on pp. 203–4.

CHAPTER 7: Poverty

1 With the kind permission of the author, I am repeating here a great deal of what has already been written by J. Murphy-O'Connor, 'What is Religious Life? Ask the Scriptures', *Supplement to Doctrine and Life* 45 (1973). The whole number is devoted to his contribution. On poverty see pp. 40–52. Even those who disagree with Fr Murphy-O'Connor must admit to the excellence of his treatment of the vows. See, for example, J. Mannion, 'What is Religious Life?', *Supplement to Doctrine and Life* 76 (1978) 202–3. The article runs from pp. 197 to 203. The structure of the chapter which follows, the passages used and a great deal of the commentary upon those passages come from Fr Murphy-O'Connor's original study. His treatment of poverty and obedience is the best biblical reflection that I know. As such, I have no hesitation in presenting my very slightly modified use of his analysis. I would urge all readers to consider the whole of his treatment of Religious life.

2. There are far too many examples of this in the Old Testament to list here. A very clear example comes from the book of Job. At the beginning of the book, Job, a man who 'was blameless and upright, one who feared God, and turned away from evil' (Job 1.1) has the blessing of God in his great material wealth (1.3–5). At the end of the book, after his faithfulness through his terrible trials: 'The Lord restored the fortunes of Job . . . and the Lord gave Job twice as much as he had before' (42.10. See vv. 11–17).

3. In fact, it is only Matthew who makes him a 'rich young man', probably because Mark (whom Matthew was following) has him say, 'All these things I have observed from my youth' (Mark 10.20). For Mark he is simply 'a man' (10.17) and for Luke he is 'a ruler' (Luke 18.18).

4. There are, of course, many nuances of these two positions. See, on these two solutions, the excellent article of J. M. R. Tillard, 'Poverty and Prayer', *Supplement to Doctrine and Life* 73 (1978) 14–28.

5. A good Greek dictionary will indicate this. See, for example, W. Bauer, W. F. Arndt and F. W. Gingrich, *A Greek-English Lexicon of the New Testament and Other Early Christian Literature* (Chicago, University of Chicago Press, 1967) pp. 257–61. There are eight columns devoted to the word '*en*'.

6. For an excellent and up-to-date survey of these various interpretations, see C. F. D. Moule, *The Origin of Christology* (Cambridge, University Press, 1977) pp. 54–69.

7. A little reflection will show that it must be so. None of us became a Christian on our own. It was given to us by people who were prepared to share what they already enjoyed, our parents or the people who drew us, by the quality of their own Christian lives, into this shared life 'in Christ'. Once 'in', to abandon this shared life is to abandon Christianity, even if we were to make our private Mass and communion every day! For a fine analysis of the biblical material which leads to this conclusion, see J. Murphy-O'Connor, *Becoming Human Together*, pp. 187–212.

8. See above, pp. 32–45.

9. Luke, the author of both the Gospel which bears his name and the Acts of the Apostles (and *exactly* who 'Luke' was we cannot really say) makes the point about the need to share throughout both of his books. See Luke 3.11; 6.3–38; 11.41; 12.13–34; 14.13, 24, 33; 16.1–31; 19.1–10; 21.1–4. On these texts, see T. Matura, *Le radicalisme évangélique*, pp. 92–107. Matura thinks that this command to share goes back to the historical Jesus. It is also found in Paul. See *ibid.*, pp. 160–3 and especially, P. Seidensticker, 'Saint Paul et la pauvreté', in *La pauvreté évangélique*, Lire la Bible 27 (Paris, Editions du Cerf, 1971) pp. 93–133.

10. See above, pp. 86–7.

11. For a magnificent presentation of this, see John Paul II's opening discourse to the Latin American Episcopal Conference at Puebla on 28

January, 1979. For the English text, see *The Tablet* 233 (1979) 119–23. Since that memorable discourse he has published his first encyclical, which also devotes a great deal of attention to this subject. See John Paul II, *Redemptor Hominis*, given at Rome on 4 March, 1979.

12. A comparison of the two versions shows that Luke's linking of the underprivileged with the Kingdom is immediate and urgent, while Matthew tends to tone this down. Luke's hand, however, can be seen in the way he organises his material. He has a balance of three beatitudes (vv. 6.20–1) with three woes (vv. 6.24–6), and this literary scheme probably reflects the skill of the Evangelist.

13. The Greek word '*christos*' is a translation of the Hebrew/Aramaic word 'messiah', which means 'anointed one'. The Greek verb 'to anoint' (*chriō*) is used here.

14. One is reminded of Dickens' *David Copperfield*, where the overdrawn but charming Mr Micawber lives happily in the midst of his nothingness, waiting for 'something to turn up'!

15. Fundamental to a study of this passage (and indeed to much of the biblical material used in discussions of Religious life) is S. Legasse, *L'appel du riche (Mc 10, 17–31 et par). Contribution à l'étude des fondements scripturaires de l'état religieuse*, Verbum Salutis 1 (Paris, Desclée, 1966).

16. See above, pp. 9–12.

17. I have already mentioned that it is only Matthew who speaks of a rich young man, but I am referring to the story by that term because it is immediately recognised under that title.

18. There is a further understandable variation here. Mark has Jesus quoting from the Law of Moses, but out of the order given in the Old Testament. Matthew and Luke correct Mark's order (and his Greek!).

19. Held by some scholars to be an authentic piece of historical material. See, however, R. E. Brown, *The Gospel according to John xiii–xxi*, The Anchor Bible 29–29a (New York, Doubleday, 1970) pp. 1085–92. Brown gives an excellent survey of this discussion, with a good bibliography (pp. 1131–2).

20. For a fine study of this passage, see M. Hengel, *Nachfolge und Charisma. Eine exegetisch-religionsgeschichtliche Studie zu Mt. 8,21f. und Jesu Ruf in die Nachfolge*, Beihefte zur Zeitschrift für die Neutestamentliche Wissenschaft 34 (Berlin, Töpelmann, 1968). Unfortunately, in the past some Congregations did universalise this passage!

21. I would like to mention here the unity which I found in a community where one of the sisters, a top-line nurse directing the operating theatre in a large city hospital, shared her table, her prayer life and her day-to-day experiences with an older sister whose main task was to wash the dishes and set the table in the community dining-room. The nursing sister found her source of strength and joy, not primarily in her success as a nurse, but

rather in the exchange of affection which she experienced in her community, and particularly in the genuine sharing of life that she had with the older sister. This is the sort of thing which makes people (in this case the rest of the medical staff in the hospital) ask: 'Why?'

22. I have used the word 'poverty' throughout this chapter, out of respect for tradition and in order not to create confusion. However, given the political, social and even emotional implications of the word 'poverty' in contemporary Western society, it strikes me that it is not really the correct term to describe the radical sharing of life just outlined as the biblical model for the vow taken by a Religious. See, on this, the observations of D. Rees and Others, *Consider your Call*, p. 205. The author(s) of the pages devoted to poverty in this excellent book have sought to avoid the difficulty by entitling the chapter 'Poverty and the Sharing of the Goods' (pp. 205–20).

CHAPTER 8: Chastity

1. The linking of chastity with angelic imagery was very popular in the late Middle Ages. See T. Matura, *Célibat et communauté*, p. 14. For the modern objections to a life of celibacy, see J. Wilcken, *Religious Life Today: A Theological and Scriptural Approach* (Melbourne, Polding Press, 1974), pp. 33–5. For Ignatius, see Ignatius of Loyola, *Constitutions of the Society of Jesus*. Translated with an Introduction and Commentary by George E. Ganff, S. J. (St Louis, The Institute of Jesuit Sources, 1970). On this single passage on the vow of chastity, see pp. 245–6, note 6.

2. It is important to notice that the tradition has always spoken of a vow of chastity – not a vow of celibacy. Again the universal call to sanctity enters. We are all called to chastity but some of us publicly profess this vow and commit ourselves to a Religious community, where we live it as celibates. Others publicly profess it in the marriage ceremony and commit themselves to a husband or wife with whom they strive to live chastely. Nevertheless, out of respect for traditional language, and again to avoid confusion, I will refer to the chastity of a Religious, rather than his or her celibacy, even though the latter is intended.

3. Behind this stands the work of such theologians as H. de Lubac who, since the 40s had been showing that the traditional distinction between the natural and the supernatural was false. The more poetic, but tremendously influential, work of Teilhard de Chardin also played a major role in the development of these ideas.

4. The problem always remains, of course, the 'authentic' love of so many married people. Where this is absent, then the parallel no longer holds.

5. 'Propter hanc concupiscentiam fit, ut etiam de iustis et legitimis nuptiis

filiorum Dei, non filii Dei, sed filii saeculi generentur' (*De nuptiis et concupiscentia* I,18,20: PL 44:424). On the whole question, see M. Flick and Z. Alszeghy, *Il peccato originale*, Biblioteca di Teologia Contemporanea 12 (Brescia, Queriniana, 1972) pp. 97–110, especially pp. 106–9. See also P. Brown, *Augustine of Hippo, a Biography* (London, Faber and Faber, 1967) pp. 388–94. For the most important texts from Augustine, see further *De nuptiis et concupiscentia* I, 24: PL 44:429; *Operis Imperfecti contra Julianum* I, 48: PL 45:1017 and III, 209: PL 45:1335. As *De nuptiis* was written in 419 and *Operis Imperfecti* in 429, both reflect the mature Augustine. He died in 430.

6. One thinks of Tertullian whose hard line on these matters eventually led him to become a Montanist (in 211–12), a heretical sect which had very negative views on marriage and sexual activity. See especially his *De Pudicitia* (PL 2:979–1030). For a general presentation of the thought of the third century on this question, see A. Fliche and V. Martin, *Storia della Chiesa dalle origini ai nostri giorni II: Dalla fine del II secolo alla pace constantiniana* (313), Terza edizione italiana a cura di Raffaelo Farina (Torino, S. A. I. E., 1972) pp. 429–31; 444–6.

7. For an excellent survey of this problem, and a balanced solution, see A. Sicari, *La gelosia di Dio*, pp. 23–65.

8. The teaching of the Council of Trent, that virginity was a superior state (see *Denziger* 1810) still reflects the earlier attitude, but must be understood as a direct answer to the criticism of celibacy by the Reformers. Once again, we must not take it out of this context to make it a universal message. On the principles to be used for the exegesis of the Tridentine texts, see A. Amato, *I pronunciamenti tridentini sulla necessità della confessione sacramentale*, Biblioteca Teologica Salesiana. Series I: Fontes (Rome, LAS, 1975) and the example of a critical use of Trent by P. Schoonenberg, *Man and Sin. A Theological View* (London, Sheed and Ward, 1965) pp. 168–77.

9. Here we have an example of a point made in the Preface (see above, p. 171, note 2). This document reflects the lack of a well-developed pre-conciliar theology of Religious life. It is not that what it says is wrong, but it is clearly a document which is strongly legal, and thus the profound theological message of *Lumen Gentium* and *Gaudium et Spes*, the products of years of pre-conciliar reflection, is not to be found here.

10. For a full-scale discussion of this passage, with more complete bibiliographical references, see F. J. Moloney, 'Matthew 19.3–12 and Celibacy. A Redactional and Form Critical Study', *Journal for the Study of the New Testament* 2 (1979) 42–60. The basic study of this passage is J. Dupont, *Mariage et divorce dans l'évangile: Matthieu 19, 3–12 et parallèles* (Bruges, Desclée de Brouwer, 1959). I have been greatly helped by this important book, even though my conclusions differ somewhat from those of Dupont.

11. We have already seen (see above, p. 11) that this practice of going

beyond the Law with the authority of his own word and person is typical of Jesus in Matthew's Gospel. What is announced is the 'higher righteousness' of the Christian vocation.

12. See any good introduction to the books of the New Testament. The best in English is W. G. Kümmel, *Introduction to the New Testament* (London, SCM Press, 1975). On Matthew, see pp. 105–19. See also R. A. Spivey and D. M. Smith, *Anatomy of the New Testament*, pp. 115–49.

13. This is one interpretation among many. It all depends upon how one translates the Greek word *porneia*, which the Revised Standard Version gives as 'unchastity'. I would be more specific in describing just what form of unchastity Matthew has in mind when he introduces his exception to the rule. Again, for a full discussion of this problem, see F. J. Moloney, 'Matthew 19.3–12 and Celibacy' mentioned in note 10. See especially pp. 43–9.

14. One should again use a good commentary. See, for example, C. K. Barrett, *The First Epistle to the Corinthians*, pp. 172–87.

15. We have already seen (see above, pp. 174, note 15) that Ephesians is most probably post-Pauline, but most scholars would see it as a direct and logical development of the later Paul.

16. This question is again dealt with in detail in my article 'Matthew 19.3–12 and Celibacy', mentioned in note 10. See especially pp. 49–53.

17. This spiralling structure is called a *mâshâl*.

18. There is plenty of contemporary evidence which presents the eunuch as syncophantic, fat, beardless, feminine but despotically cruel. According to Deut. 23.1 a eunuch could not belong to the people of God. For a good survey of this material see J. Schneider, Art. *'eunouchos'*, *Theological Dictionary of the New Testament* 2 (1964) 765–8.

19. This suggestion was first made by J. Blinzler, *'Eisin eunouchoi*, Zur Auslegung von Mt. 19,12', *Zeitschrift für die Neutestamentliche Wissenschaft* 48 (1957) 254–70.

20. In fact, this way of understanding Matt. 19.12 is the only explicit piece of historical evidence that we have in the whole of the New Testament on the celibacy of Jesus. It is enough, as it gives backbone to a number of more implicit indications.

21. This practice has not died out over the centuries. Most cultures and languages have terms of abuse which refer to a man's sexual capacity. My own Australian 'popular culture' is extremely rich in such expressions!

22. A 'religious experience' is a technical term. It does not refer to what happens to religious people in church. The term refers to those experiences, which all men and women have, which are somehow greater than them. The most common of these experiences is, of course, falling in love.

23. On this, see the very fine article of R. Balducelli, 'The Decision for

Celibacy', *Theological Studies* 36 (1975) 219–42.

24. Further reflections on this element would lead us into the eschatological significance of the vow of chastity. This is well spelt out already in *Perfectae Caritatis* 12.

25. J. Murphy-O'Connor, *What is Religious Life?*, p. 59. See also T. Matura, *Célibat et communauté*, pp. 62–7; 117–21.

26. Here the question of close friendships among celibates arises. This question needs a detailed treatment which cannot be offered here. I would merely like to lay down three principles which I have found to be basic to such relationships.

(i) They must not be condemned out of hand. The fear of 'particular friendships' should be a thing of the past, although difficulties and mistakes will be found here, as in all aspects of our lives.

(ii) These friendships must never be sought out. They must arise and happen in a context of mutually shared prayer, work and ideals.

(iii) They should be directed by people *outside* the relationship because self-direction always leads to self-deception.

For an excellent contribution on this issue, see Y. Raguin, 'Chastity and Friendship', *Supplement to the Way* 19 (1973) 105–17. This article is, to my mind, still the best treatment available. See also the useful book of C. Kiesling, *Celibacy, Prayer and Friendship. A making-sense-out-of-life Approach* (New York, Alba House, 1978). Unfortunately, Kiesling still tends to present celibacy as primarily 'freeing for service'.

CHAPTER 9: Obedience

1. Again I am depending heavily upon the treatment of J. Murphy-O'Connor, *What is Religious Life?*, pp. 23–30.

2. As I pointed out above, p. 174, note 15, Ephesians may have been written by a follower after Paul was dead. However, there is a continuity of Pauline thought, and the personality of Paul is not lost. Thus, I will continue to speak of 'Paul', even though this critical problem exists.

3. This is not a new concept in the history of Religious life. It stands at the heart of St Benedict's treatment of 'What kind of man the Abbot ought to be' in chapter 2 of his rule. See, for example: 'He is believed to hold the place of Christ in the Monastery.' 'He should show forth all goodness and holiness by his deeds rather than his words.'

See O. Hunter Blair, *The Rule of St Benedict* (Fort Augustus, Abbey Press, 1948⁵) pp. 15–23. The quotations are from pp. 15–17. See, on this, D. Rees and Others, *Consider your Call*, pp. 86–9. This tradition came to Benedict from the very earliest moments of monastic life. See *ibid.*, pp. 77–9. In an interesting recent article, R. F. O'Toole has attempted to show from Acts

25–6 that this theme was not only Pauline, but also Lucan. See R. F. O'Toole, 'Luke's Notion of "Be Imitators of Me as I am of Christ" in Acts 25–6', *Biblical Theology Bulletin* 8 (1978) 155–61.

4. '*Gloria enim Dei vivens homo*'. The passage then goes on to argue that man is fully alive, however, only when he lives in the presence of God: '*Vita autem hominis visio Dei*' (PG 7:1057).

5. This means, in practice, that many of the criteria which are commonly used for the appointment of superiors should be revised. Often a superior is chosen because he has a strong personality, because he knows about building construction, because he is able to handle the lay staff with skill etc. As is quite obvious, these criteria are used because Religious life is seen as primarily concerned with 'getting a job done', and the people best equipped to do that are given authority to make sure that it does 'get done'. The upward call to life in Christ is rarely used as the major criterion for the choice of a superior. Surely, the 'tasks' could be shared throughout the community, to our mutual enrichment and growth in the sense of a shared responsibility. The personal one-to-one encounter with the upward call into Christ cannot, however, be reduced to a shared ideal. It must be historical, i.e. made flesh and blood in a concrete, historical personality.

6. See also J. Murphy-O'Connor, 'The Contemporary Value of Pauline Moral Imperatives', *Doctrine and Life* 21 (1971) 59–71, and his further development of this in *Becoming Human Together*, pp. 217–37.

7. J. Murphy-O'Connor, *Becoming Human Together*, p. 54. See his whole chapter: 'Christ the Criterion' (pp. 33–55).

8. Again, this practice is found in the earliest forms of organised Religious life. See the Rule of St Benedict, chapter 3: 'Of calling the Brethren to council'. See O. Hunter Blair, *op. cit.*, pp. 25–7. See, for example: 'We have said that all should be called to council, because it is often to the younger, that the Lord reveals what is best' (Hunter Blair, p. 25).
See on this, D. Rees and Others, *Consider your Call*, pp. 69–75.

CHAPTER 10: Disciples of Jesus

1. This problem stood at the centre of the discussion which arose around Fr Murphy-O'Connor book. He argues that community living was the *raison d'être* of Religious life. See, *What is Religious Life?*, pp. 3–15. However, the discussion has not been limited to English-speaking Religious. It has been widely felt. As the Salesian Society attempted to rewrite their rule in their special General Chapter of 1971, they found that they could not move until they resolved the dilemma of what they called consecration or mission. It boils down to the same thing as community and apostolate.

2. It should be pointed out that Fr Murphy-O'Connor's position has been

somewhat caricatured by those who argue with him. As he himself insists: 'It goes without saying that members of religious communities will continue to render service. I am not advocating that they should sit and simply *be*' (*What is Religious Life?*. p. 14).

3. I argued this somewhat sketchily in Francis J. Moloney, 'Asking the Scriptures about Religious Life', *Supplement to Doctrine and Life* 58 (1975) 3–12. The reply of Fr Murphy-O'Connor to my article, on pp. 13–24 of the same number, is a fine reflection on the relationship between community and apostolate. The very title of the article answers the problem raised: 'Community: the possibility of discipleship'.

4. The problem of the disciples in Mark's Gospel has been the subject of a great deal of study. A very good recent article on the subject is C. Focant, 'L'incompréhension des disciples dans le deuxième évangile', *Revue Biblique* 82 (1975) 161–85. This excellent article has been translated, unfortunately in a much abridged form, as 'The disciples' blindness in Mark's Gospel', *Theology Digest* 24 (1976) 260–4. Another excellent scholarly work is E. Best, 'The Role of the Disciples in Mark', *New Testament Studies* 23 (1976–7) 377–401. A most useful popular book on the subject is R. C. Tannehill, *A Mirror for Disciples: A Study of the Gospel of Mark* (Nashville, Discipleship Resources, 1977). A very recent popular presentation of discipleship can be found in R. Schnackenburg, *Nachfolge Christi – heute: Antworten und Weisungen aus dem Neuen Testament*, Herderbücherei 595 (Freiburg, Herder, 1978²). There is also a book of meditations on the theme which some readers may find helpful: G. Appleton, *The Way of a Disciple* (London, Collins, 1979). See also the beautiful, and biblically sound, reflections of M. T. Winstanley, 'Discipleship and Loneliness: A Marcan Meditation', *Review for Religious* 38 (1979) 13–20.

5. The story of the rich man (Mark 10.17–22 parrs.) is a further example. We have already considered this story (see above, pp. 193–5) and the reader will remember that the rich man takes the initiative: 'What must *I* do?' (Mark 10.17). When Jesus attempts to take the initiative by asking the man to bind himself radically to him, the man refuses – and thus refuses discipleship, which can only be based on Jesus' terms.

6. See J. Donaldson, ' "Called to Follow". A Twofold Experience of Discipleship in Mark', *Biblical Theology Bulletin* 5 (1975) 67–77.

7. H. Anderson, *The Gospel of Mark*, New Century Bible (London, Oliphants, 1976) p. 86.

8. Although the stories are quite different, one can already see the close verbal links between Mark 1.16–20 and Luke 5.1–11.

9. This may, of course, explain the hostility!

10. Again the contacts with the Marcan stories are clear.

11. There is a never-ending debate about the historicity of the original

group of 'the twelve'. Some say that such a group never existed, but was invented by the early Church, the new Israel, in the light of the twelve tribes of the Old Testament people of God. There is not sufficient reason to doubt the historicity of the group. See the excellent discussion in V. Taylor, *The Gospel according to Saint Mark: A Commentary on the Greek Text* (London, Macmillan, 1959) pp. 619–27.

12. Again we have a critical problem, as the order of the names, and the names themselves, vary in the parallels from Matthew and Luke (Matt. 10.1–4; Luke 6.12–16). This need not detain us here. An interested reader will find it discussed in any good commentary. See, for example, H. Anderson, *Mark*, pp. 117–19.

13. Particularly important in this school of thought are N. Perrin, 'Towards an Interpretation of the Gospel of Mark', in H. D. Betz (ed.), *Christology and a Modern Pilgrimage: A Discussion with Norman Perrin* (Missoula, Scholars' Press, 1974) pp. 1–52, and Perrin's students. See especially T. J. Weeden, *Mark – Traditions in Conflict* (Philadelphia, Fortress Press, 1971) and W. Kelber (ed.), *The Passion in Mark: Studies on Mark 14–16* (Philadelphia, Fortress Press, 1976).

14. There is a serious difficulty with the text here, and it may well read 'seventy-two others'. An interested reader should see the commentaries, especially I. H. Marshall, *The Gospel of Luke. A Commentary on the Greek Text*, New International Commentary (Exeter, Paternoster Press, 1978) pp. 414–16. Here I am following the Revised Standard Version. See the Jerusalem Bible for the other reading.

15. I am continuing with the Revised Standard Version, but the term 'apostles' is misleading here. It is the only place in the whole Gospel of Mark where the term *apostolos* appears (here in the plural), and it simply means 'the ones sent out'. As yet it does not have the technical sense which it received at the hands of Paul and Luke.

16. See above, pp. 64–5.

17. I use the term 'blindness' deliberately, as the miracle story of the blind man in Bethsaida in 8.22–6, which immediately precedes our passage, is clearly used by Mark as a sort of example of what is to happen in vv. 27–33 (see also v. 18). At first the blind man has to be 'brought to him' (v. 22). He is completely blind. This is the situation of those who say that Jesus is a precursor.

18. Returning to our model in 8.22–6, this is paralleled by the blind man's arriving at a partial but distorted vision: ' "I see men; but they look like trees walking" '(v. 24).

19. Again returning to our model of a gradual progression to sight from blindness, this intervention from Jesus himself is paralleled by his intervention in v. 22, where he lays his hands upon the man and 'he saw

everything clearly'.

20. One should not make too much of the term 'satan'. Peter is not identified with the devil. The Greek word transcribes the Hebrew, which means 'stumbling-block, obstruction'. Peter, an obstruction to Jesus as he goes along his God-given 'way', must 'get behind' Jesus. This is the correct place for any disciple.

21. This is also the point of the negative statement in 8.38. The Son of Man will be ashamed of those who are ashamed of the way of the Son of Man 'when he comes in the glory of his Father with the holy angels'. This means, implicitly, that the opposite will be the case for those who are prepared to take the risk of discipleship. The idea of a way of suffering humbly accepted as God's way, in the faith and hope that it will lead to vindication and ultimate glory is, in my opinion, central to Jesus' identification of himself as 'the Son of Man', a term which he took from Dan. 7.13. See, for a fuller explanation of this, F. J. Moloney, *The Johannine Son of Man*, pp. 216–17; 221–47, and also M. D. Hooker, 'Is the Son of Man problem really insoluble?', in E. Best and R. McL. Wilson (eds), *Text and Interpretation: Studies in the New Testament Presented to Matthew Black* (Cambridge, University Press, 1979) pp. 155–68. Prof. Hooker's essay offers an excellent critical survey of current discussion of this very important christological title.

22. This aspect of Mark's treatment of the disciples of Jesus is entirely overlooked in the work of Weeden (see above, note 13). Perrin sees it (and indeed I am indebted to Perrin for much of this section) but he does not evaluate it as in any way positive.

23. See above, pp. 56–60.

24. Although I have limited myself to the actual passion predictions and their immediate contexts where it is particularly clear, the teaching about discipleship is found in three blocks of material which run from 8.22–9.1 (the Cross), 9.2–50 (servanthood) and 10.1–52 (the Cross and servanthood). This has been well presented by N. Perrin, 'Towards an Interpretation of the Gospel of Mark', pp. 6–21. I interpret the material somewhat differently, however. Perrin, who sadly died of cancer in November 1976, was a most perceptive scholar. He was working on a full-scale commentary on the Gospel of Mark for the Hermeneia series, published by Fortress Press, Philadelphia. It is hoped that the volume, which is certain to be of great value, will still be published.

25. This prediction, so full of details taken from the Marcan passion story, has clearly been formulated in the Marcan tradition *after* it all happened. As I mentioned above, pp. 184, note 10, Jesus would have spoken of his coming death in terms of Mark 9.31: 'The Son of Man will be delivered into the hands of men, and they will kill him' (see also Luke 9.44). The

early Church filled out these predictions in the light of what had in fact happened.

26. It appears that Jesus addressed his prayer to God by speaking to him as 'abba'. This is an Aramaic term of endearment which would have been used only in the context of a loving Son-Father relationship. Modern Hebrew still uses the same term when a son addresses his father. See especially J. Jeremias, *The Prayers of Jesus*, Studies in Biblical Theology, Second Series 6 (London, SCM Press, 1967) pp. 11–65.

27. It is universally admitted that Mark 16.9–20 is a later addition to Mark's Gospel. See, for example, the note in the Jerusalem Bible, chapter 16, note c. Did the Gospel end at 16.8, or have we lost an original ending which contained resurrection appearances? For many reasons, based on textual criticism and Marcan theology, I believe that Mark concluded his Gospel at 16.8. For a brief but telling presentation of this case, see N. Perrin, *The Resurrection Narratives: A New Approach* (London, SCM Press, 1977) pp. 20–2. There is now a valuable comprehensive study of the whole question. See J. Hug, *La finale de l'Evangile de Marc (Mc. 16.9–20)* Études Bibliques (Paris, Gabalda, 1978).

28. The words translated in the Revised Standard Version as 'quite openly and freely' (Greek: *meta pasēs parrēsias*) also carry with them the idea of courage and fearlessness.

29. For the universal significance of the Gospels' discipleship material, see T. Matura, *Le radicalisme évangélique*, pp. 199–202.

30. For a presentation of the Pauline concept of life leading to resurrection, see J. Murphy-O'Connor, *Becoming Human Together*, pp. 70–8. See also John Paul II, *Redemptor Hominis*, 20. For a fine treatment of the central role of the Eucharist in the Benedictine tradition, most of which should be applied to any form of Christian community living, see D. Rees and Others, *Consider your Call*, pp. 228–37.

31. See John Paul II, *Redemptor Hominis*, 21. See also *Mutuae Relationes* 15–23;

CHAPTER 11: Prophets of the Lord

1. There is a growing recognition of the centrality of this function of Religious life within the universal call to sanctity. See, for what follows, S. C. Doyle, 'Religious Life: Prophetic Charism', *Review for Religious* 36 (1977) 49–56 and J. Murphy-O'Connor, *What is Religious Life?*, pp. 3–15. See also F. Smith, 'Selon le plan de Dieu', *Donum Dei* 4 (1962) 51–62; J. M. R. Tillard, 'Dans le sillage de la vie sacramentaire', *Donum Dei* 4 (1962) 63–83, especially pp. 77–80. See, most recently, Canadian Religious Conference, 'The Prophetic Role of Religious', *Donum Dei* 23 (1977). The whole issue

is devoted to the question, but see especially, the first two papers by F. Larivière. Very recently there has been a collection of essays published on the theme of the vocation to prophecy in the New Testament and its relevance today. Although somewhat technical, the papers in the collection are valuable. See J. Panagopolous (ed.), *Prophetic Vocation in the New Testament and Today*, Supplements to Novum Testamentum 45 (Leiden, E. J. Brill, 1977).

2. Even in this solution we find another 'loose end'. At the conclusion of the meeting a letter is sent to all the Christians with instructions about what should be retained from Judaism in the admission of non-Jews to their ranks (see Acts 15.23–39). These recommendations are never heard of again. There is a specific recommendation about abstaining from food sacrificed to idols (v. 29), but Paul seems to know nothing of this in I Cor. 8, where he has recourse to the concept of conscience and the example offered to others.

3. See above, pp. 13–15.

4. To what extent it is found in the New Testament, and what is meant by 'the Church' there, is a much discussed question. For a sure guide through these questions, see R. Schnackenburg, *The Church in the New Testament* (London, Burns and Oates, 1965).

5. For an excellent and well-documented historical presentation of the development of Religious life, see A. Veilleux, 'Evoluzione della vita religiosa nel suo contesto storico-spirituale', in A. Favale (ed), *Per una presenza viva dei religiosi nella Chiesa e nel mondo* (Torino, LDC, 1970) pp. 13–56.

6. Albright pointed this out, passingly, in his little book, *The Biblical Period from Abraham to Ezra*, Harper Torchbooks (New York, Harper and Row, 1963) p. 44. In many ways, Albright was well qualified to make such a comparison. Although a devout Protestant throughout his distinguished life, he has a son who became a Catholic and worked for many years as a missionary Religious Brother in South America.

7. It is interesting to notice that behind the story of Israel's request for a king, there are clearly two different traditions. Some of the story reflects a pro-monarchy stance (see, for example, I Sam. 9.1–10.8), while other parts of it are anti-monarchy (see, for example, I Sam. 8; 10.9–27). The final redaction of these two opposing lines of thought, however, is deeply concerned with the threat to Israel's unique covenant with God.

8. Robert North, a specialist in Old Testament history and archeology, suggests that the revolt of Jeroboam in 921, which led to the division of the land into Northern and Southern Kingdoms, was the result of enforced slave labour and the generally bad social situation of the people from the North. Particularly important in this was the enslavement of Hebrews for the building of Solomon's Temple. See R. North, *Reges* (Rome, Biblical

Institute: Class notes, 1971) pp. 87–93.

9. Elijah and Elisha 'cycles', as they are called, have been inserted into this series of disastrous kings by the deuteronomic author, but this in no way invalidates the point I am making. It is exactly the same point which the authors of I–II Kings were making. See B. W. Anderson, *The Living World of the Old Testament*, pp. 249–58.

10. On prophets and prophecy see, above all, G. von Rad, *The Message of the Prophets* (London, SCM Press, 1968). See also E. Heaton, *The Old Testament Prophets* (London, Darton, Longman and Todd, 1977) and B. Vawter, *The Conscience of Israel: Pre-Exilic Prophets and Prophecy* (London, Sheed and Ward, 1961). There is also an excellent introductory synthesis in B. Vawter, 'Introduction to Prophetic Literature', *Jerome Biblical Commentary*, pp. 223–37.

11. As this is the case, it can be seen that Deuteronomy is also a prophetic work. See above, pp. 50–1.

12. For the full text, which is most interesting, see PL 49:1094–1100. The citation comes from column 1096. See also his *Institutiones coenobiorum* II, 5 (PL 49:84–88).

13. See, on this, J. Murphy-O'Connor, *What is Religious Life?*, pp. 13–14; J. M. R. Tillard, 'Le fondement évangélique de la vie religieuse', pp. 940–55; H. Schürmann, 'Le groupe des disciples de Jésus', *Christus* 50 (1966) 184–209. For an excellent and well-documented analysis of these earliest years of organised Religious life in the Church, leading to the point just made, see R. McCulloch, 'Monks, Bishops, Society in 4th and 5th Century Empire', *Tjurunga* 17 (1979) 57–76. Concluding his analysis, McCulloch writes: 'In the fourth and fifth century when the episcopacy was having to come to grips with a world-maintaining role, monasticism presented a balancing corrective by upholding a world view which was otherworldly in inspiration and goal. In their world view they retained an insight vital to Christianity as a check upon the principles and effects of accommodation. Monasticism acted as a bridle upon the structured church which had emerged with Constantine' (p. 72).

14. By the time of Jesus, it appears that Deut. 18.18 was understood in Judaism as the promise of a new and perfect Moses who would usher in the messianic era. This belief stands behind the many confessions of faith in Jesus as 'a prophet'. See, for example, Mk. 8.28 and John 4.19; 9.17.

15. S. C. Doyle, 'Religious Life: Prophetic Charism', p. 53. I am following his treatment closely here.

16. See John Paul II, *Redemptor Hominis*, 8 for an analysis of this phenomenon in our era. See further, J. Murphy-O'Connor, *Becoming Human Together*, pp. 81–143 for the Pauline criticism of such a situation. See also *ibid.*, pp. 9–14 for Murphy-O'Connor's severe criticism of some contem-

porary Christian attempts to side-step this problem.

17. See, on this, J. Murphy-O'Connor, *What is Religious Life?*, pp. 9–10. I am following his treatment closely here.

18. This task has been well described by *Lumen Gentium* 46: 'Religious should be careful to consider that through them, to believers and non-believers alike, the Church truly wishes to give an increasingly clearer revelation of Christ.' See also *Mutuae Relationes* 10: 'The consecration of those professing religious vows is especially ordained to this purpose, namely the offering to the world visible proof the unfathomable mystery of Christ.'

19. This 'thorn in the side' role of the Religious, which is one of its outstandingly prophetic functions, has been well developed by J. B. Metz, *Followers of Christ: The Religious Life and the Church* (London, Burns and Oates, 1978). Once again, this has been clearly taught by *Lumen Gentium* 44: 'The profession of the evangelical counsels, then, appears as a sign which can and ought to attract all the members of the Church to an effective and prompt fulfilment of the duties of their Christian vocation . . . The religious state reveals in a unique way that the kingdom of God and its overmastering necessities are superior to all earthly considerations. Finally, to all men it shows wonderfully at work within the Church the surpassing greatness of the force of Christ the King and the boundless power of the Holy Spirit.'

20. Although I have stated these situations baldly, I am well aware that all the non-Christian attitudes do not belong to one side only in these terrible divisions. An analysis of those questions is both outside my scope and ability. See John Paul II's criticism of this 'accepted' situation in *Redemptor Hominis* 16.

21. One must not be too pessimistic. There have been some wonderful initiatives in this area. My own Salesian family has set up a system whereby *any* confrère, no matter how important to the local apostolate, *must* be freed if he wishes to work among the poorer Churches. This is only one prophetic example among many.

22. See John Paul II's plea for a reasonable self-criticism within the Church in *Redemptor Hominis* 4; 15–17. Given the Pope's Polish background, it must be seen as significant that he should mention this need, even though in more attenuated terms than *Lumen Gentium* 8.

23. The most useful book of T. Matura, *Célibat et communauté* argues that celibacy is the identifying characteristic of Religious life. It seems to me that both the tradition and the biblical evidence give a different answer. See the reflections of H. A. Williams, *Poverty, Chastity and Obedience: The True Virtues* (London, Mitchell Beazley, 1975) which are somewhat parallel to my own. I am well aware that a certain monastic tradition does not formally

take public vows of poverty and chastity. This was largely caused by historical reasons. See D. Rees and Others, *Consider your Call*, p. 128. This same tradition, which does take the vow of obedience, sees chastity and poverty as involved in the public commitment to '*conversio morum*'. See *ibid.*, pp. 154; 205. The treatment of the vows in this book (especially chastity) is particularly well done. See pp. 154–220.

Bibliography

The bibliography which follows merely gives the full details, in alphabetical order, of the publications used in this book. It is in no way a complete list of contemporary reflections on Religious life. Given the never-ending volume of publications in this area, I doubt if such a survey exists. For an excellent bibliography up to 1970, see A. Favale, 'Orientamento biblio-grafico post-conciliare sulla vita religiosa', in A. Favale (ed.), *Per una presenza viva dei religiosi nella Chiesa e nel mondo* (Torino, LDC, 1970) pp. 887–930. For more recent indications, one should consult the review *Claretianum*, and the annual bibliographies published by the Carmelites at the Theresianum, Rome.

AA. VV., *The God of Israel, The God of the Christians* (New York, Desclée, 1961).

Abbott, W., *The Documents of Vatican II* (London, Geoffrey Chapman, 1965).

Albright, W. F., *The Biblical Period from Abraham to Ezra*. Harper Torchbooks (New York, Harper and Row, 1963).

Amato, A., *I pronunciamenti tridentini sulla necessità della confessione sacramentale*. Biblioteca Teologica Salesiana. Series I: Fontes (Roma, LAS, 1975).

Anderson, B. W. , *The Living World of the Old Testament* (London, Longmans, 1978³).

Anderson, H., *The Gospel of Mark*. New Century Bible (London, Oliphants, 1976).

Appleton, G., *The Way of a Disciple* (London, Collins, 1979).

Aubry, J., *Teologia della vita religiosa alla luce del Vaticano II* (Torino, LDC, 1969).

Auge, M., 'L'abito religioso', *Claretianum* 16 (1976) 33–95, 17 (1977) 5–106.

Balducelli, R., 'The Decision for Celibacy', *Theological Studies* 36 (1975) 219–42.

Barrett, C. K., *The Epistle to the Romans*. Black's New Testament Commentaries (London, A. and C. Black, 1957).

Barrett, C. K., *The First Epistle to the Corinthians*. Black's New Testament Commentaries (London, A. and C. Black, 1971).

—*The Second Epistle to the Corinthians*. Black's New Testament Commentaries (London, A. and C. Black, 1973).

Bauer, W., Arndt, W. F. and Gingrich, F. W., *A Greek-English Lexicon of the New Testament and Other Early Christian Literature* (Chicago, University of Chicago Press, 1967).

Best, E., 'The Role of the Disciples in Mark', *New Testament Studies* 23 (1976–7) 377–401.

Bittlinger, A., *Gifts and Graces. A Commentary on I Corinthians 12–14* (London, Hodder and Stoughton, 1973).

Blenkinsopp, J., 'Deuteronomy', in *The Jerome Biblical Commentary* (London, Geoffrey Chapman, 1969).

Blinzler, J., '*Eisin eunouchoi.* Zur Auslegung von Mt. 19.12', *Zeitschrift für die Neutestamentliche Wissenschaft* 48 (Berlin, Töpelmann, 1957) 254–70.

Bornkamm, G., *Jesus of Nazareth* (London, Hodder and Stoughton, 1960).

—*Paul* (London, Hodder and Stoughton, 1971).

Bright, J., *Jeremiah.* The Anchor Bible 21 (New York, Doubleday, 1965).

Brown, P., *Augustine of Hippo: a Biography* (London, Faber and Faber, 1967).

Brown, R. E., *The Birth of the Messiah. A Commentary on the Infancy Narratives in Matthew and Luke* (London, Geoffrey Chapman, 1977).

—*The Community of the Beloved Disciple* (London, Geoffrey Chapman, 1979).

—*The Gospel According to John.* The Anchor Bible 29–29a (New York, Doubleday, 1966–70).

Bruce, F. F., *Paul: Apostle of the Free Spirit* (Exeter, Paternoster Press, 1977).

Bultmann, R., *Jesus and the Word.* Fontana (London, Collins, 1958).

—*Jesus Christ and Mythology* (London, SCM Press, 1960).

Burchill, J. P., 'Biblical Basis of Religious Life', *Review for Religious* 36 (1977) 900–17.

Cambier, J., 'Realtà carismatica ed ecclesiale della vita religiosa', in A. Favale (ed.), *Per una presenza viva dei religiosi nella Chiesa e nel mondo* (Torino, LDC, 1970).

Canadian Religious Conference, 'The Prophetic Role of Religious', *Donum Dei* 23 (1977). The whole number.

Cassem, N. H., 'A Grammatical and Contextual Inventory of the Use of *kosmos* in the Johannine Corpus with Some Implications for a Johannine Cosmic Theology'. *New Testament Studies* 19 (1972–3) 81–90.

Dalman, G., *The Words of Jesus* (Edinburgh, T. and T. Clark, 1902).

Davies, W. D., *The Sermon on the Mount* (Cambridge, University Press, 1966).

—*The Setting of the Sermon on the Mount* (Cambridge, University Press, 1963).

Dodd, C. H., *The Founder of Christianity* (London, Collins, 1971).

Donaldson, J., 'Called to Follow. A Twofold Experience of Discipleship in Mark', *Biblical Theology Bulletin* 5. (1975) 67–77.

Doyle, S. C., 'Religious Life: Prophetic Charism', *Review for Religious* 36 (1977) 49–56.

Dunn, J. D. G., *Jesus and the Spirit: A Study of the Religious and Charismatic*

Experience of Jesus and the First Christians as Reflected in the New Testament (London, SCM Press, 1975).

—*Unity and Diversity in the New Testament. An Enquiry into the Character of Earliest Christianity* (London, SCM Press, 1977).

Dupont, J., *Mariage et divorce dans l'évangile: Matthieu 19, 3–12 et parallèles* (Bruges, Desclée de Brouwer, 1959).

Eichrodt, W., *Theology of the Old Testament* (London, SCM Press, 1961).

Eissfeldt, O., 'Jahwe, der Gott der Väter', *Theologische Literaturzeitung* 88 (1963) 481–90.

Fliche, A. and Martin V., *Storia della Chiesa dalle origini ai nostri giorni II: Dalla fine del II secolo alla pace constantiniana (313)*. Terza edizione italiana a cura di Raffaelo Farina (Torino, S. A. I. E., 1972).

Flick, M and Alszeghy, Z., *Il peccato originale*. Biblioteca di Teologia Contemporanea 12 (Brescia, Queriniana, 1972).

Focant, C., 'The disciples' blindness in Mark's Gospel', *Theology Digest* 24 (1976) 260–4.

—'L'incompréhension des disciples dans le deuxième évangile', *Revue Biblique* 82 (1975) 161–85.

Furnish, V. P., *The Love Command in the New Testament* (London, SCM Press, 1973).

Galot, J., 'Le fondement évangélique du voeu religieux de pauvreté', *Gregorianum* 56 (1975) 441–67.

Genovesi, V. J., 'The Faith of Christ: Source of the Virtue of the Vows', *Review for Religious* 38 (1979).

Heaton, E., *The Old Testament Prophets* (London, Darton, Longman and Todd, 1977).

Hengel, M., Nachfolge und Charisma: Eine exegetisch-religionsgeschichtliche Studie zu Mt 8,21f. und Jesu Ruf in die Nachfolge. *Beihefte zur Zeitschrift für die Neutestamentliche Wissenschaft* 34 (Berlin, Töpelmann, 1968).

Hooker, M. D., 'Is the Son of Man problem really insoluble?', in E. Best and R. McL. Wilson (eds), *Text and Interpretation: Studies in the New Testament Presented to Matthew Black* (Cambridge, University Press, 1979) pp. 155–68.

Houlden, J. L., *A Commentary on the Johannine Epistles*. Black's New Testament Commentaries (London, A. and C. Black, 1975).

Hug, J., *La finale de L'Evangile de Marc (Mc. 16.9–20)*. Etudes Bibliques (Paris, Gabalda, 1978).

Hunter Blair, O., *The Rule of St. Benedict* (Fort Augustus, Abbey Press, 1948[5]).

Ignatius of Loyola, *Constitutions of the Society of Jesus*. Translated with an Introduction and Commentary by George E. Ganff, S. J. (St Louis, The

Institute of Jesuit Sources, 1970).

Jacob, E., *Theology of the Old Testament* (London, Hodder and Stoughton, 1958).

Jeremias, J., *The Prayers of Jesus*. Studies in Biblical Theology, Second Series 6 (London, SCM Press, 1967).

Jukes, J., 'A Commentary on the *Notae Directivae* for the Mutual Relations between Bishops and Religious in the Church', *The Clergy Review* 63 (1978) 472–7.

Kiesling, C., *Celibacy, Prayer and Friendship. A making-sense-out-of-life Approach* (New York, Alba House, 1978).

Kelber, W. (ed.), *The Passion in Mark: Studies on Mark 14–16* (Philadelphia, Fortress Press, 1976).

Kümmel, W., *Introduction to the New Testament* (London, SCM Press, 1976).

Laplace, J., *Prayer according to the Scriptures* (Brighton, Mass., Religious of the Cenacle, no date).

Legasse, S., *L'appel du riche (Mc 10.17–31 et par.): Contribution à l'étude des fondements scripturaires de l'état religieuse*, Verbum Salutis 1 (Paris, Desclée, 1966).

Leslie, E. A., *Jeremiah: Chronologically arranged, translated and interpreted* (New York, Abingdon, 1954).

Lindars, B., *The Gospel of John*. New Century Bible (London, Oliphants, 1972).

Mackenzie, R. A. F., *Faith and History in the Old Testament* (New York, Macmillan, 1963).

McCulloch, R., 'Monks, Bishops: Society in 4th- and 5th-Century Empire', *Tjurunga* 17 (1979) 57–76.

Mannion, J., 'What is Religious Life?', *Supplement to Doctrine and Life* 76 (1978) 197–203.

Marchel, W., *Abba Vater! Die Vaterbotschaft des Neuen Testaments* (Düsseldorf, Patmos Verlag, 1964).

Marshall, I. H., *The Gospel of Luke: A Commentary on the Greek Text*, New International Commentary (Exeter, Paternoster Press, 1978).

Matura T., *Célibat et communauté. Les fondements évangéliques de la vie religieuse* (Paris, Editions du Cerf, 1967).

—*Le radicalisme évangélique. Aux sources de la vie chrétienne*, Lectio Divina 97 (Paris, Editions du Cerf, 1978).

Metz, J. B., *Followers of Christ: The Religious Life and the Church* (London, Burns and Oates, 1978).

Milton, J. P., *Prophecy Interpreted* (London, Geoffrey Chapman, 1974).

Moloney, F. J., 'Asking the Scriptures about religious life', *Supplement to Doctrine and Life* 58 (1975) 3–12.

—'The Communities of the Early Church', *Supplement to Doctrine and Life* 50

(1974) 24–30.

—'From Cana to Cana (John 2.1 – 4.54) and the Fourth Evangelist's Concept of Correct (and Incorrect) Faith', *Salesianum* 40. (1978) 817–43.

—'The Johannine Son of God' *Salesianum* 38. (1976) 71–86.

—*The Johannine Son of Man*, Biblioteca di Scienze Religiose 14 (Roma, LAS, 1978²).

—'Matthew 19.3–12 and Celibacy'. A Redactional and Form Critical Study', *Journal for the Study of the New Testament* 2 (1979) 42–60.

—'Why Community?', *Supplement to Doctrine and Life* 49 (1974) 19–31.

—*The Word Became Flesh: A Study of Jesus in the Fourth Gospel* (Cork, Mercier Press, 1979).

Moule, C. F. D., *The Origin of Christology* (Cambridge, University Press, 1977).

Murphy-O'Connor, J., *Becoming Human Together* (Dublin, Veritas, 1977).

—'Community: the Possibility of Discipleship', *Supplement to Doctrine and Life* 58. (1975) 13–24.

—'The Contemporary Value of Pauline Moral Imperatives', *Doctrine and Life* 21 (1971) 59–71.

— 'The New Canon Law versus the Gospel: a critique', *Supplement to Doctrine and Life* 63 (1976) 38–57.

— 'What is Religious Life? Ask the Scriptures', *Supplement to Doctrine and Life* 45 (1973). The whole number.

Murphy-O'Connor, J. and Others, *What is Religious Life? A Critical Reappraisal* (Dublin, Dominican Publications, 1977).

A New Catechism: Catholic Faith for Adults (London, Burns and Oates, 1970).

North, R., *Reges* (Rome, Biblical Institute: Class notes, 1971).

O'Toole, R. F., 'Luke's Notion of "Be Imitators of Me as I am of Christ" in Acts 25–26', *Biblical Theology Bulletin* 8 (1978) 155–61.

Panagopolous, J. (ed.), *Prophetic Vocation in the New Testament and Today.* Supplements to Novum Testamentum 45 (Leiden, E. J. Brill, 1977).

Perrin, N., *The Resurrection Narratives: A New Approach* (London, SCM Press, 1977).

—'Towards an Interpretation of the Gospel of Mark', in H. D. Betz (ed.), *Christology and a Modern Pilgrimage. A Discussion with Norman Perrin* (Missoula, Scholars' Press, 1974).

Raguin, Y., 'Chastity and Friendship', *Supplement to the Way* 19 (1973) 105–17.

—*L'Esprit sur le monde,* Collection Christus 40 (Bruges, Desclée de Brouwer, 1975).

—*La Profondeur de Dieu,* Collection Christus 33 (Bruges, Desclée de Brouwer, 1973).

Ratzinger, J., *Introduction to Christianity* (London, Burns and Oates, 1969).

Rees, D., and Others, *Consider your Call: A Theology of Monastic Life Today* (London, SPCK, 1978).

Renckens, H., *The Religion of Israel* (London, Sheed and Ward, 1967).

Rowley, H. H., *The Faith of Israel: Aspects of Old Testament Thought* (London, SCM Press, 1956).

Rudolph, K., *Jeremia, Handbuch zum Alten Testament*, Erste Reihe 12 (Tübingen, J. C. B. Mohr, 1968[2]).

Sanders, J. T., *Ethics in the New Testament: Change and Development* (London, SCM Press, 1975).

Schnackenburg, R., *The Church in the New Testament* (London, Burns and Oates, 1965).

—*Nachfolge Christi – heute: Antworten und Weisungen aus dem Neuen Testament*. Herder Bücherei 595 (Freiburg, Herder, 1978[2]).

Schneider, J., Art. '*eunouchos*', in *Theological Dictionary of the New Testament* 2 (1964) 765–68.

Schoonenberg, P., *Man and Sin: A Theological View* (London, Sheed and Ward, 1965).

Schürmann, H., 'Le groupe des disciples de Jésus', *Christus* 50 (1966) 184–209.

Seidensticker, P., 'Saint Paul et la pauvreté', in *La pauvreté évangélique*, Lire la Bible 27 (Paris, Editions du Cerf, 1971).

Senior, D., *Jesus: A Gospel Portrait* (Dayton, Pflaum, 1975).

Sicari, A., *Matrimonio e verginità nella rivelazione. L'uomo di fronte alla 'Gelosia di Dio'*, Già e non ancora 31 (Milano, Jaca Book, 1978).

Skinner, J., *Prophecy and Religion: Studies in the Life of Jeremiah* (Cambridge, University Press, 1922).

Smith, F., 'Selon le plan de Dieu', *Donum Dei* 4 (1962) 51–62.

Snijders, J., 'Bishops and Religious: A Vatican Document on the Mutual Relations between Bishops and Religious in the Church', *The Australasian Catholic Record* 56 (1979) 192–203.

Soggin, J. A., *Introduction to the Old Testament* (London, SCM Press, 1976).

Spivey R. A., and Smith, D. M., *Anatomy of the New Testament: A Guide to its Structure and Meaning* (London, Macmillan, 1974[2]).

Stendhal, K., *The School of St Matthew* (Philadelphia, Fortress Press, 1966[2]).

Tannehill, R. C., *A Mirror for Disciples. A Study of the Gospel of Mark* (Nashville, Discipleship Resources, 1977).

Tanquerey, A., *The Spiritual Life: A Treatise on Ascetical and Mystical Theology* (Tournai, Desclée, 1930).

Taylor, V., *The Gospel according to Saint Mark: A Commentary on the Greek Text* (London, Macmillan, 1959).

Tillard, J. M. R., 'Dans le sillage de la vie sacramentaire', *Donum Dei* 4 (1962) 63–83.

—*The Gospel Path: The Religious Life* (Bruxelles, Lumen Vitae, 1977³).

—'Poverty and Prayer', *Supplement to Doctrine and Life* 73 (1978) 14–28.

—'Le propos de pauvreté et l'exigence évangélique', *Nouvelle Revue Théologique* 100 (1978) 207–37.

—*Les religieux au coeur de l'Eglise* Problèmes de vie religieuse 30 (Paris, Editions du Cerf, 1969)

—*There are Charisms and Charisms: The Religious Life* (Bruxelles, Lumen Vitae, 1977).

—*Devant Dieu et pour le monde.* Cogitatio Fidei 75 (Paris, Editions du Cerf, 1975).

—'Le fondement évangélique de la vie religieuse', *Nouvelle Revue Théologique* 91 (1969) 916–55.

Tillard, J. M. R. and Congar, Y. (eds), *L'adaptation de la vie religieuse. Decret 'Perfectae Caritatis'.* Unam Sanctam (Paris, Editions du Cerf, 1967).

van Cangh, J. M., 'Fondement évangélique de la vie religieuse', *Nouvelle Revue Théologique* 95 (1973) 635–47.

van Steenkiste, J.-A., *Sanctum Jesu Christi Evangelium secundum Mattheum*, (Bruges, C. Begaert, 1903⁴).

Vawter, B., *The Conscience of Israel. Pre-Exilic Prophets and Prophecy* (London, Sheed and Ward, 1961).

—'Introduction to Prophetic Literature', in *The Jerome Biblical Commentary* (London, Geoffrey Chapman, 1969).

—*On Genesis: A New Reading* (London, Geoffrey Chapman, 1977).

Veilleux, A., 'Evoluzione della vita religiosa nel suo contesto storico-spirituale', in A. Favale (ed.), *Per una presenza viva dei religiosi nella Chiesa e nel mondo* (Torino, LDC, 1970).

Volz, P., *Der Prophet Jeremia* (Leipzig, A. Deichert, 1922).

von Rad, G., *Deuteronomy* (London, SCM Press, 1966).

—*Genesis* (London, SCM Press, 1976²).

—*The Message of the Prophets* (London, SCM Press, 1968).

—*Old Testament Theology* (Edinburgh, Oliver and Boyd, 1962).

Weeden, T. J., *Mark: Traditions in Conflict* (Philadelphia, Fortress Press, 1971).

Wilcken, J., *Religious Life Today: A Theological and Scriptural Approach* (Melbourne, Polding Press, 1974).

Williams, H. A., *Poverty, Chastity and Obedience. The True Virtues* (London, Mitchell Beazley, 1975).

Winstanley, M. T., 'Disciples and Loneliness': A Marcan Meditation', *Review for Religious* 38 (1979) 13–20.

Index of Biblical References

Old Testament

New Testament

Index of Authors